Revolution and Church: The Early History of Christian Democracy, 1789–1901. Hans Maier.

The Overall Development of Chile. Mario Zañartu, S.J., and John J. Kennedy, eds.

The Catholic Church Today: Western Europe. M. A. Fitzsimons, ed.

Contemporary Catholicism in the United States. Philip Gleason, ed.

The Major Works of Peter Chaadaev. Raymond T. McNally.

A Russian European: Paul Miliukov in Russian Politics. Thomas Riha.

A Search for Stability: U. S. Diplomacy Toward Nicaragua, 1925–1933. William Kamman.

Freedom and Authority in the West. George N. Shuster, ed.

Theory and Practice: History of a Concept from Aristotle to Marx. Nicholas Lobkowicz.

Coexistence: Communism and Its Practice in Bologna, 1945–1965. Robert H. Evans.

Marx and the Western World. Nicholas Lobkowicz, ed.

Argentina's Foreign Policy 1930–1962. Alberto A. Conil Paz and Gustavo E. Ferrari.

Italy after Fascism, A Political History, 1943–1965. Giuseppe Mammarella.

The Volunteer Army and Allied Intervention in South Russia 1917–1921. George A. Brinkley.

Peru and the United States, 1900–1962. James C. Carey.

Empire by Treaty: Britain and the Middle East in the Twentieth Century. M. A. Fitzsimons.

The USSR and the UN's Economic and Social Activities. Harold Karan Jacobson.

INTERNATIONAL STUDIES OF THE

COMMITTEE ON INTERNATIONAL RELATIONS

UNIVERSITY OF NOTRE DAME

Chile and the United States: 1880–1962. Fredrick B. Pike.

East Central Europe and the World: Developments in the Post-Stalin Era. Stephen D. Kertesz, ed.

Soviet Policy Toward International Control and Atomic Energy. Joseph L. Nogee.

The Russian Revolution and Religion, 1917–1925. Edited and translated by Bolesław Szcześniak.

Soviet Policy Toward the Baltic States, 1918–1940. Albert N. Tarulis.

Introduction to Modern Politics. Ferdinand Hermens.

Freedom and Reform in Latin America. Fredrick B. Pike, ed.

What America Stands For. Stephen D. Kertesz and M. A. Fitzsimons, eds.

The Representative Republic. Ferdinand Hermens.

Theoretical Aspects of International Relations. William T. R. Fox, ed.

Catholicism, Nationalism and Democracy in Argentina. John J. Kennedy.

Christian Democracy in Western Europe, 1820–1953. Michael P. Fogarty.

The Fate of East Central Europe. Stephen D. Kertesz, ed.

German Protestants Face the Social Question. William O. Shanahan.

Soviet Imperialism: Its Origins and Tactics. Waldemar Gurian, ed.

The Foreign Policy of the British Labour Government, 1945–1951. M. A. Fitzsimons.

Diplomacy in a Whirlpool: Hungary between Nazi Germany and Soviet Russia. Stephen D. Kertesz.

Bolshevism: An Introduction to Soviet Communism. Waldemar Gurian.

The Church
and Social Change
in Latin America

The Church
and Social Change
in Latin America

HENRY A. LANDSBERGER, *Editor*

CONTRIBUTORS

Emanuel de Kadt • Cecilio de Lora Soria, S.M.

François Houtart • John J. Kennedy • Henry A. Landsberger

Mark G. McGrath, C.S.C. • Fredrick B. Pike

Renato Poblete, S.J. • Richard Shaull • Ivan Vallier

UNIVERSITY OF NOTRE DAME PRESS

NOTRE DAME — LONDON

Library of Congress Catalog Card Number: 77-85355
Manufactured in the United States of America by
NAPCO Graphic Arts, Inc., Milwaukee, Wisconsin

CONTENTS

ix

CONTRIBUTORS

CECILIO DE LORA SORIA, S.M., is a Marianist priest, ordained in 1957, with a Ph.D. in Social Sciences from Gregorian University, Rome, 1964, and an M.A. from Columbia University, 1961. He has been the assistant to the secretary general of CELAM (the Latin American Bishops' Council) and at the present time is the executive secretary of the Department of Education of CELAM. He has several books published in Madrid, chief among which is *The Process of Socialization of Contemporary Spanish Youth*, and numerous magazine articles.

EMANUEL DE KADT is fellow in sociology at the Institute of Development Studies, University of Sussex, and Latin American research specialist at the Royal Institute of International Affairs, London. He is the author of *Catholic Radicals in Brazil* and editor of *Patterns of Foreign Influence in the Caribbean*, both to be published by Oxford University Press in 1970.

FATHER FRANÇOIS HOUTART is secretary general of the International Federation of Institutes of Social and Socio-Religious Research, and served as expert advisor to the Commission on the Church in the Modern World at the Second Vatican Council. He holds degrees from Louvain University and the International Institute for Urban Studies in Brussels, has been a visiting professor at various European, North American, and South American universities, and has published twenty books, which have been translated into ten languages.

JOHN J. KENNEDY, director of the program of Latin American Studies at the University of Notre Dame, is currently with the Fundación Rockefeller in Cali, Colombia. He is the author of *Catholicism, Nationalism and Democracy in Argentina* and co-editor of *The Overall Development of Chile*.

HENRY A. LANDSBERGER is professor of sociology at the University of North Carolina. He spent four years in Chile on a program jointly sponsored by the University of Chile and Cornell University. He has written on politics, labor, and peasants in Latin America, as well as on various general sociological topics.

THE MOST REVEREND MARK G. McGRATH, Archbishop of Panama, is also Second Vice President of the Council of Latin American Bishops. He was a member of the Doctrinal Commission at the Second Vatican Council, and is a member of the Post-Conciliar Vatican Council of the Laity and Consultant to the Post-Conciliar Vatican Secretariat for Non-Believers. He has studied at the University of Notre Dame, Holy Cross College, and the Catholic Institute of Paris, and holds a doctorate from the Angelicum in Rome.

FREDRICK B. PIKE is professor of history, University of Notre Dame and author of *Chile and the United States, 1880–1962* (Notre Dame, 1963; Bolton Prize, 1964), *The Modern History of Peru* (London and New York, 1967), and some sixty articles in scholarly journals of various countries. He has also edited *Freedom and Reform in Latin America* (Notre Dame, 1959, 1967), *Latin American History: Identity, Integration, Nationhood* (New York, 1969), and other books. He was awarded a Doherty Foundation grant for research in Chile, 1959–60; a Social Science Research Council grant for research in Peru, 1963–64; and a Guggenheim Foundation grant for research in Spain, 1968–69.

FATHER RENATO POBLETE, S.J., is at present professor of sociology at the Catholic University of Santiago, Chile. He is also director of the Bureau of Religious Sociology of the Chilean Episcopate and of the Institute for Social and Socio-Religious Research (FERES) in Chile. He is a member of the executive committee of the Catholic Inter-American Cooperation Program (CICOP) and was one of the organizers of the Conference of Latin American Bishops in Mar del Plata and in Medellín. Father Poblete has published several books on the problem of the Latin American Church including *La Iglesia en Chile* (FERES), *Crisis Sacerdotal*, and others.

M. Richard Shaull is on the faculty of the Princeton Theological Seminary, and is an ordained minister in the United Presbyterian Church. He has taught in Presbyterian seminaries in Colombia and Brazil and has lived for over twenty years in Latin America. He has published several articles on Protestantism in Latin America, and he has been particularly interested in the student movement in Brazil, and more generally in revolutionary changes in Latin America.

Ivan Vallier, Ph.D. (Harvard, 1959) is currently professor of sociology, Crown College, University of California, Santa Cruz. He was formerly a member of the faculty at Dartmouth College and Columbia University, and is the author of articles on the Israeli kibbutzim, the Mormons, theories of development, religious elites and Latin American institutions. A book examining Latin American Catholicism—*Religion, Social Control, and Modernization*—is being published in 1970 by Prentice-Hall.

Part I:
Introduction

1: INTRODUCTION

Henry A. Landsberger

Latin America and Latin American institutions have undergone greater and historically more continuous change than generally accepted views suggest. Latin America was not suddenly shaken out of a centuries-old slumber by the depression of the 1930's or by World War II or by the example of the postwar independence movements in the European colonies in Africa and Asia. These events—and the diffusion of new consumption expectations and revolutionary ideologies that occurred at the same time—merely accelerated changes that had long been underway in Latin America, as they were elsewhere.

One consequence of breaking the bonds of Spanish mercantilism, for example, was the creation of a limited, but socially and politically important, sector of Latin America's economy, in a process that spanned the nineteenth century. Since this sector was oriented to trade with Europe and North America, European and counter-European ideologies and immigrants came with it, as did changes in the composition of ruling elites, shifts in the relative importance of geographical regions, the establishing of professional military strata, the growth of small-scale middle and working classes, and expansion in the educational system. Though perhaps slower in pace than in certain parts of Europe, there has always been change in Latin America. This change cannot always be described as progressive. But the prevalent idea that Latin American institutions literally have been static over long periods is surely incorrect.

The Catholic church in Latin America, like religious institutions everywhere, reflects the society in which it is rooted, but, of course, by no means is it a mirror image of that society. Change in the Latin American Catholic church has sometimes been less rapid than change

3

in the society around it. Portions of the historical chapters in this collection, particularly that by Fr. Poblete, seem to support this interpretation. Yet the widening gap to which such a discrepancy gives rise may itself cause accelerated transformation in the church in a subsequent period, when the church, or elements of it, seem to overtake other institutions. As Vallier points out, in the chapter that follows, certain streams of Catholic thought in both Brazil and Chile are today as advanced, if not more advanced, than those of Belgium, France, and Germany, from which countries they received their progressive inspiration originally.

The present decade is clearly a period of accelerated transformation in the church of Latin America. For this reason, the decade is of enormous interest to those who are concerned, academically or for other reasons, about Latin America. Indeed, it is of concern to all who are interested in religious institutions as such and in the process of social change.

There are at least four reasons to support an assertion of the church's importance in the Latin American context. First, at the level of ideology, it is perhaps the most creative and, for that reason alone, one of the most fascinating streams of Latin thought. I believe it is at present *the* most original ideology in Latin America.

This estimate should not be construed as especially partisan or positive. In the first place, it is possible that each of the many problems facing Latin America has a solution that is as much related to the problem's nature as to ideology of any kind; that solutions should be more technical than philosophical. Were that the case, the deduction of specific solutions from general ideologies would be a strategy of limited value. There are certainly a vast number of specific ideas of a relatively non-ideological kind that have been offered for the problems that face the continent. We are merely asserting that, insofar as ideologies are concerned with solutions that harmonize with their philosophies, Catholicism lags behind none, including Latin American Marxism. Marxism has produced many ideas on how and when to make a revolution and has come up with stimulating critiques of existing systems and provocative interpretations of the past. But, except for the Cuban experiment, about which little is known and which has probably been forged by experience as much as by doctrine, Marxism has come up with no set of guiding principles for a new society in the manner of Catholicism.

Second, by way of caution, Catholic thought is clearly open to challenge on the appropriateness and, hence, the social usefulness of its ideas. Yet, creativeness and originality, which Catholicism has undeniably shown, are a *sine qua non* for viable new solutions. Hence, the ideas being proposed by Catholicism should be given very careful scrutiny. What may at one time have been their chief defect—their underemphasis of institutions and overemphasis of the unchanging nature and psychology of man—is perhaps today a point of strength. Current solutions are too often based on a logic of institutions that does not take into sufficient account the characteristics of man, the importance of which Catholicism has always recognized.

Third, the importance of Catholicism in Latin America rests on the number of persons it influences. We make reference not only to those who participate in the ritual life of the church. We include all members of Christian Democratic parties (e.g., in Chile, Peru, Venezuela); of trade unions or employers' associations in some way based on Catholic doctrine; of Catholic-controlled community groups in the slum areas of large cities; and of Catholic family associations. Even students, for example, who vote for a Catholic-inspired leader rather than for his rival, although they may feel no link with Catholic ideology, may be to some degree influenced by Catholic doctrine, as are those perhaps who ponder its propositions and reject them. In this broad sense, Latin American Catholicism is active and effervescing and deserving of very serious study.

Fourth, Catholicism is important because of its organizational strength. Aside from the nation states themselves, it is the most highly organized entity in Latin America. Vertically, it often extends downward effectively into regions and to levels where the state's bureaucracy does not function at all. In many isolated villages the choice is between a form of theocracy, often unsought by priest or bishop, and no government at all. Upward, the church has built mechanisms, at the level of Latin America as a whole, for consultation, service, and communication with other parts of the world that are unrivaled in the private sphere.

The church extends not only geographically but functionally. It is the only entity, excepting governments, that inspires and sponsors organizations devoted to education, health, politics, community organization, collective bargaining, culture, recreation—practically the entire range of human life and activity. These organizations, often related to Catholicism only in a general and tenuous way, should not be seen as signs of unified direction or of a well thought-out master plan or the embodiment of the old nightmare of a state within the state. They do mean that new ideas put forth within the "Catholic world," loosely defined, have a higher probability of finding existing organizations to implement them or the resources—in or outside Latin America—to establish new organizations than do ideas of other non-governmental provenience.

Given, then, the vitality and importance of Catholicism in Latin America, and the evident changes it is undergoing, it was decided as part of Cornell University's Latin American Year (1965–66) to bring together a number of clerical and lay individuals who have been close to these changes. They include those who had been participants in or even highly responsible for crucial events. The guests were deliberately invited to come at different times to give more opportunity for individual meetings.

The major statements of the visitors, and essays written later at the editor's invitation, are collected in this volume. Books of this kind are far from perfect and cannot hope to be systematic. Yet, this collection has the virtue of juxtaposing two very different types of writing: there are the chapters by men of policy, who must necessarily be somewhat cautious, but whose words are revealing when studied carefully and when contrasted with the past declarations of others in similar positions. They reveal great powers of reflection and dynamism; they are in many ways personal documents of high interest. On the other hand, there are the chapters written by scholars who, having less immediate responsibility for events, have more freedom to enter into detail. A second virtue of the volume is, perhaps, its considerable scope. It may be seen as an interim progress report on change in certain critical spheres.

We first meet Ivan Vallier's systematic analysis of the various forms of church influence, the sequential stages of their development, and an analysis of the conditions determining the passage from one stage and type of influence to the next. There follow three historical chapters: a general view of the chief events in the history of the Catholic church in Latin America by Renato Poblete, S.J.; a more detailed account of church history in Argentina, Chile, and Peru during the past sixty years by Fredrick B. Pike; and a chapter by myself that concentrates on the timing and persons involved in Chilean change, ending with an account of doctrinal change there, thus making a bridge to the third section of the book. Professor Pike's discussion of Chile centers on political philosophy as sustained by the laity, and my own focuses on social doctrine as formulated by the hierarchy.

The third section deals chiefly with doctrinal and lay ideological developments. Two of the chapters, by Msgr. Mark McGrath and Abbé Houtart, respectively, look outward—as one inevitably must—to the Second Vatican Council. The third, by Richard Shaull, compares two Latin American countries, one of which, Brazil, had experienced the emergence of a more radical stream of thought than the other, Chile, at least at the time of Dr. Shaull's lecture.

The final section deals with topics that have long been of critical importance to the church: the relationship to the state (J. J. Kennedy); the growth of CELAM, the Latin American Episcopal Conference, and its imposing list of subsidiary activities (Cecilio de Lora, S.M.); and finally an account by Emanuel de Kadt of the development and increasingly greater independence of Catholic lay action groups in Brazil.

The editor thanks the persons and institutions who have helped to implement the idea of this sequential symposium: William H. Mac-Leish, Director, Cornell Latin American Year; Professors Donald K. Freebairn, Tom E. Davis, and J. Mayone Stycos, at that time Directors of Cornell's Latin American Program; and Dean David G. Moore and Professor James O. Morris of the Cornell School of Industrial and Labor Relations, who, as usual, willingly supported a novel undertaking.

2: EXTRACTION, INSULATION, AND RE-ENTRY: TOWARD A THEORY OF RELIGIOUS CHANGE

Ivan Vallier

Outlooks and initiatives emanating from Vatican II are leading to insightful and often penetrating diagnoses of the church's internal life. New perspectives are being gained on problems of leadership, the nature of the Christian community, and the roles that laymen can assume in liturgy, social action, and decision-making. But this energetic phase of collective self-analysis is doomed to an early and unfruitful end unless attention is shifted more centrally to the church's relationships with society and how these interdependencies affect both its own programs of reform and its role in social change.

I do not want to suggest that churchmen are taking no cognizance of trends and events in the world, nor that they see no significance in bringing the church in closer touch with society. One of the major documents prepared and ratified by Vatican II, the Pastoral Constitution on the Church in the Modern World (*Gaudium et Spes*), is an unambiguous call to the church to dialogue with the world, to confront it, to live within it, and to influence it. In O'Dea's words, the constitution is "a most striking attempt to take the world of secular man seriously and to relate it in depth to the concerns and teachings of the Church."[1] Nor do I maintain that the church has abandoned its missionary vocation vis-à-vis the world. The past half-century of apostolic concerns has generated a whole series of specialized programs and experimental institutions, such as Catholic Action, the worker-priest movement, the Legion of Mary, the Papal Volunteers for Latin America—all of which operate on the boundaries between church and society. The wider society has been and remains a major preoccupation of both church leaders and the rank and file. Yet this challenge has tended to be articulated mainly at two levels: the theo-

9

logical and the motivational, with little or no concern for the complex institutional and structural aspects of the church's relationships to, embeddednesses in, and interdependencies with corporate secular groups, class strata, political bodies, educational systems, and economic bases. It is in terms of these variables that the church is, and always will be, part of society; it is through these ties and connections that the church either achieves its goals or fails in its mission.

These issues are particularly relevant to Roman Catholicism in Latin America, for it is within the boundaries of that great geo-cultural region that we may observe some of the most complicated patterns of church-society interdependencies. These interdependencies must be taken into account both by students of the religious situation and by those who concentrate on facilitating changes in the political, social, and economic realms.[2] Since it is naive to think that the church will disappear overnight or abandon its interests in human society, questions need to be raised as to how a given national church, or parts thereof, can be stimulated to forego traditional emphases and take up positions that will help facilitate social change. This, to me, seems to be a problem that is worth working on and one that bears centrally on many aspects of development and modernization in Latin America.

STATEMENT OF THE PROBLEM

Theologically inspired enthusiasms and ideological fervor are not valid indicators of change in the church, and change in the church—if it is at all significant—cannot go very far unless changes occur in the relationships between church and society. Thus my first working hypothesis: if a church, say at the national level, defines its responsibilities as those of facilitating basic changes in society, it must, of necessity, confront the problem of reworking its relationships with power groups, central institutions, and cultural frameworks. This leads to a second hypothesis: the ways in which a church is involved with or connected to external systems of power and control significantly affect its adaptive modes and problem-solving styles, i.e., the way it handles threats, competition, and crises. My third hypothesis is no less important: the responses of the church to problem-solving, especially in Latin America where it occupies a very prominent public position, carry important implications for the integration and change of the wider society. Its major policy decisions carry repercussions far beyond the sanctuary. This should be obvious.

The extensive institutional scope of the church in Latin America makes it one of the pivotal systems of influence and control. In most countries Roman Catholicism dominates the religious sphere and thereby stands very high in these societies' overall hierarchies of organized, corporate life. The church also holds a visible and influential position in the political system of many countries and maintains significant ties with regional and national governments. It is also a principal, and in some places an almost monopolistic, educational system, promoting curricula that are heavily overlaid with moral and religious emphases.

As an administrative and pastoral system, the church encompasses the total territory that falls within the boundaries of Latin America. It is organized in terms of more than 500 ecclesiastical jurisdictions (dioceses and mission territories). Its local programs of a liturgical, sacramental, and pastoral nature are centered in more than 15,000 parishes. On a more symbolic or expressive level, the church displays intimate connections with a religio-Catholic "culture" composed of general beliefs, conceptions of divine personages, and eschatological paradigms. Interspersed between the formal church and this broader religious culture stands a staggering array of Catholic-inspired movements, social action programs, and charitable agencies. So far-reaching are the arms of the church that no aspect of Latin American life is free from its influence.

However, the sociological bases of church influence are variously organized and differ in their overall implications. If a church holds an established legal position in society, draws financial support from the public treasury, consorts with the upper class, and defines the role of the clergy as one of diffuse, public authority, then it is likely that church leaders will attempt to meet competition and threats by defending the political status quo. Since the church leaders realize that their position of dominance in society depends, to a large extent, on legal-political arrangements, these become extremely important and will be defended, even if it means assuming a direct political stand against other groups. If this occurs, the society is likely to be torn by political conflicts that are fed by primordial, religious sentiments. The church becomes politicized, antichurch forces assume aggressive positions, the entire basis of social order is broken, or at least severely disrupted, and broader processes of change are blocked.

On the other hand, we can think of a church that stands autonomous from legal privileges, eschews political alignments, and focuses its efforts to influence people around pastoral activities, specialized programs of religious education, and the participation of the laity in decision-making processes. This church's linkages with society are twofold: at the cultural level it articulates and fosters frameworks of belief and meaning in terms of contemporary problems; at the motivational level, i.e., the member or layman, it attempts to generate commitments in terms of general religious principles that can be applied by the individual to many different contexts, including secular roles. In times of threat or in situations of strong competition this church is forced to rely on either its symbolic capacities at the cultural level or the principled religious actions of laymen who live and work in secular society. Neither of these bases is directly political, nor do they predispose the church leaders to court the support of conservative political groups. Furthermore, the leaders of this second church are aware that legitimacy and influence depend on their capacities to develop religious perspectives and local structures that have meaning for a changing society. The interests of church leaders tend to coincide with the interests of secular groups who favor change and modernization.

These are hypothetical cases, of course, but the point should be clear enough: the kinds of linkages a church holds with society affect its problem-solving strategies, and these actions, in turn, carry direct and indirect consequences for social processes.[3] Thus the sociological problem of a changing Catholicism is one of identifying the conditions that place the church under institutional anxiety as well as those conditions that give rise to structural developments (new roles, new bases of influence, new relationships with society) that reduce the likelihood that it will turn to reactionary, conservative strategies.

This point needs to be clarified a little more. Although the contemporary church has lost none of its ambitions, it has lost many of its traditional sources of legitimacy and, concurrently, important structural connections with secular power groups. This combination of high ambitions and low legitimacy breeds anxiety and fear. Churchmen recognize that major losses have occurred, yet have no ready solutions for counteracting these trends. The resultant anxiety has a number of consequences: it generates autocriticism, even to the point of calling basic assumptions about authority and purpose into question. This internal anxiety also stimulates an "experimental mood" at the levels of concept formation, procedural norms, and influence strategies. Entrepreneurship and innovation begin to draw singular rewards, yet the ferment of experimentation also breeds new fears: How far should experimentation go? Who has the best solution? What will be the long-range outcome of adopting a certain institutional policy? This internal anxiety also steps up the interest of church elites in objective knowledge about the external situation and about the availability of internal resources (membership commitments, the state of mind among the clergy, the effectiveness of educational programs, etc.). This search for new knowledge breeds a specialized corps of researchers and consultants. As their power grows within the total elite group, theologians and other traditional specialists become uneasy. They see the new men as usurpers and even dangerous. This leads officials to withdraw legitimacy from certain kinds of adaptive efforts, increasing the width of the cleavage between innovators and traditionalists.

But the combination of high ambitions and low legitimacy also carries external consequences. In its search for new bases of control and influence in society the church may turn to safe political groups who will protect it. Or it may try to outdo secular political movements of the left by demonstrating that the church can be an agent of revolutionary change. Various intermediary positions are clearly possible, and in many places quite evident. The anxiety of the church's corporate elites in the wider society may also lead it to seek social rewards that come with the establishment of fashionable programs. Lacking legitimacy and not knowing what the future holds, the church turns to a number of short-run projects that give it momentary prestige (at least among certain political groups) but weaken its capacities to determine its own course of action or to speak for all men. Under these conditions it tends to take up defensive, reactionary, and blocking strategies—interfering with legislative processes, holding fast to government subsidies, fomenting ideological strife in local situations, and doing its best to see that favorable votes are turned in at election time. However, these defensive, reactive responses are not a direct product of the church's central teachings, nor do they stem from a particular bishop's or cardinal's personal philosophy. Instead the sources of the conservative, reactionary church lie in the kinds of structural ties it holds with society, or sectors thereof, and in the types of influence apparatus it uses to bolster its power and prestige. The church, according to my hypothesis, is not conservative "by nature." Its tendencies and record in that direction, instead, are to be found mainly in the kinds of interdependencies it holds with society and how these either block or short-circuit its capacities to create and institutionalize new roles and structures.

If these assumptions are valid, then I suggest that one of the problems of development in Latin America is to work out theories or models that can be used to guide the church toward structural bases that will reduce its tendencies to "go conservative."[4] Development is not just a stimulation of behaviors and changes that are deemed positive, e.g., values of occupational achievement, administrative effectiveness, etc. It is also a problem of extricating institutions from structural bases that breed counter-developmental pressures. How can this be done? What are the developmental, or extricating, principles to be followed? Which sectors of the church are probably most susceptible to such proddings? These are questions that seem to me to be critical for current work on Latin American Catholicism. The purpose of this essay is to explore some of the possible answers.

Three sections divide the essay. The first section presents an evolutionary typology of church systems, with particular attention to changing patterns of church-society relationships. Section two analyzes the basic sequence of extraction, insulation, and re-entry, and notes some of the conditions that accompany this sequence. The final section discusses several of the practical implications of the theory.

A STAGE-BASED TYPOLOGY

Several possibilities exist for identifying strategic changes in church-society relationships. At the level of the membership, inquiries could be made regarding changes in the class composition of faithful churchgoers as well as in the status characteristics of seminarians. Such studies would provide an over-time perspective on the church's major clientele and sources of leadership. Other gains could be realized by systematic studies of the status network of church elites or through inquiries into the various arrangements that are consolidated between hierarchies and governmental groups. It would be equally important to identify the ways in which the church is making efforts to align itself with the urban poor, student groups, and the peasants.

We also need to formulate typologies that condense historical and cross-national configurations. Changes in church-society relationships are expected to proceed in clusters or interrelated patterns. By constructing types that bring out these combinations, we may be able to grasp, if only preliminarily, the nature of underlying themes and processes. I shall follow the typological approach in this essay. In it I place primary emphasis on the church's relationships to society and how these linkages or interdependencies undergo change and affect its capabilities for influence. Five types of church systems are identified: the monopoly church, the political church, the ghetto church, the servant church, and the pastoral church.

Stage 1: The "Monopoly" Church—Territorial Dominance and Legal Privilege

The monopoly church possesses legal guarantees and political support to the extent that Catholicism constitutes the state religion or holds a position as the established church. The monopoly church is protected, totally or in part, from certain kinds of religious competition, and its elites consider themselves the moral arbiters of national life. In this stage the clergy are essentially civil bureaucrats or employees of the state, and the hierarchy is legally subject to traditional forms of civil surveillance and control. The principle of the "patronato" and the exercise of the *placet* on papal communications are observed. The church as a national organization is centered around the major urban see, with the other dioceses existing in relative isolation as small ecclesiastical kingdoms. Since legislative decisions are a primary concern of the prelates, their attention is directed horizontally to the political arena rather than downward through the parishes to the membership.

Formal education is virtually in the hands of the church. Even though state schools operate, their curricula include religious courses, and the clergy or religious are permitted to provide Catholic instrucion. Beyond the school system the church exercises influence through diffuse controls, privileged access to functional spheres, and indirectly through its clergy being members of elite groups and having connections with upper-status individuals.

Laymen are viewed as charges or as ritual clients. Their religious needs are serviced through the formal schedule of the sacraments; pastoral activity is weak and intermittent. Consequently, many extra-ecclesial styles of "Catholic" activity emerge—devotional cults, fiesta patterns, etc.—each one bound up with particular localities or ethnic traditions. Since one of the main concerns of the clergy is to augment and maintain a Catholic hegemony, special care is given to the rite of baptism and the sacrament of marriage.

The "monopoly" church configuration has prevailed throughout most of Latin America's history since the sixteenth century, though with many unique variations in time and place. Even today this model operates extensively, not only in the minds of many churchmen but also institutionally. Most observers tend to place the Colombian church in categories that approximate the monopoly position, even though not all of the conditions mentioned above hold. Certainly the situation in Brazil to the end of the Empire in 1889 would fit this pattern, as would many other nineteenth-century configurations. But it is not my intention to use the types outlined here as shorthand descriptions for this or that national church. This is not the intellectual purpose of heuristic types. Instead they are devices for throwing into relief features or sequences that facilitate thinking about concrete units. My references to particular historical periods or to contemporary national situations are to be taken, then, as illustrative rather than conclusive.

Stage 2: The "Political" Church—Short-Run Coalitions and Clerical Threats

One of the most significant sequences that emerges from the pages of historical works involves a shift in the position of the church from a monopoly role to one that is political and conservative. Most of such sequences took place in the third and fourth quarters of the nineteenth century. As liberal political forces gained strength and began to capture legitimate positions of power, the church experienced sharp curtailments in its privileges and freedoms. Having relied on formal arrangements as major bases of influence and control, these changes automatically brought deep anxieties to churchmen. The typical response was to move quickly to the side of the political conservatives, a stance which inevitably drew the church into partisan conflicts and lengthy political struggles.

The case of Chile is instructive. Although some tensions between the church and the Conservative rulers had emerged before the 1870's, it was then that the Liberals and Radicals gained control of the government. Reform measures affecting the church were susbequently adopted, including an elimination of obligatory religious instruction in the schools, doing away with the "fuero ecclesiastico" for all civil and criminal infractions, the opening of the cemeteries for Protestant burials, and the abolishment of the tithes arrangement.[5] These issues stimulated open opposition on the part of the clergy, led, as Mecham reports, by the Archbishop of Santiago, Rafael Valentín Valdivieso, "who even proceeded to the limit of excommunicating those who had supported the laws."[6]

Subsequent restrictions on the church occurred during the Liberal Republic (1871–91), and the "theological questions" continued to incite serious political battles. Gil quotes the Chilean historian Galdames as follows: "The political struggle degenerated . . . into a religious struggle, and the Conservative Party was transformed into a clerical or 'ultra-montane' group. . . ."[7] These struggles marked the end of the monopoly phase of the church in Chile. Mecham summarizes the effects as follows:

> The *reformas téologicas* seriously weakened the Chilean Church; in a formal encounter it had been defeated and humiliated; its prestige was shaken and thereafter it was placed on the defensive.[8]

Other variations on the Chilean pattern occurred in Latin America, taking on more violent proportions in Mexico but creating fewer incidents in places like Brazil. But not all of the national church systems have fully passed through this phase. In Colombia, for example, the intense struggles between Conservatives and Liberals actually led to a separation of church and state in 1853, being "the first act of separation in Latin-American history."[9] But this was not permanent. Under Rafael Núñez, elected to the presidency as a Liberal in 1880, the church gained a new position of traditional power. For this "Liberal turned Conservative . . . [R]estoration of the power and influence of the Catholic Church in Colombia was a cardinal feature of the new policy. . . ."[10] A new constitution was adopted in 1886 which presented "God as the supreme fountain of all authority" and indicated that "Roman Catholicism was to be respected as an essential factor of the social order."[11] Within two years a singularly important concordat had been signed with the Holy See which, still largely in effect, provides the church both a monopoly status and institutional independence from the "patronato." Colombia, then, represents a case wherein changes got underway very early in the independence period, but events led to significant reversals.

STAGE 3: THE GHETTO CHURCH—INSULATION AND OFFENSE

Once the legal guarantees are broken and the political alliance with the conservatives becomes problematic, the church tends to move back away from society and to develop structural barriers, insulative strategies, and specialized "missionary" programs. It wants to hold what it has and to co-opt, so far as possible, individuals or groups that possess significant positions in society. This is a phase of confessional defense, bureaucratic growth, and concern with ideologies and procedures of apostolic action. The church is viewed as a beleaguered and victimized institution, beset on every side by enemies. Hierarchical authority is tightened; specialization is increased along lines having to do with offense and defense; emphasis is placed on training the younger generation to the faith and bringing the laity under the direct supervision of the clergy. The usual rewards associated with ritual conformity are supplemented by another reward system for those who go beyond the formal requirements to assume corporate responsibilities for the defense of the church. Thus Catholic youth who take the church's influence into the factory or university are defined as collaborators with the hierarchy. Direct political involvements are eschewed, and even forbidden, for the laity who represent the church as worldly missionaries. There is, then, a withdrawal from the political arena, especially at the formal and governmental levels, accompanied by a specialized emphasis on ideological formation of the Catholic laity and its organization into militant cadres.

Sequences approximating these patterns have occurred in the churches of Mexico, Chile, Brazil, Guatemala, and Cuba, with varying degrees of explicitness, while partial developments along these lines have taken place in Argentina, Colombia, and Peru. Initiatives in Chile, Brazil, and Argentina were started during the second and third decades of this century, preparing the basis for later developments in Catholic Action. This process began later in Guatemala and

Mexico. In other countries, such as Ecuador and Venezuela, these kinds of developments have been weak.

Adams' description of recent changes in the Guatemalan church may serve as an illustration.[12] Between the close of the 1930's and 1960 three new dioceses were established by the initiative of the Holy See; foreign clergymen were brought in to supplement the local supply; schools, clinics, and cooperatives were built and developed; the internal organization of the church was strengthened; the number of religious orders increased; the work of the seminaries was upgraded; and the church actively promoted Catholic Action movements, the revitalization program known as the cursillos, and the work of catechists. These, along with other changes and emphases, reshaped the church as an organization and deeply modified its relationships with society. Instead of looking to formal, legal arrangements as guarantees of ecclesiastical privilege or relying on open coalitions with organized political groups, the church began to fortify its internal bases and complemented these with specialized, but clerically supervised, programs in society.

It may seem too simple to gather all these initiatives under a single principle or concept, such as "controlled contact with society" or "parallelism." Yet, a definite sequence does occur in church-society relationships which differs fundamentally from the shift of the church from a monopoly to the political stage. The sequence appears to involve a two-level change: on one level the institutional church withdraws from organized politics and promulgates a strong a-political norm of religious action; on another level the church undertakes to resocialize the laity, to guard them from secular forces, and to mobilize them into specialized missionary groups.

What stimulates this stage of church-society relationships and what are its sociological implications? As I see it, the political church reaches a point where leaders begin to recognize that short-range coalitions and public defeats divide the laity, cast doubt on the church's claim to religious legitimacy, block its access to rising status groups of liberal persuasion, and undermine the internal structure of authority and communication. The main corollary of these internal problems is anxiety about the weakened position of Catholicism as a religious system and the falling away of the masses. These conditions typically give rise to a strategy of influence that combines confessionalism with the establishment of specialized structures that are to insulate Catholics from secular forces. Thus, "parallelism" consists of developing specialized confessional organizations and Catholic programs for every major institutional sphere of society: Catholic trade unions, Catholic youth groups, Catholic schools, Catholic charities and welfare programs. These organizational emphases are accompanied by explicit efforts to "revitalize the laity" and to mobilize them into specialized missionary cadres. This latter mechanism is focused on purely spiritual or religious goals, such as the evangelization of the urban workers. Political involvements on the part of Catholic organizations are forbidden, and each point of contact with society is guarded by a hedge of Catholic rules and principles. In the movement from the political stage into the confessional-insulative stage the church's bases of influence and control follow a general withdrawal of the religious system from diffuse, unguarded relationships with society as well as a decided pullback from political alignments. Lines of vertical control are tightened; specialization takes place along functional lines having to do with offense and defense; laymen are drawn more fully into the clerical system and named as hierarchical collaborators. In brief, the church disengages itself from many of its traditional interdependencies with society and enters a period of institutional consolidation and religious activity.

STAGE 4: THE "SERVANT" CHURCH—SOCIAL DEVELOPMENT AND INSTITUTION-BUILDING

The break between stages three and four is one of fundamental proportions. It is essentially a change from defensive and antagonistic relations with society to an acceptance of responsibility for facilitating social goals. This does not mean that the church elites abandon an interest in building up the Catholic faith or achieving influence in society. The overall objective remains, but the specific goals of religious action and the procedures for realizing them undergo basic modifications. Social needs and religious aims are viewed together and given a central place in planning and organization. This is the beginning of re-entry into society and the main instrument for regaining visibility and legitimation is service programs that are aimed at relieving social problems or helping better the living conditions of marginal, dispossessed groups. Entrepreneurial initiatives of reform-minded priests and the technical-professional skills of militant laymen are combined to foster organized programs. These, in turn, are shaped and legitimated with reference to a Catholic-Christian ideology of social change and national development.

Direct political alliances and legislative battles are self-consciously avoided, even though the service programs being sponsored symbolize a progressive political position. Laymen are urged to engage themselves politically as citizens, not as representatives of either the church or Catholic-related associations. Internal rewards and social prestige go to those who succeed in fusing the social principles of Catholicism with concrete programs of human betterment. Controversies among church elites unfold along several lines; between those who hold traditional or conservative outlooks and the new men of change; between those who emphasize rational planning, organization, and specialization versus those who promote a full-fledged revolutionary church that must confront the political opposition directly; and between those who want to pursue militant programs of proselytizing and those who emphasize the need for material and social changes in the fabric of society. During this stage secular movements of social reform and radical political groups take on signal importance as reference groups for church elites.

Major developments in the direction of the "servant" church have occurred during the past fifteen years: literacy programs in the rural areas of Brazil, Chile, and Colombia have been developed with reference to principles of national development and social service. Similar emphases are displayed in the efforts that have gone into building cooperatives and fostering community growth. The Chilean church's experiments in land reform represent another instance of allocating resources to assist in the solution of social problems.[13] Many other instances of aid, assistance, and social reform could be cited. Undoubtedly the Northeast section of Brazil represents the area of most concentrated work along these lines, though certainly within the context of other emphases equal in importance.

STAGE 5: THE PASTORAL CHURCH—RELIGIOUS LEADERSHIP AND
      CONGREGATIONAL FORMS

The fifth stage gives rise to a church that holds no legal guarantees to shore up special privileges. It is not hemmed in by insulative devices of its own making, and it does not allocate its main energies to social development and economic programs. Instead its main center of gravity is found at two levels: in the local church which is focused on meeting the spiritual-social needs of the laity and, second, at the cultural level, involving the development of ethical norms and symbolic frameworks that tie Catholic teachings to the values of a modern society.

Correspondingly, it attempts to provide members opportunities for meaningful religious experiences in various types of settings:liturgical, social-expressive, educational. The bishop functions mainly as a socio-ethical spokesman, emphasizing the charismatic content of the church's teachings and the Catholic's responsibilities in secular society. In turn, the priest becomes increasingly the spiritual leader and human relations expert. His roles within the local church are extended beyond that of ritual specialist and church administrator (transferring the latter to laymen) to include that of task leader, pastoral counselor, and a facilitator of communal activities.

The "pastoral" model is only beginning to emerge in Latin America, but I think it is due to gain rapidly in significance. The changes occurring in the worship service throughout many parishes are only one sign of this trend. New efforts to develop small groups for scriptural study, such as biblical circles, represent another important shift. It is also clear that many priests are relearning their roles and placing greater emphasis on close relations with the laity, meaningful preaching, and communal forms of religious solidarity in the world. In Chile and Brazil, where the Protestant Pentecostals have made considerable gains, the principles of congregational life have assumed an obvious place in church planning and programming. Although many current attempts to restructure local church life stand at the experimental stage, I expect these problems to gain a central and continuing place in pastoral activities.

It is also clear that many bishops are beginning to place more emphasis on symbolic leadership and socio-ethical problems. The few men who initiated these trends, prior to Vatican II, were viewed as out of step and of a revolutionary mind. Traditional bishops believed that they would destroy the church. However, the general mood has changed, with the result that a pastoral conception of the episcopacy and the idea that the church holds a responsibility to facilitate socio-ethical development have become basic norms. Through the vehicles of the Latin American Episcopal Council (CELAM) and the national

TABLE I

STAGES OF CHURCH-SOCIETY RELATIONSHIPS AND TYPICAL EMPHASES

	Monopoly	Political	Insulated	Social Servant	Cultural-Pastoral
1. Basis of Church/society relationship	structural fusion	opposition and dependency	withdrawal and controlled contact	involvement in national change	integrated autonomy
2. Major mechanism of religious control	secular power	political bargaining	protective organizations	co-optation of marginal groups	religio-cultural leadership
3. Secondary mechanism of religious control	withholding of religious sacraments	clerical threats	ideological indoctrination	social action opportunities	communal identification
4. Degree of tolerance of social change	low	none	low	moderate to high	high
5. Church's role vis-à-vis societal change	opposition	opposition and regressive	opposition and neutralizing	facilitation and legitimation	initiation and legitimation

episcopal conferences the church's changing teachings on social problems, economic reform, supranational integration, and citizenship
responsibilities have been widely disseminated. The new bishop is a
man who has moved away from ecclesiastical rules and disciplinary
conceptions of authority toward the problems of human community
and social change.

These five sequences are mere sketches of immensely complicated
processes, and accordingly I view them as very tentative.[14] However,
I have taken the risk of oversimplification in order to throw into relief
the directional changes in church-society relationships. When the five
stages are viewed together, a rough descriptive model begins to
emerge. A monopoly stage is succeeded by a political stage, then follows a confessional-insulative stage, next a social-servant configuration,
and finally the cultural-congregational stage. In each of these stages
the church rests its reputation and fortunes on specific combinations
of integrative and adaptive mechanisms which, correspondingly,
result in specific types of relationships with society. As a means of
bringing the five stages together and showing their differences, I have
worked out a preliminary table.

According to this model the church's basic mechanisms of religious
and social control undergo decisive changes as it passes from one stage
to another. Similarly its tolerance of and role in the processes of a
wider social change undergo modifications. At stage five—the cultural-
pastoral stage—the church exhibits a high tolerance for change and
plays a dual role in change: an initiator of changes at the level of
values and symbol systems and a legitimator of institutional changes
in secular spheres.

This typological framework suggests that the church's relationships
to society require taking account of at least three levels of analysis: the
church's sociological bases in society, its primary strategy of influence,
and the structural units that operate as instruments of that influence.
With regard to the first—the church's sociological bases in society—
a monopoly church combines reliance on elite groups and folk sentiments with public involvements. Its main strategy of influence is
political, since its security hinges largely on its capacity to maintain
legal privileges and constitutional guarantees. The key adaptive structures are informal systems of communication and pressure that extend
among and through the formal power structure and traditional elite
groups. The ghetto church, quite dissimilar, is tied principally to the

active faithful, made up mainly of middle- and upper-class groups. It does not instrumentalize its relationship with these groups in ways that characterize the monopoly church. Instead, the emphasis is on religious formation and indoctrination, the building up of confessional structures (parallelism), and the organization of clerical, supervisory roles at the apertures that emerge at the boundaries between church and society. Its main strategy of influence is thereby organized defensive and selective missionary efforts in secular spheres. Confessional, clericalized organizations with specialized functions become the primary structural units, and prestige is conferred on those clerics and laymen who lead, elaborate, and maintain them.

The ghetto stage typically breeds a preoccupation with secular society. Specialists engage in empirical research having to do with demographic trends, occupational structures, decision-making centers, and rising status groups. These endeavors, in conjunction with theological works that begin to incorporate variables having to do with the nature and evolution of contemporary societies, tend to confront strategists with the problem of social change and how the church can be linked to these processes. The visible social problems that emerge in modernizing societies are perceived as opportunities for achieving a transition from a ghetto position to one that will provide re-entry into society. Having learned certain things about the hazards and disabilities that go with direct political involvements, the re-emerging church takes up social problems within a dual framework of meanings. At one level, social problems (or national development issues) are defined as responsibilities of the church, since the gospels emphasize the value of each man and the sacred nature of social justice. These emphases allow the church to assert a religious position and to draw social responsibility upon itself. On another level, that of concrete organization, this newly articulated social responsibility gives rise to service-types of church action: community development programs, literacy training, agrarian projects, and vocational schools.

The basic transitional process from the ghetto stage to the servant stage may be viewed as a re-entry into society via the cultural sphere and service activity. Neither of these linkage mechanisms are directly political, since the cultural emphasis allows the church to speak for all men and to voice support for the welfare of the total society, while the organized service programs, even though initiated frequently by clerics, symbolize the church's readiness to facilitate change and to render assistance without reference to religious or confessional criteria.

These re-entry bases into society generate roles, religious orientations, and national structures (such as the national episcopal conference) that provide possibilities for moving the church into the
pastoral-congregational, or charismatic, stage. As the church gains a
new linkage with the values and cultural emphases that are fostering
societal change and as it begins to discover principles for dealing with
human needs generated by a changing society, its leading elites gain
a new confidence in their religio-ethical capacities. These elites also
become conscious of the necessity continually to transfer the church's
service programs to public, secular, or governmental agencies. If it
stays too long in the organized servant stage, it begins either to
court political conflict or to wind up as the guardian of new types of
confessional programs. It is from these kinds of institutional dilem-
mas that the possibility arises for the church to move fully into the
pastoral-charismatic stage.

In this fifth type of church the principal sociological bases in
society are the cultural system and the Christian-citizen. The cultural
level provides the church's key leaders an open and symbolic framework within which to create, articulate, and consolidate broad principles of religio-ethical meaning. At this level, charismatic influence
can be exercised without reference to particular groups or political
positions. At the other end of the sociological spectrum, or at the level
of individual action, the responsibility for fusing religious principles
with concrete behaviors falls to the layman. As a member of both the
church and society he becomes the primary structural unit for linking
the two spheres. This linkage, of course, depends on the emergence
of laymen who have internalized general religious norms and who are
capable of applying these to everyday situations flexibly and autono-
mously. Whether or not this type of layman emerges depends, to an
important degree, on what takes place in the local church. If the local
church becomes an arena for meeting the felt needs of members—
expressive, social, and spiritual—then it is likely that religious involvements will emerge voluntarily and become one of the reference points
for laymen in defining their roles in society. Although the church as
a formal organization will involve a less salient position in the layman's total orientations than formerly, his ties to its religious life will
be deeper and more principled.

Religious influence, correspondingly, will be realized, not by the supervisory and regulative mechanisms that typify clerical dominance, but through a combination of the Christian-citizen who makes his way in society and a socio-religious leadership at the cultural-symbolic level. These two levels do not exist in separation but become linked through a series of pastoral, coordinative, and educational structures that emerge within the total church. The pastoral-congregational church holds a position of integrated autonomy with society: integrated in the sense of being part of a changing culture and simultaneously in touch with all parts of the social structure through laymen; autonomous in the sense of being free from dependencies on power elites and governmental agencies or on any other external supports that may damage its possibilities for self-determination.

Each of the church types faces the political problem, but the vulnerabilities in relation to the political sphere differ. The monopoly church depends on and is inserted in the political system. Since the basis of its position in society is guaranteed by legal provisions which are supported by political power, its fortunes are tied to events and changes in government. The defensive or ghetto phase, on the other hand, is explicitly non-political. Manifest steps are taken by the hierarchy to insulate the church's agents and activities from the political arena. In moving into the servant, or public, phase the church once again takes some politically related positions, though not in terms of a particular party but in relation to the issue of national change and social mobilization. This phase, if successful (i.e., public leadership is developed without the church becoming identified with a particular political party or political movement), gives the church a new set of ties with societal values and provides it a new conception of the Catholic member's role in society. These developments, in turn, prepare the ground for the church to enter the stage of integrated autonomy. The church moves from an agent of social mobilization into a position as a pastoral and religious system—standing both in society and also differentiated from it—yet without any direct political ties.

EXTRACTION, INSULATION, AND RE-ENTRY:
THE BASIC CHANGE PROCESS

The five-stage typology presented above may be viewed, at a higher level of abstraction, as a single change sequence in church-society relationships. Between stages one and five a church system moves from an original position of deep fusion and multiple interdependencies with society to a position of specialized involvement at the cultural and the associational levels (e.g., local congregational units). In the course of making this transition the church follows a path of extraction–insulation–re-entry. In order for a church to reach stage five—the cultural-pastoral stage—it must pull away from certain traditional bases in society (extraction), undergo a phase of internal consolidation and fortification in relative aloofness from society (insulative stage), and then re-open negotiations with society on other than traditional bases and at different levels of socio-cultural reality (re-entry).

This transformative process—extraction, insulation, and re-entry—involves not only basic shifts in the types of interdependencies a church holds with society but also shifts in the levels of contact and functional activity. This last condition is particularly important, since it is a question not only of the degree of church-society interdependency but the levels at which this interdependency occurs. There is a significant sociological difference between a church that is bound up with governmental, political, and economic structures and one that is bound up with value systems and religio-socio associations. It is that kind of difference that separates churches found at the monopolistic and political stages from those situated at the cultural-pastoral stage.

The process of extraction disconnects the institutional church from traditional embeddednesses in the structure of society. It frees it from short-run political involvements, disengages it from particularistic class ties, brings about autonomy from the government, and pulls the clergy back from their traditional roles as diffuse, authority figures in the community. Such changes are fraught with tension, and thus the probabilities of "retrogressive" sequences are always quite high. More than one group of church elites, upon being confronted with disestablishment decrees, has attempted to re-fuse the church with the state and governments. In Brazil, as Bruneau's study shows,[15] the fact of church-state separation in 1890 stimulated deep ambivalences among leading prelates. Although they heralded the advantages of their newly gained autonomy, they subsequently tried to restore a de facto, if not legal, pattern of fusion (and partially succeeded). In Colombia, as noted earlier, the achievement of church-state separation in the 1840's lasted only into the 1880's, at which time a remarkably strong union of church and state was arranged. The Argentine hierarchy also displays marked ambivalences about the church's relationship to the state. Even though the principle of the "patronato" was discarded in 1966, the links between the two systems continue to be deep and pervasive.

The process of extraction appears to be facilitated and accelerated under certain conditions, e.g., with the rapid rise of organized, anti-Catholic (not just anticlerical), grass-roots movements that promote humanitarian values and back this ideology up with militant political action. Against these challenges a church's traditional mechanisms of influence and its traditional ties with power structures and old elites are impotent. Its leaders recognize that attention must be directed to both the religious life of the masses and the problems of internal organization and ideology. These imperatives stimulate a move toward the insulative stage and push church elites to prepare for a new phase of re-entry into society. Old solutions and props are largely jettisoned, new dioceses and apostolic organizations are established, instructional and formative activities are developed to enliven the commitments of the heretofore neglected laymen, and the significance and number of strategists, planners, and ideologists rise within the professional strata of the church.

It is well to keep in mind that the traditional church system in Latin America is not organizationally tight nor preoccupied with boundaries, apostolic endeavors, and long-range strategies. The degree of bureaucratization tends to be low, the vertical line of authority is much flatter or shorter than is typical of the church in the United States or France, and there is little attempt to mobilize the Catholic laymen as religious cadres. Consequently, the shift into the insulative stage, in which the church consolidates itself organizationally and motivationally, represents a new ecclesiastical trajectory. If this phase is successful, or relatively so, then church elites possess a well-structured and manipulable system that can be linked in specialized ways to a complex society. The insulative, or "ghetto," stage is thus a period of institutional resocialization that completes the extraction process and readies the system for selective types of re-entry into society.

Some churches are forced into a segregated position by political force, e.g., as a result of a major revolution. Both the Mexican church and the Cuban church have experienced such changes. On the other hand, the church in Chile proceeded along a more evolutionary path: a reduction of privileges and public scope in the 1870's and 1880's; a peaceful legal separation of church and state in 1925, followed by a period of growth in diocesan structures, a turn to organized programs of Catholic Action, and corollary emphases on reforms in certain important seminaries. In the midst of these changes in the 1930's strategic types of re-entry got underway, e.g., the rise of a progressive, lay-controlled political party—the "Falange Nacional" (later to become the Christian Democratic party)—and the first phase of priest-led programs of social service. By the beginning of the 1960's an important group of bishops had assumed a progressive, cultural role in society on behalf of rapid social change and human justice. During the same period various kinds of organized programs of socio-economic reform were initiated in the cities and the countryside to reach and facilitate change among marginal groups. These programs have given way, in part, to new emphases on pastoral work, liturgical changes, and the development of a more congregational type of local church. In short, the Chilean church has undergone a metamorphosis over the past 90 years that approximates the sequence of extraction, insulation, and re-entry that I have identified. The Chilean church's emerging linkages with the wider society are cultural and associational, rather than those based on governmental protection, upper-class support, and political structures. Its main bases of influence must be gained, in this emerging stage, from its leaders' religio-ethical capacities at the level of values and symbols and from the strength of the laity's religious motivations. I judge that its major phase of serving as an agent of socio-economic change has passed and that it must now accept the imperatives that go with the cultural-pastoral model.

What kinds of conditions facilitate a shift from the social servant stage into the cultural-pastoral? Here the patterns are not very clear, since this latter stage is only beginning to take shape. Yet certain factors do appear as significant:

1. The church's limited "technical capacities." Although progressive church elites may play important, innovative roles in developing socio-economic programs and service institutions (vocational schools, credit cooperatives, land reform experiments, etc.), the church is not equipped—economically, organizationally, or ideologically—to sustain these enterprises beyond a kind of "demonstration point." Funds are scarce, trained personnel are hard to recruit and hold, and latent political dimensions begin to crowd out religious emphases. As the national government begins to initiate public programs of agrarian reform, housing for the urban poor, and new types of educational services, the church loses its visibility and influence in the socio-

economic sector. It seems, then, that the role of the church in socio-economic betterment is limited, in most instances, to the first, pilot phase. Once that has passed, it is forced to seek new avenues of organized action.

2. The demands of the laity for religious and communal leadership. Although many laymen endorse the socio-economic emphases of the church and assume roles in the development of such programs, their religious sentiments and spiritual expectations remain tied to the local church. They ask for closer relations with the clergy, for more participation in the liturgical and administrative activities of the church, and for a greater emphasis on community and religious fellowship. These demands help to draw portions of the clergy into new types of pastoral work. Preaching, group work, home visits, and the teaching of the Bible begin to overshadow traditional emphases on formal, sacramental activities.

3. New forms of competition at the levels of cultural meaning and national purpose. Socio-economic changes and political development not only bring new collective ideologies but also place new burdens on traditional frameworks of values, symbols, and beliefs. Earlier loyalties to something called the "Catholic" religion lose meaning and relevance. In such circumstances the church is stimulated to develop new theologies and to recast its ethical emphases. These efforts inevitably push the referents of normative concern away from the local and the particular and toward the more universal, collective aspects of human society. Bishops are expected to assume roles as socio-ethical spokesmen and to help clarify moral priorities. Instead of placing first emphasis on administrative authority and doctrinal-sacramental conformity, such "new bishops" begin to articulate general, normative principles that are relevant to "all men" and to the directional development of human society. This type of leadership role moves the church, as a religious system, back into society, yet it does not make it hostage to partisan political groups.

There may be other conditions that serve to shift a church from the stage that emphasizes social service and economic change to the cultural-pastoral stage. My thoughts are merely suggestive. It is also well to bear in mind that the stages I have adduced are abstract and ideal-typical. No church system follows a neat, progressive trajectory in its historical development. Nor is it necessary to assume that a church which has moved into one or another of the phases will simply proceed to the next as though some general law was operating.

PRELIMINARY APPLICATIONS

Many other aspects of the contemporary church could be analyzed, and I think with gains in clarification and understanding, by taking account of its changing relationships with society and by emphasizing the ways in which problems of control, influence, and legitimation underlie such changes. I have merely set a direction of thinking about these issues; much more remains to be done before steps can be taken to identify the conditions under which variations occur. In the meantime, however, it may be useful to reflect on the implications that my discussion holds for planning and policy decisions, both for those within the church and for secular or governmental elites. As I indicated in the introductory pages, the church is a public actor, and its behaviors hold ramified consequences for non-religious spheres. Developmental models for national or regional systems might then benefit from inserting variables that pertain to the adaptive styles and organized activities of the church. What does this mean specifically? I have three suggestions.

1. Church-state relationships. Since establishment clauses and other types of legal privileges concerning the church are indicators of the monopoly phase, and since the monopoly phase in my judgment breeds political involvements on the part of the church, which in turn create traditional forms of political conflict and cleavage, I think it should be evident that separation of church and state is one of the priorities in future programs of change. The sooner the church is required to make its own way, and to confront open competition, the greater the possibilities for basic changes in other spheres of society. The high degree of political embeddedness that the church evidences in some countries is then a development problem for the total society, not just for the church. If the significance of this embeddedness is understood, both by church elites and secular elites, then it is not unlikely that the process of extraction can proceed without major political turmoil. But if this alternative is not feasible, when tried, then other means may be necessary.

2. The church as an instrument of social reform. Public officials and politicians are inclined, under certain circumstances, to draw the church into their developmental programs and to allocate it responsibility for facilitating secular change. This may occur, as an instance, when a government becomes aware that the education of the peasants

is a crucial problem. Lacking facilities and personnel, the government turns to the church. The church, in turn, anxious about its relationships with society and eager to gain a legitimate basis for approaching the long-neglected peasants, agrees to undertake responsibility for the educational program. Public funds are made available to the church to finance the program. Yet such alliances are extremely hazardous, both for the church and for the government. The church, because of its financial weakness and because of its uncertain prestige, falls prey to a new form of political dependency; moreover, by being associated, openly or indirectly, with a particular government, it loses its capacities for symbolizing and articulating an autonomous religious position. The government, in turn, may gain some short-run advantages, mostly of a political nature, but stimulates, as well, another phase of clerical-anticlerical conflicts. When the political opposition learns that the government is sponsoring the church for its political ends, then all of the latent sentiments connected with the religio-political syndrome are activated. Political conflict takes on religious or ecclesiastical dimensions, which, as numerous periods of Latin America's history show, tends to disrupt society in ways that are defeating for all major social groups and political parties. I may be inclined to overestimate the latent negative implications of church involvement in government programs of change, though I doubt it. In any case, those who hold the responsibility for decisions of this nature would be well advised to dwell at length upon the long-range consequences of turning to the church for assistance.

3. The development of the new layman. The new churchmen want a laity that is committed to the church on the basis of voluntary choice and also an integral, participating member of society. They want an active laity, a responsive laity, and a responsible laity, one that is neither defensive in the face of ideological opposition nor triumphal in posture toward less dominant religious groups. Various norms and theologies have been devised to provide a general framework for orientating laymen to this new, complex role. Yet, few attempts are made to think out the kinds of sociological and psychological processes that would make this role possible. Here I shall indicate briefly some of the considerations that, in my judgment, would go into such a developmental enterprise.

First, there needs to be a transfer of responsibility to laymen for corporate decisions. The church has shown an exceptional willingness over the past forty years to transfer apostolic responsibility to laymen, but this reallocation of duties has not been accompanied by corresponding amounts of decision-making power.[16] In short, the officials have created a classical sociological problem—responsibility without power—and have had to live with the consequences. But it is worth reflecting on the importance of delegating power. If subordinates are expected to take a personal interest in an enterprise, they should be given an opportunity to shape and affect the course of that enterprise. Laymen who feel that they have capabilities for running organizational affairs often do if given a chance. Some of these capabilities may come from training and experience in secular occupations, others may come from public or social involvements, and others may inhere in natural leadership abilities. My aim is not to identify where talent springs from so much as that of suggesting that organizations which lack coercive powers and that also seek to gain personal commitments forget, at their own peril, the importance of distributing decision-making power.

The church does possess, within its own range of possibilities, the basis for reallocating decision-making powers of certain types. It can, on the initiative of its designated leaders, transfer certain degrees and types of power (and implicitly corporate responsibility) to laymen, e.g., by making them responsible for the temporal life of the local church, by assigning them educational work, by allowing them. to initiate programs related to social or religious interests, and so on.

A second consideration has to do with expressive emotion and the release of religious tension. The church has always been wary of religious impulses and free-floating religious charisma, especially among the laity. It has therefore taken explicit steps to forestall and channel these impulses by organizing devotional societies, encouraging apostolic enterprises, and fostering special retreats. But it is not unlikely that residues of religious charisma, finding no place in the church, take on political forms and breed spasmodic adventures that help maintain the split between reactionaries and revolutionaries. I do not think it is farfetched to think of Catholics as highly attuned to politics and susceptible to intense politicization. Although this is expected to differ by time and place, culture and circumstance, I suggest that it has its roots, at least in part, within the church and more specifically in the church's established constraints against the expression of religious impulse. As the church learns to give these tendencies expression, either through developing smaller congregational units or by allocating religious leadership repsonsibilities to laymen, it may find that the voluntary interests of laymen in its programs will rise and the laity's tendencies continually to seek political bases of recognition will decrease. There are probably many more dimensions to this problem, since it is indeed complex.[17] However, I think it may be worth further consideration and study.

SUMMARY

I shall now summarize briefly my major arugment. The Latin American church is a major corporate entity, and its actions, in many ways, directly affect public interests. The decisions of its elites hold consequences not only for internal affairs but also for the political, economic, and educational spheres of external society. Since these consequences are often negative for national developmental goals, the church's problem of change becomes a public concern, or at least a relevant issue in national planning and government initiatives. But in order to understand how changes in the church can be brought about so as to reduce the likelihood of regressive and reactionary swings, we need to know more about the processes that move it away from traditional problem-solving styles and into new types of relationships with society. I have offered a stage-based typology to illustrate the kinds of changes that seem to be involved in shifting the church's underlying strategies of influence. This typology assumes that the church is not simply going to fade away or leave the scene. It will continue to hold an important place in Latin American societies. The question, of course, is whether that position of influence should be conservative and interruptive of change or more on the side of modernization and development. The pastoral-cultural church that represents the fifth stage in the typology is one that has a place in contemporary society and, correspondingly, is not a block to the achievement of non-religious goals. The extractive–insulative–re-entry principle of change that I have identified may then serve as one guide to both churchmen and secular elites for formulating policies to guide religious development. It should be obvious, of course, that my thinking is preliminary, and we need to engage in a great deal more discussion on these problems.

Part II:
History

3: THE CHURCH IN LATIN AMERICA:
A HISTORICAL SURVEY
Renato Poblete, S.J.

He was wise who said that what we most take for granted deserves our closest scrutiny. For too long the Latin American continent has been shrouded in a mist of romance, encouraged by the tourist trade. We have called it a Catholic continent and statistics can be quoted to support that description: over 200 million faithful, one-third of the entire Roman Catholic population in the world, live in Latin America. If we add the four-and-one-half centuries of undisputed influence by the church of Rome, the argument appears very impressive. It is too impressive, however, to be taken for granted.

What myth-dispelling facts seriously challenge this too-facile reading of superficial data? First, the continent of Latin America has the lowest proportion of priests per Catholic population in the world, lower than Africa, which is considered, in greater part, a missionary continent. Second, religious affiliation on the basis of active participation in church ritual is extremely low. Moreover, the social and economic inequality of so many millions of Latin citizens stands forth as evidence of an enfeebled social conscience.

Latin America is a continent of baffling paradoxes that may be resolved only if viewed in the light of the past.

I. THE EVANGELIZING CHURCH AND ITS
SOCIAL ROLE IN COLONIAL TIMES

The Christianization of Latin America began in 1493 with Columbus' second expedition to the New World. The arrival of the first missionaries inaugurated a period that is comparable in many respects to the church's early activity among the Frankish tribes. Their methods were, in substance, almost identical to those that had been recommended by Pope Gregory the Great more than eight hundred years before when he sent Augustine and forty Benedictine monks on a pioneer mission to pagan England. They were instructed not to destroy pagan temples or the culture that produced them but, instead, to use pagan elements in their apostolate, patiently leading the neophytes at their own pace gradually to a more profound understanding of the true God.[1] However well-conceived such missionary tactics may appear, they contained pitfalls that were not always recognized or avoided.

In Latin America the actual transition from paganism to Christianity was accomplished with a minimum of struggle, since the religious structure of both Aztecs and Incas was hierarchically apt. Both religions recognized, of course, many gods, but worshipped one supreme deity that ruled the destinies of men and lesser gods. The concepts of life after death and veneration of saints were already honored in their tribal liturgies. It remained but for the friar missionaries to "baptize" these elements for Christian use by altering their content. The methods by which this was accomplished included the use of such institutions as the "fiscales," "alférez," and the "doctrineros," in which laymen were placed in charge of groups of Indians and mestizos in order to prepare them for baptism. The actual function of these laymen included the repetition of doctrine to the catechumens with a view to memorization, leading these community groups in prayer, and, occasionally and according to circumstances, baptizing infants. There was, however, a notable absence of any true catechetical preparation before these mass baptisms. Statistics on conversion were impressively high; Bishop Zumárraga in his ecclesiastical report of 1531 attributed more than a million Indian baptisms to the Franciscans alone. One may rightfully question the depth of these conversions in the light of known facts.[2] Obviously, the resulting undesirable syncretisms have left their mark on all future generations of Latin Americans.

A happier chapter in the early colonial history of the church was its championing the Indian cause. The Spanish conquerors were proud, ambitious, and often avaricious men whose treatment of the conquered Indian was too often divorced from Christian principles.

The church, however, through the social action of her missionaries demanded that the Indians be treated with respect as human beings. Among the strongest voices raised in defense of the conquered natives was that of Antonio de Montesinos, whose preaching severely opposed Spanish abuses in Santo Domingo. It is, however, to Bartolomé de las Casas that history awards the title "defender of the Indians." Himself a colonist and an owner of Indians, de las Casas recognized the degradation imposed on the natives by the *encomienda* system, under which they were little more than slaves. Having renounced his holdings, he pleaded the Indians' cause before Cardinal Cisneros, Regent of the King of Spain. The result was a considerable amelioration of colonial legislation affecting the Indians and a modification of the abuses of the *encomienda* system, in accordance with which natives were allocated not to individual colonists but to a sacred village trust, supervised by a friar.

Not every struggle for social justice met with equal success, for Spanish officials were often obdurate in their policies. History, however, assigns to the church the honor of having been the sole defender of the Indian cause before the Spanish king. "The conquest of America was launched in violence and consummated in a degree of mercy. The men of the Cross finally proved mightier than the men of the sword. The soldiers won battles but the friars won hearts."[3]

II. THE CIVILIZING ROLE OF THE CHURCH

A. EXPERIMENTAL MISSIOLOGY

Historians differ in their judgments of the reservations established by Spanish Jesuit missionaries in the Spanish colonies. Experimentation —and the social and cultural mobility that it symbolizes—is a refreshingly healthy phenomenon in any society. The settlements and reservations that dotted Lower California and parts of the Latin American continent for the religious and cultural education of the Indians were well in advance of their time.

According to the historical records of the Society of Jesus, the most famous of these reservations seem to have been concentrated in the area of the River Plata, including the greater part of Paraguay, northern Argentina, southern Brazil, and a section of Uruguay. In structure the reservations resembled tight-knit mission villages. Indians were given intensive instruction in the faith, trained at some skilled labor, and protected against slave-hunting colonists. By 1731 the Jesuit reservations had reached the climax of their development, numbering over 141,240 Christian Indians within their structures alone.[4] It is understandable that these groups were the objects of attacks, verbally by outraged public officials jealous of their authority and physically by the Paulistas, or Brazilian slavers.

It is difficult to measure the impact of these village structures on the Indians, but it is certain that the missions prospered both in respect to the promulgation of the faith and the social and economic progress of the inhabitants. Every generation judges the past in the light of the present. Undoubtedly, the reservations were, by present standards, paternalistic, but they were, despite modern attempts to explain them away, successful ventures. The experiment came to an abrupt end in 1767, with the expulsion of the Society of Jesus from the Spanish empire.

B. Intellectual Life and Social and Economic Development

The history of colonial Latin America offers numerous instances to prove that the Catholic church has never tolerated for very long any opposition between man's spiritual needs and his preparation for and progress in human society. The Dominican and Franciscan friars, among others, dedicated their extensive apostolate to an intensive preaching of the Gospel, and the Society of Jesus by leaving its mark on the socio-economic and intellectual dimensions of colonial life identified the church with progress. Agriculture prospered through Jesuit introduction of irrigation canals; horticulture was extended by addition of new varieties of trees from Europe; and the import of fine cattle improved breeding. So, too, were these same priests responsible for the first organized colonial industries: "their flour mills and bakeries supplied the cities . . . they manufactured lime, made rope, pottery, tanned leather and in some places had a virtual monopoly on drugs and medicine."[5]

The economic ventures of the Jesuits, though extensive and enduring, were however secondary to their intellectual contribution to Latin American colonial society. In Mexico 300 priests directed 22 colleges, 19 schools, and 10 seminaries, while in Chile, a territory possessing at that time only 400,000 inhabitants, there were 400

Jesuits at work. In many places institutions for the training of the clergy were entrusted to the Society of Jesus, and their acclaimed libraries laid the foundation for some of the best collections in Spanish and Portuguese America.[6] In all respects this was a golden age for the Latin American church, and its splendor, now dimmed, can still be glimpsed in the magnificent cathedrals of Mexico, Quito, and Lima. Her lasting glory, however, is best revealed in such men and women as the Saints Rose, Martín de Porres, and Turibius in Peru, Peter Claver in Colombia, and Anchietas and Nobrega in Brazil, whose outstanding lives reflect the depth of the church's penetration of colonial society.

III. THE END OF AN ERA

A. The Expulsion of the Jesuits

To attempt a full analysis of the church's loss of influence during the late eighteenth and nineteenth centuries would require space far beyond the scope of this essay. There are, however, elements that are universally accepted as contributing factors. In chronological terms, the expulsion of the Jesuits in 1767 initiated the church's decline. The extensive labors and undeniably powerful influence of the Jesuits provoked the jealousy of civil authorities both in Spain and Latin America and led to the sudden and unjust order to abandon, with only a few hours' notice, all Spanish and Portuguese colonies. The Society had been responsible in great part for the church's prosperity, and the departure of the Jesuits was a profound blow and plunged the continent into the crisis of its first serious shortage of priests and deprived the colonies of their intellectual leadership.

B. The War for Independence

Approximately in 1810, demonstrations began to spread rapidly across the Latin American continent. These demonstrations were the first serious break in the monotonous regularity of colonial life. Spain had given her colonies three centuries of peace, but with the passing of years the complaints against the crown had become increasingly common. Creole grievances centered on trade restrictions that limited their economic advancement, but grievances of this kind were not alone responsible for the outbreaks of violence that occurred in widely separated centers on the continent. The causes are related to events and ideas that were neither Spanish nor of Spanish American origin. The North American and French Revolutions had given substance to man's longing for liberty, and the doctrines of eighteenth-century European rationalism condemned what was called superstition and intolerance. Rousseau and other writers proscribed by the Inquisition and smuggled in by young Creole students returning from Europe became increasingly popular in the colonies. With such inspiration it was unlikely that the movement for independence would find complete acceptance within the church. And so it was that some bishops openly favored the movement, whereas others abandoned their dioceses[7] and with disaffected Spanish officials returned to Spain, thereby expressing their sharp disagreement with the revolutionary cause. In some areas, including Mexico and Argentina, the native clergy fought with and even led the revolutionaries. In Mexico more than one hundred priests headed battalions; in Argentina seventeen priests were present at the first meeting of the assembly in May, 1810;[8] and sixteen priests were members of the congress of Tucuman.[9]

Although such instances suggest an identification of the church with the struggle for independence, the revolution itself weakened church structures. Separation from Spain caused a stop in the constant flow of clergy from the Iberian Peninsula, while vacancies could not be filled locally as a result of the total disorganization of the seminaries caused by the war. Many dioceses were without bishops for several years. The need to fill these posts was at the bottom of one of the deepest antagonisms between the church and the new republics.

C. Patronage and the Struggle for Power

The new republics, liberal as they considered themselves to be, were anxious to take to themselves the old privilege of patronage. The Spanish crown had enjoyed the right to name and appoint new bishops;[10] but Rome, suspicious of all liberal governments, was unwilling to renew the privilege. Prolonged and complex negotiations left the entire continent in a state of ecclesiastical disorder with some bishops in voluntary exile, others expelled, and with vacancies resulting from deaths unfilled; in some areas church property was expropriated, the clergy was scattered, and foreign priests were prohibited the exercise of their ministry. By 1829, there was not a single bishop in Mexico, and the anticlerical measures of O'Higgins in Chile and Rivadavia in Argentina accentuated the growing bitterness felt on both sides in this struggle for power.

It is difficult to evaluate the extent to which this anticlericalism was also an antireligious movement. The division into conservative and liberal camps in post-revolutionary society was, in fact, the heart of the matter. The conservatives were devoted to the maintenance of continuity and stability in the social order. Since the church was at that time identified with tradition, by virtue of its opposition to the revolutionary concept, conservatives supported this symbol of the stability that favored their prosperity. The liberals, who strove for freedom and progress, were consequently enemies of conservatism and, thus, unfortunately, of the church. The church's monopoly of education, hospitals, orphanages, cemeteries, and the keeping of vital statistics became the target of efforts by the state to ensure its own autonomy, and indeed not until the early part of the twentieth century was this problem solved. The result of this long and turbulent period was the church's loss of any identification with progress. Many of Latin America's intellectuals, convinced of the liberal future of the continent, ceased to practice their faith, thereby laying the foundation for a pluralistic society.[11]

IV. THE CHURCH AND THE MODERN CHALLENGE

Despite the laudable propensity of men to begin anew, to change the course of history, we are willy-nilly the heirs of the past. Groaning under such inherited handicaps as have been outlined, the Latin American church was totally incapable at the beginning of the twentieth century of meeting the challenge of the new era. To attempt to analyze the entire situation facing the church in the modern world would be an engrossing but enormous task. The basic problem can be appreciated, however, if looked at in the light of the two factors that are shaping the destiny of the continent today.

A. THE DEMOGRAPHIC EXPLOSION

Population statistics for the past sixty-five years offer an astonishing index to understanding Latin America's demographic problems. From 63 million in 1900, the population rose to 100 million in 1924, 165 million in 1950, and to more than 210 million in a recent census. This unprecedented growth has left an unmistakable mark on all social structures and human activities, as the failure of efforts to satisfy the needs of an ever-growing populace creates continual tension.

Because of inherited structural flaws,[12] the church is among the institutions most deeply affected by population growth. When, for example, it is realized that the number of dioceses, parishes, and priests is smaller now than any derived from eighteenth-century ecclesiastical records and the population is now almost four times what it was in 1900—the gravity of the situation is evident. Today, there is one priest for every 5,700 Latin Americans, and national differences range from 3,000 in Chile and Colombia to 12,000 in Guatemala and 15,000 in Honduras. Differences among Latin American countries are too often overlooked, and the concept of the equal intensity of priestly shortages throughout Latin America is one of the unfortu-

TOTAL NUMBER OF PRIESTS AND NUMBER OF INHABITANTS
PER PRIEST BY COUNTRY (1965 APPROX.)

	Total Priests	Inhabitants per Priest
Argentina	4,922	4,064
Bolivia	581	5,958
Brazil	9,116	7,766
Chile	2,357	3,114
Colombia	3,841	3,679
Costa Rica	235	4,983
Cuba	730	9,310
Ecuador	1,170	3,400
Haiti	463	7,570
Honduras	119	15,899
Mexico	6,512	5,373
Nicaragua	190	7,773
Paraguay	426	4,150
Panama	141	7,482
Peru	1,496	7,257
Puerto Rico	400	5,902
Dominican Republic	246	12,252
El Salvador	310	8,067
Uruguay	688	4,109
Venezuela	1,249	5,371

nate generalities that this approach spawns. The table shows the total number of priests in each country and also the ratio of inhabitants and priest.[13]

The number of priestly vocations is another index of a people's religiosity. Here, again, with the exception of Colombia, the number of seminarians and newly ordained is smaller than the rate of general population increase. During the last fifteen years the continent has experienced an increase of 12,000 priests and a population increase of fifty million. In the last five years alone population increase has been twice that of priests and seminarians. Only the assistance of foreign clergy has enabled a few countries to preserve some proportion between this population growth and the priestly ministry.

The resulting state of affairs produces tension throughout the religious structure, for the modern challenge presents problems that cannot be solved by the cumbersome, traditional structures of yesterday. The whole parochial concept must be examined with an eye to the size of areas, the numbers served, and the methods to be employed. These areas at present cover territories of 100–600 square miles and contain parochial populations that vary in national averages from 10,000 in Paraguay and Ecuador, and 25,000 in Honduras, to a probable 32,000 in Cuba. Statistics disclose, moreover, a number of cities with over 50,000 inhabitants per parish. The preceding facts become all the more pessimistic in the light of a pastoral approach that has been almost exclusively clerical and has allowed for little lay or religious participation.[14]

It is not sufficient, however, to limit this structural problem to population explosion and priestly shortage, acute as they are. Today's pluralistic society, under the impact of secularization, provides a cultural context in which the modern priest is seriously hampered in the transmission of the Christian message. We cannot rest on the assumption that all is well because Latin American Catholicism has the weight of four centuries of tradition behind it. Census figures alone show a serious decrease in the number declaring themselves Catholics as level of education rises. Whereas 90 per cent of those with one or two years' attendance at grammar school consider themselves Catholics, only 67 percent of those who have attended universities do so.[15] Tradition, then, in itself is not sufficient to communicate values, attitudes, and norms. The message of Christianity must be proclaimed to every age through the channels provided by society.

B. Secularization and Latin American Society

Among the most evident characteristics of the modern era are the collapse of the concept of traditional religion and a basic change in the way man comprehends reality and life itself. Man is exchanging the mythological and traditional conceptions that were central in his thoughts for a new center of gravity in himself. Some modern theologians see this new world concept bereft of myth as one where responsibility is emphasized, where man has truly become lord of creation. This secularizing process is looked upon then as the liberation of man from the religious or metaphysical conception of the material universe that dominated his reason and permeated his language. Max Weber chose to define secularization as a growing inclination toward a rational understanding of the world about us through a greater systematizing of science, technology, and art. He identified this process with rationalization.

This disenchantment of the world was actually made possible by the Judeo-Christian religion that had sought to liberate man both from the oppression of the material and the taboo of paganism. Although soon contaminated by dualistic heresies, the Christian religion is still, in fact, the origin of all that is acceptable in the present process of secularization. Notable efforts on the part of theologians have been made in past decades and, more specifically, in recent Conciliar deliberations to approve and sanctify the advances of science and technology.[16] (They have learned, in any case, that no number of ecclesiastical decrees can put a stop to social upheavals.) Theological studies, too, are taking orientation from modern conditions and are now dedicated to an elaboration of a theology of the temporal, a synthesis of science and faith.

The presence of secularization is a sign of the existence of pluralism in a culture, an indication of the end of its monolithic era. This fact is of profound importance for the role of the church in society. The transmission of the Christian message during the monolithic past was a comparatively simple procedure, since it was accomplished within a culture possessing a framework of Christian values. In such a society all the agencies of socialization transmit the same norms and value system. What is said by the church is repeated in the schools, lived in family life, accepted by the community, and reinforced by social pressures expressed in uniform behavior patterns and the punishment of dissidence. Such a vertical system of authority exercises a pressure that is accepted without much personal analysis by those under its sway. In today's pluralistic society, however, there is no coincidence of social and religious structures, of cultural and Christian norms and values. There is, rather, competition, even conflict, between the norms and values transmitted by different social groups representing secularism, communism, and laicism. The church, school, and family no longer represent the same thinking, and an egalitarian and democratic society refuses any imposition of ideas or customs, preferring rather to analyze, to discuss, and to participate in their formation, a fact that in itself evidently impedes transmission. The mystical aspects of traditional Catholicism no longer satisfy the requirements posed by the new values of an urban and technical civilization.

Secularization has brought the Latin American continent face to face with a peculiarly complex problem. There are rural areas that are still basically untouched by this process; pluralism has not penetrated them, and a certain kind of Christian culture is still dominant in them. At the same time, however, urban concentrations exhibit a very rapid tendency toward secularization, although masses of the population are only partially affected by the process. The Catholic church, then, finds itself obliged to direct its labors toward three quite distinct groups in Latin American society in its effort to meet the problem of secularization. The work of evangelization, however, does develop on a positive Christian foundation in the population. Of course, there is massive Christianity that has all the characteristics of a more primitive religion; it does not for this reason cease to be Christian, or at least to be open to the basic Christian concepts of love and service to one's fellowmen. Indeed, these concepts are often more formative than is generally believed. Large masses of the population evince religiosity that cannot be dismissed offhandedly. Every survey made has proved that Latin Americans conserve certain values, certain relations to the church, and certain numerous educable traits upon which a Christianity appropriate for the masses can be constructed.

Every organized church must eventually find itself facing a dilemma. Its being a church rather than a sect gives its desire to convert men a universal scope; at the same time this somewhat dilutes its message and causes the loss, to a degree, of its spontaneity and informal and charismatic qualities. This is the price of all institutionalization. Doubtless, there are sentiments, images, rites, and religious expressions of the natural man that might be termed impure. The Christian message is meant to purify them. But what of those possessed by dreams of an absolutely pure Christianity for an elect group? Is such a "pure Christianity" possible? Man does not experience his religion in a vacuum, but rather within a determined social and cultural context. A feeling of deep esthetic pleasure, for example, does not detract from a true religious experience; the existence of purely religious motivations is difficult to prove. The existence of popular religious expressions and beliefs is a fact in Latin America. Although it is true that many Christian rites and practices have virtually been divested of their religious context and have been converted to cultural and folkloric elements, it remains possible to reincorporate these religious symbols and to enrich them with their true Christian significance.

V. THE RESPONSE TO CHALLENGE

The social and cultural challenge of our times demands an immediate and clear response from the church. The new orientations of modern man demand of a Christian a sincere preoccupation with the milieu in which he finds himself, an intelligent use of mass communications, and a living testimony to a positive image of the church. Human relations of a more democratic kind are drawing us toward a revision both of ecclesiastical government and of the use of authority in religious communities. There is a growing demand for the greater participation of all members in a more collegial government, such as outlined by Vatican Council II. At the same time the universalist tendency reminds us that, despite the autonomy and authority given to bishops, there can be no true diocesan pastoral action that is not integrated and coordinated at national and even international levels. This is a reinforcement of the necessity for episcopal conferences where collegiality is most truly experienced.

Latin American society has embarked upon a journey toward secularization. This process is not everywhere taking place with the same rhythm. Moreover, in addition to characteristics generally observed in other parts of the world, secularization has acquired certain elements peculiar to the Latin American socio-cultural milieu.

Sociologists of various research centers are in the process of specifying the characteristics related to religious behavior. They will need direction from theologians to prevent their seeking "the religious" exclusively in typically cultural acts and to encourage their appreciation of it in the more profound attitudes of justice, generosity, and charity. Theologians, aided by sociological findings, can compare contemporary religious conduct with attitudes of faith and religion offered by Christianity both in biblical sources and its own tradition.

Secularization and pluralism are helping to form a church of openness and dialogue, where pastoral action will no longer be directed toward a multiplication of closed structures. Such groups, where Catholics have access only to other Catholics, are "ghettos" without future in the secular, pluralistic society now forming. How then is the church to respond within the major spheres of its influence? In treating of temporal spheres, such as politics and unions, the present doctrine of the Second Vatican Council insists that ample liberty be given and that the church not accede to the temptation of using them for apostolic purposes of evangelization.

Another sphere open to the church's influence is education. Although Catholic schools are dedicated to a synthesis of secular knowledge and religious faith, they are not the only medium by which this synthesis can take place. It will be necessary to take into consideration the equally important temporal end of these institutions and impress this upon their personnel.

In regard to the apostolic sphere the church's response must be as decisive as it is swift. The members themselves must unite in a common effort to live, cultivate, and propagate their faith. An elite group, they will enter into contact with the masses about them without any of that false "angelicalness" that pretends to the role of leaven and refuses contact with the dough. In this way the church's members will ccasc to be a symbol whose meaning is obsolete or forgotten, and they will not fear institutionalization because of the risks involved. Such is the vision of the church of the future, the reality of which is already taking shape in today's Latin America.

In his discourse to the bishops of Latin America,[17] Paul VI spoke of a dual orientation in the pastorate of the church. He called first of all for a revitalization of the church's Christian community as such, a return to the role of leaven in the masses.

Together with the revitalization of the Christian community, the Pontiff commended to the Latin American bishops the labor of elevating and purifying the latent religiosity of the masses. Elevate "the true and good present among them," whether it be an explicit desire for God, or prayer, or one hidden under the form of a longing for justice, honesty, love, equality, and human solidarity. Purify religion of all elements that cannot be Christianized. This purification, however, is not to be identified with a destruction of those forms used by the mass of people to express their relationship with God. As has already been said, these forms must be revitalized with authentic evangelical content centered in the paschal mystery, "signs" explained by the Gospel.

The double line of action outlined by Paul VI focuses again on the pastoral labor of Latin American priests and gives form to the church's response to the modern challenge.

4: SOUTH AMERICA'S MULTIFACETED CATHOLICISM: GLIMPSES OF TWENTIETH-CENTURY ARGENTINA, CHILE, AND PERU

Fredrick B. Pike

THE DIVERSE MANIFESTATIONS OF ONE FAITH

Essentially, there has been one church in the three southernmost Spanish-speaking republics of the American hemisphere. Yet there has never developed what could remotely be considered a monolithic ecclesiastical structure whose directors, except in the limited realm of doctrine, simultaneously pursued identical or even intimately related policies. Instead, the different facets of South American Catholicism and the divergent results of the interplay of spiritual and temporal forces are strikingly illustrated by twentieth-century developments in Argentina, Chile and Peru.

Differences between Argentina and Chile, on the one hand, and Peru, on the other, are to be expected. Since Argentina and Chile are essentially *Latin* American republics and Peru is a leading representative of *Indo* America, inevitably there has resulted a diversity rather than similarity in their institutions, including their major religious institution, the Catholic church. Ethnic considerations, however, are not the overriding influence that certain determinists still like to contend. In the two countries that pride themselves on having no "Indian problems," Catholicism has evolved through quite different stages, although the evolution has seemed similar occasionally. In the mid-1960's Catholicism as a spiritual, intellectual, and social force in a Chile that bitterly resents consideration in the same terms as the "turbulent, Indian republics" appeared strikingly like the Catholicism of Peru, whose Indians constitute nearly 40 per cent of the population —and this in spite of the fact that at isolated moments Chilean Catholicism seemed to be evolving along significantly different lines from those in Peru.

ARGENTINA: THE EARLY INTERPLAY OF RELIGION AND POLITICS

The stereotype of a ruling triumvirate in Latin America during the nineteenth century made up of the church, the military, and the land-owning oligarchy had some truth for Argentina only during the period of the Juan Manuel Rosas dictatorship (1829–32 and 1835–51). By the mid-1850's, however, a group of liberal, anticlerical ideologues and politicians had gained the upper hand over defenders of traditional Catholic values, and the church had definitely been ousted from the ruling triumvirate. An expanding, state-controlled educational system sought to instil secular values, and, when a Córdoba prelate and a papal nuncio sought in the 1880's to challenge this situation, they were expelled from the country.

Three of the most influential Argentines in the second half of the nineteenth century, the *pensador* Juan Bautista Alberdi and the presidents Bartolomé Mitre (1862–68) and Domingo Faustino Sarmiento (1868–74), were agreed in believing that Argentina had to be restructured according to the norms and values then in vogue in the more progressive countries of Western Europe and in the United States. These three planners of Argentine modernization regarded reduction of the church's temporal power as essential to clearing the way for nation-building projects. And if Alberdi did not realize his dream of populating Argentina largely with non-Catholic immigrants, at least the newcomers who arrived in waves from Europe in the late nineteenth and early twentieth centuries were often religiously indifferent and anticlerical. Indeed, anticlericalism was one of the few concepts which the traditional, *criollo* landowning aristocrats who dominated the Partido Autonomista Nacionalista shared with Argentina's largely middle sector- and immigrant-controlled Unión Cívica Radical. By 1900 *criollos* and immigrants, aristocrats and middle sectors, land-owners and emerging urban businessmen seemed to agree that in the ideal Argentina the church would have to be a relatively unimportant social institution. Above all, it was to be denied the power to impede progress by imposing allegedly archaic, medieval values on the temporal order.

ARGENTINE RELIGION AND POLITICS IN THE FIRST HALF OF THE TWENTIETH CENTURY

Early in the twentieth century the Argentine oligarchy found its power seriously threatened by the rising might of the middle sectors and their party, the Unión Cívica Radical. Increasingly concerned over how long they could keep a majority party out of power through electoral manipulations and fraud, many traditional elements responded approvingly to the right-wing nationalism that prominent Catholic leaders, both clerical and lay, had begun to preach.

Spokesmen of right-wing or reactionary Catholic nationalism were fond of harking back to a golden age that had supposedly existed in the colonial period and, to some degree at least, during the rule of Rosas.[1] It was pictured as a time when society had been structured hierarchically. Each class, it was asserted, had been content in its proper place, in part because citizens had been dedicated to the values of Catholicism and were not consumed by worldly ambitions of rising beyond their proper life stations. In the golden age, moreover, the aristocracy had, supposedly, cared solicitiously for the masses, animated by the church's teachings on charity and paternalism. Solidarity rather than destructive class struggle had characterized social relations.

Deterioration had begun, it was charged, with the advent of massive immigration. Foreigners introduced materialism and initiated a process of social leveling that engendered class struggle. Moreover, the political liberalism attributed to the immigrant influence had, by eroding the structure of the political hierarchy, thrown the scale of human values totally out of balance. Owing to the forces of political liberalism, uncouth and essentially uncivilized individuals were admitted into positions of power and influence. These individuals were incapable of protecting the higher cultural, esthetic, and spiritual values of life. If Argentina was to be redirected toward worthwhile and exalted national goals, the higher values of life would have to be protected through a system of authoritarianism that was to be the political manifestation of a hierarchical social structure.

The real need, as right-wing nationalist and *pensador* Manuel Gálvez saw it, was to spiritualize Argentina, to replace obsessive concern for material gains with intense devotion to the values of Catholicism, which had been uppermost in the colonial and early independence periods but which had subsequently been repudiated by hordes of undesirable immigrants. In one of his best-known works, Gálvez declared:

> Our strong and beautiful Argentina lives these moments in her supreme hour: the hour in which her best intellectuals and truest hearts must seek the spiritualization of the national conscience. . . . The skeptical materialism of today is a recent thing, for it has appeared along with the fever for riches and, as such, has come from Europe. The conquering immigrant through his enormous success in acquiring wealth has introduced into the nation a new concept of life. He brought no other proposition save that of getting rich, and thus it was natural for the Argentines to become contaminated by an over-riding obsession with material considerations. . . . To the memory of my Spanish ancestors . . . I dedicate this book in a concrete act of homage toward the admirable Spain; the Spain where there still endures an intense spiritual life; the profound and marvelous Spain; the Spain which is for us Argentines the ancestral and proud home we should love. . . . We should take the spiritual teachings of Spain as a simple point of departure, as a seed which is transplanted to the moral climate of our country and in it takes root with new vigor and new form.[2]

The true, the good, the noble Argentina, as Gálvez saw the situation, was the *criollo* Argentina before 1853. Therefore, he exhorted *criollo* elements, depicted as still loyal to the values of the past, to forge a true Argentine nation by enforcing the exalted values of bygone days on newly arrived elements. Only through the authoritarian rule of an elite, guided by the institution that remained most steadfastly loyal to the genuine values of human existence, the Catholic church, could so vast a transformation be accomplished.

Other Argentine intellectuals, especially Leopoldo Lugones, maintained that the elite could rely not only upon the church as its ally in civilizing the immigrant hordes; it must rely as well upon the army, which had also maintained a proper concern for hierarchical organization. The military must combine with and perhaps even become the state and proceed then to mold a nation by imposing the values of *criollo* Argentina and eliminating the errors of political liberalism and anticlericalism. Lugones contended that the contempt toward "the country of our elders," manifested by liberally-inclined "sons of foreigners, especially writers and university students," had brought the country to the verge of armed civil conflict. Only the establishment of authoritarian military rule, he asserted, could avert actual civil war in Argentina.[3]

The secular priest Julio Meinvielle was one of the most persistent spokesmen of Argentine right-wing nationalism. The world, as he saw it, had begun to deteriorate about the time of the Protestant Reformation. The Reformation, he stated, "gave free rein to the spirit of greed, to the old sin of avarice" and thus had destroyed the harmonious equilibrium of the Middle Ages, when Christianity repressed the lust for material gain.[4] Argentina's demoralization, according to Father Meinvielle, began around 1853 with attempts to introduce the liberal concepts of the bourgeois world. Men like Manuel Gálvez, Leopoldo Lugones, and Julio Meinvielle agreed that Juan Bautista Alberdi, Bartolomé Mitre, and Domingo Faustino Sarmineto were the great villains and cultural traitors.

The cure, according to Father Meinvielle and his fellow right-wing nationalists, was Catholicism:

> The country as a human reality must be informed by a doctrine and spirit. This, in our country, is either the laicism of liberalism and socialism which leads to communism, or it is Catholicism. The liberal-socialist current has constituted a divisive element within the country; it has weakened the country's conjunctive fabric. . . . Catholicism, on the other hand, has strengthened its men and the fundamental institutions of family, property, and State.[5]

Argentina's *criollo* aristocracy, hard-pressed especially after 1916 by the economically rising and politically dominant middle sectors, naturally found the right-wing nationalism preached by Gálvez, Lugones, Meinvielle and their disciples very much to its liking. Especially from the writings of the priest, the aristocracy (and middle groups that identified with the elite) would draw, during the second third of the twentieth century, theological justification for regaining and tenaciously clinging to political power, through armed force if necessary.

Right-wing Catholic nationalism, developed by a few ideologues and enthusiastically embraced by a beleaguered elite and some middle-sector allies, was an important factor in bringing on the military revolution of 1930 that overthrew Hipólito Irigoyen, the personification of Argentina's somewhat tired radical movement. Installed in the presidency shortly after the fall of Irigoyen, General José Félix Uriburu sought to introduce the corporate state, the political system favored by right-wing nationalists as the means to destroy the majoritarian democracy of liberalism. When Uriburu failed in this endeavor, right-wing nationalists were forced to seek a new political leader. In the mid-1940s some thought he was Juan Domingo Perón.

Shortly after the 1946 election that brought Perón to the presidency, Father Meinvielle saw him as about to liberate the masses from the myths of liberalism, socialism, and communism. This development would present the "national group," that is the *criollo* aristocracy and its partisans, who understood the true traditions of the country and could formulate an integral nationalism, with an opportunity to penetrate the masses and lead them toward acceptance of a genuinely Argentine and Catholic conception of life.[6]

Explaining his hopes and those of many fellow Catholic reactionary nationalists in Argentina, Meinvielle stated:

> The President of the Nation, General Perón, has manifested on repeated occasions that his social policy is as far from capitalism as from communism. In his judgment, the submission of men' to the exploitation of capital and to the exploitation of the State are equally intolerable. He has declared that his policy will be to find a third position which avoids the two preceding evils. . . . General Perón has also insistently stated that in social matters he will inform his actions of government with the doctrines of the papal encyclicals. . . .[7] Today there are only the crude, crass materialistic conception of life, which is Soviet communism, the libertarian materialism, which is the Anglo-Saxon system, and the sane, healthy spiritualism which is the Hispanic-Latin tradition. Perón . . . has rendered homage to the last tradition of life, which has been responsible for the greatness of Western Christendom. And in the moment of crisis for the people of the world he has pointed out the proper path, avoiding the double pitfalls of Soviet and Anglo-Saxon imperialism. In this he merits our most profound approval.[8]

Perón, of course, quickly disappointed Argentina's right-wing nationalists. He placed, from their point of view, too much interest on the material comfort and security of the *descamisados* and in the process began to threaten the oligarchy's political dominance. For a time Perón even seemed intent upon replacing a system of hierarchical paternalism with one of social pluralism within which the masses would possess sufficient power to force from the aristocracy what they considered their due. Social solidarity thus was threatened by the specter of class struggle.

Equally significant in causing a break between Argentina's reactionary nationalists and the administration was the fact that Perón, in seeking a broadly-based program, by 1951 had decided that Catholicism could not be the exclusive element of Argentine nationalism. In this the dictator showed far greater understanding of the realities of Argentine life than did the right-wing Catholic nationalists.

Perón seemed to sense that Argentina could not be forged into a nation by encouraging the defenders of traditional, *criollo* values to impose their viewpoints, *in toto*, on the inhabitants of the country. Anticlericalism, religious indifference, and preoccupation with material gain were values that had been too firmly entrenched, not only among middle sectors of immigrant extraction, but among some members of the landowning aristocracy as well. The whole body of traditions associated with late nineteenth- and early twentieth-century anticlericalism could not readily be dissolved. Thus, Hispanic Catholicism could not constitute, as many right-wing elements demanded, the sole informing spirit of Argentine nationalism. Instead, a nationalistic program had to be devised that would allow the church some social influence but would at the same time incorporate some anticlerical national traditions. Only such a program, it was felt, could constitute the basis of an Argentine nationalism capable of widespread support among diverse sectors throughout the country. Seeking a third position between clericalism and anticlericalism—actually, a most enlightened endeavor—Perón soon hopelessly alienated the extremist champions of right-wing, Catholic nationalism who had at one time seen him as their savior.

As early as 1949 Father Meinvielle and many of his associates began to attack Perón for not embracing an exclusively Catholic nationalism. They rejoiced at Perón's fall from power in 1955 and resumed their demands for an administration that would embrace Catholicism as the all-important, virtually exclusive element of nationalism. Concluding a rather typical peroration in 1956, Meinvielle stated: ". . . in virtue of its transcendancy, Catholic doctrine and spirit must inform and vivify human societies and ultimately political societies."[9]

After the fall of Perón, Catholicism turned out to be incapable of exercising the powerful influence that right-wing nationalists desired. The Perón administration had bitterly divided Argentina between passionate defenders and intemperate critics. The church had evinced an ambivalence vis-à-vis Perón, at first supporting him, later breaking with him. Thus, it could scarcely hope to wield great influence among either supporters or foes of the fallen dictator. Its position was further compromised by the general failure of its leaders to criticize the authoritarian features of Perón's rule that had antagonized the considerable number of Argentines who sincerely believed in liberal democratic principles and who thought that these principles deserved a place in a truly representative program of Argentine nationalism.

More significant still in undermining Catholicism's strength in mid-twentieth-century Argentina was the church's deep involvement in the most agonizing of all the debates waged by the country's intellectuals and statesmen. On the question of whether the true Argentina was the country of pre-immigration times and of *criollo* values (real or imagined) or the country of post-1853, immigrant values (actual or alleged), the church had clearly chosen its side. In identifying itself with *criollo* Argentina, it seriously alienated the post-1853 population elements and all who associated (and associate) with their values. It will be some time before the church can overcome the consequences of identifying with but one of the country's cultural elements in this long-standing debate, which is argued more on emotional than rational grounds. Meanwhile, the church will probably be able to exercise only limited influence in Argentina's quest for an eclectic nationalism that can be broadly shared among all population elements.

CHILEAN RELIGION AND POLITICS IN THE FIRST HALF OF THE TWENTIETH CENTURY

As in Argentina, Chile's Catholic spokesmen in the early twentieth century began to express grave misgivings about liberalism. In many ways, however, their attacks on liberalism were more temperate than those of their Argentine counterparts. Moreover, in condemning liberalism Chilean clerical and right-wing elements in general did not vent their spleen primarily against immigrants in their midst. In Chile immigrants were hardly numerous enough to be charged with primary responsibility for the ills of the country. To a much greater extent than in Argentina, moreover, immigrants had been absorbed into *criollo* Chilean society through business partnerships and marriage with established families. Rather than attacking those in their midst and thus contributing to bitter divisiveness within the state, Chilean conservatives tended to direct their wrath against the errors of foreign lands, such as the United States, and to point out the dangers of introducing alien models into Chile.

Liberalism, its Chilean critics were wont to observe, made sense and produced whatever good it could only when introduced in a milieu characterized by open socio-economic structures, in which stratification was disappearing, urbanization and industrial and commercial revolutions were already well under way, and mass education programs had begun to exercise influence. When introduced into a socially stratified, largely pre-industrial environment and among a mass of illiterates totally unprepared to protect their interests, liberalism, charged its conservative opponents in Chile, served only to foment a degree of social and economic exploitation previously unknown.

By 1920 even Chilean liberals were willing to concede the social evils of classical liberalism. In its 1920 campaign platform Chile's Liberal Alliance, headed by presidential candidate Arturo Alessandri Palma, proposed to correct glaring social problems by introducing a system of government supervision of capital and protection of working classes. A basic assumption of the Liberal Alliance was that the operation of this system would be entrusted to the government bureaucracy in Santiago, made up largely of emerging middle sectors.

In the program that they profferred to alleviate the social evils allegedly spawned by liberalism, Chile's leading Catholic spokesmen generally favored a system of private rather than government paternalism. In their view, paternalism should be administered through company unions and various semi-autonomous associations on a relatively decentralized basis. Politically, this structure would rest ultimately on a corporate state in which unions and other semi-autonomous groups would enjoy functional representation. A system such as this, many of Chile's Catholic leaders felt, was a better means of safeguarding the masses than entrusting them to the mercies of a centralized government bureaucracy dominated by middle sectors. One advantage to be expected from the approach of semi-autonomous associations was that within them the workers would have the chance to develop skills in decision-making processes that would be denied them were they to become anonymous members of a massive, nation-wide labor organization largely controlled from the top by government bureaucrats.

Chile's advocates of the corporate state may well have been justified in doubting the willingness of a bureaucracy consisting largely of newly-risen middle sectors to provide sincere leadership in the quest for better working-class conditions. Emerging middle sectors, not yet secure in their position, aspiring to reach upper-class status and not resigned to their present position on the social ladder, often regarded the lower classes with greater disdain and fear than had the aristoc-racy.[10] They were at least a generation, or much longer, away from a sense of association with the lower mass. Perhaps the endeavor of the aristocracy to establish close ties with the lower classes through a political system based on the corporate state has been improperly maligned by writers of a traditional liberal bias. This endeavor, quite different from that of European fascism, whose major consideration seems to have been the desire of a middle class to protect itself against the rising power of a proletariat, might well have been the soundest possible approach to socio-economic reform in the Chile of the 1920's.

Many of Chile's partisans of the corporate state were high-minded, dignified, and positive in their approach. Among men of this type was Juan Enrique Concha, whose efforts were dedicated to social solidar-ity.[11] To a considerable degree he, and others associated with him in Catholic Action groups, succeeded in persuading the wealthy to give of their money—in building adequate housing facilities for workers—and of their time—in visiting, advising, and establishing warm rela-tions with the poor. A significant portion of the social and labor legis-lation introduced by Concha and his associates in the congressional sessions of 1919 was actually approved in 1924, following pressure from the military, and incorporated the next year into the country's new constitution. Still, the main thrust of the new Chilean social codes came from the Liberal Alliance program of the 1920 compaign. Chile's principal efforts to provide social justice were entrusted to a centralized, middle-sector bureaucracy.

Frustrated by this development, Catholic spokesmen continued to demand the corporate-state approach. As they did so, many became less restrained and less positive than Concha and his followers had been. A fanatic streak appeared in Chile's *criollo* fascism and some of its advocates became as insistent as Argentina's Manuel Gálvez, Leopoldo Lugones and Julio Meinvielle in urging the total suppression of democratic principles, in insisting that only Catholicism could form the basis of an authentic Chilean nationalism, and in demanding the total elimination of such alien influences as Masonry and Judaism.[12]

By no means all prominent Catholic leaders accepted the corporate state and fascism as the ideal socio-politico-economic structure. Some championed a form of humanistic socialism that owed much more to Karl Marx than to fascist ideologues. That many Catholics in the early 1930's were inclined favorably to socialism seriously concerned the conservative priest Raimundo Morales. It was this that led him to assert that a socialist could not be a Catholic.[13]

Other Chilean Catholic intellectuals, both clerical and lay, without embracing socialism began in the mid-1930's to criticize fascism's ideological basis. Jesuits like Jorge Fernández Pradel and Alberto Hurtado, as well as Catholic laymen like Eduardo Frei and other founders of the National Falange (later to develop into the Christian Democratic movement), began to question the notions of paternalism, of a stratified social structure, of a closed society, and of political authoritarianism. They argued that social justice could be provided only through an open, pluralistic society and through political democracy. Thus, even before World War II brought international disgrace to fascism and the idea of the corporate state, some Chilean Catholics had begun seriously to challenge basic fascist tenets. There was a serious split among Chilean Catholic spokesmen, between a group advocating paternalism and socio-political hierarchy and a group defending pluralism and democracy. For a number of years after the war, this split weakened the effectiveness and influence of the Catholic church in Chile.[14]

In the long run, though, this fissure in the unity of the church redounded to the advantage of Chilean Catholicism. Far more than in Argentina, where Catholicism entered into a close relationship with right-wing nationalism, Chile's Catholic opponents of fascism were strong enough to prevent the church from being identified with what, by 1945, had become a discredited cause in most of the world. In planning for the future, Chilean Catholics could utilize the foundation constructed in the 1930's for building a program of social justice, national reform and national renewal that conformed to the fashions prevailing in the postwar era.

From the 1930's on, moreover, the leaders of Chile's incipient

Christian Democratic movement sought to build upon both the Catholic and the nineteenth-century liberal traditions of their country. They did not assert that traditional Latin Catholicism was the only important ingredient of nationalism. Instead they recognized the claims of liberalism as valid for a place in Chilean nationalism. Although they rejected classical economic liberalism, they accepted the political aspects of liberalism and advocated democratic rather than authoritarian usages. To a certain extent Christian Democrats also accepted some of the anticlerical features associated with traditional liberalism as an established part of the national scene that could not be eradicated—anticlericalism in Chile had probably been an even more powerful intellectual force among nineteenth- and early twentieth-century upper-class and middle-sector groups than in Argentina. Christian Democratic leaders accepted, for example, the concept of religious pluralism, avoided direct ties with the church, and sought guidance in the spirit of Christian humanism rather than in sectarian Catholicism.

The willingness of Chile's ecclesiastical leaders by the beginning of the 1960's to accept these concepts and to allow the new political party to remain independent of the church contributed enormously to the notable victories scored by Christian Democrats in the presidential election of 1964 and the congressional elections of the year following. In Chile the tradition of anticlericalism was still strong enough to create serious difficulties for a party that maintained close official bonds with the church. Chilean clergymen at the very highest levels of authority accepted this fact. Few of their Argentine counterparts have been willing to do so.

PERUVIAN RELIGION AND POLITICS IN THE FIRST HALF OF THE TWENTIETH CENTURY

The Catholic church was never so curtailed in Peru on temporal matters as it was by the liberal, anticlerical movements in Argentina and Chile.[15] Nevertheless, the church's intellectual influence had by the late nineteenth century been significantly weakened under the impact of positivism. In the early twentieth century, however, Peruvian Catholicism, as happened elsewhere too in Latin America, began to benefit from a humanistic, Hellenistic reaction to positivist and utilitarian concepts. Leading intellectuals and statesmen became increasingly concerned for protecting the higher human values, by which they meant cultural, moral, esthetic, and spiritual values. Although this move was begun and at first popularized largely by Catholic Peruvians who had fallen away from the church and were convinced that humanism was adequate foundation for the higher values they extolled, a new pattern emerged between, roughly, 1910 and 1930. The leaders of the spiritual reaction to the utilitarian and mechanistic criteria began increasingly to return to the Catholic church, persuaded that if the higher human values were to prevail, a theological underpinning was required.

A Catholic University was established in Lima in 1917. It was primarily concerned with forming an elite that could appreciate, guard, and nourish the most exalted human values. Practical studies were largely eschewed. By the 1930's the new Catholic University had greater social standing than the venerable national institution of San Marcos that, under pressure from the university reform movement begun at Córdoba (Argentina) in 1918, was beginning to open its doors to students of humble origin. In contrast, the Catholic University reserved its places for members of the aristocracy.

During the 1920's, moreover, church leaders, perturbed by heightened social tensions and the dissemination of such radical ideologies as anarchism, socialism, and communism, began to form Catholic Action groups. The primary purpose of Catholic Action was to awaken the social conscience of the upper classes and to induce them to mitigate, through paternalistic measures, the material suffering of the masses and thus re-establish social solidarity.[16]

At the same time the Catholic church in Peru received favorable treatment from the dictator, Augusto B. Leguía, who ruled from 1919 to 1930. A shrewd opportunist who wished to preserve the main features of capitalism and was apprehensive over the rise of extremist movements, Leguía saw the church as an important ally in opposing drastic change. He established a warm relationship with the somewhat naíve and overly receptive Archbishop of Lima Emilio Lissón y Chávez and co-operated fully with Catholic Action programs.

Peruvian Catholicism was further strengthened, temporarily at least, by the vogue of fascism in many intellectual and political circles. The church's flirtation with fascism produced rather different results than in Chile and Argentina. Especially in Chile, criollo fascism had at first exhibited many positive features, in part because it was not directed against the influence of a significant population element within the country. In Argentina, on the other hand, fascism introduced new divisiveness because it was used to justify a crusade against the alleged influence of middle sectors of immigrant origin. In Peru, too, fascism produced divisive and negative results, for the new ideology was injected into an already centuries-old debate concerning identity. The crisis of identity in Peru did not involve *criollo* vs. immigrant values but centered upon the clash between indigenous and Spanish cultures. Enthusiastically embraced by Hispanophiles, fascism in Peru soon came to be associated with strong anti-Indian prejudices.

In part because of the intimate relationship between Peruvian fascism and Catholicism, the Catholic University became one of the most important intellectual centers for the dissemination of fascist ideology.[17] The views of the university's student leaders were clearly manifested at the Second Ibero-American Congress of Catholic Students, which met in Lima in 1939. In their statements the Peruvian representatives emphasized the need to return to the glorious traditions of motherland Spain, which had at last found a modern defender in General Franco. In exalting hispanism, one speaker claimed "Spanish culture is so infinitely superior to that of the Indians of Peru that the Indian culture has to be destroyed to make possible the introduction of morality and progress." The speaker continued:

> Hispanidad represents the permanent spiritual community of the Hispanic peoples and is based upon the values of Catholicism, hierarchy, and the brotherhood of Iberian peoples. . . . This brotherhood obliges us to fight for the social order of Christian justice, rejecting as equally bad liberal capitalism and Marxist collectivism.[18]

The essence of Peruvian fascism is also clearly revealed by some of the pronouncements of the eminent historian José de la Riva Agüero during the 1930's. With justification, Riva Agüero wrote: "I enjoy the honor of having raised in Peru the cry against the pseudo-democratic lies, the cry in favor of fascist Italy and the true concept of social distributive justice."[19] Having returned to Peru from a self-imposed exile after the fall of Leguía, Riva Agüero began—in tones that were occasionally wild and ranting—to denounce a capitalism that "New York City, the revolting center of international Jewry," had helped impose upon the world.[20] Democracy and liberalism, the historian said, led inevitably to communism. Although for many years a freethinker, Riva Agüero ceremoniously announced his return to the church in 1932 and began to preach that only Catholicism and fascism could contain the communist menace. "Up with Catholicism," he wrote, "up with the corporate state and fascism, with order, hierarchy, and authoritarianism." Riva Agüero developed a line of reasoning that had much in common with the pronouncements of Gálvez, Lugones, and Meinvielle in Argentina:

> Liberalism, capitalism, and democracy, all based on utilitarianism and materialism, destroyed the hierarchy of classes and values and led to the reign of mediocrity and in general so befouled human existence that they spawned communism as a reaction and supposed remedy. The only solution is to return to the medieval, Catholic, Hispanic tradition as now embodied in facism.[21]

Catholic fascism in Peru waxed increasingly vitriolic and fanatical, in part because of the extremism of its foes. Marxian socialism and related movements during the 1920's proclaimed a message of virulent anticlericalism, if not of actual atheism, advocated a leveling social revolution, and the imposition by force upon coastal, westernized Peru of the allegedly superior Andean or Indian way of life.[22] The Andean, Indian way of life was invariably identified with socialism by its proponents.

An active leader in the Peruvian socialist-Indiophile crusade of the 1920's was Luis E. Valcárcel, a gifted and indefatigable student of Indian culture who more recently has attenuated some of his youthful views. At the time, Valcárcel insisted that only the Indian, clinging allegedly to pre-Columbian socialist practices and values, could redeem and regenerate Peru. He saw the future not in terms of mestizaje, the synthesis of European and Indian cultural and ethnic elements, but in the imposition by the Indian of his civilization, pure and uncontaminated, on all Peru and all Latin America, or, as he preferred to call it, Indo America. "European culture," he wrote, "has never truly affected the Indian. Peru is Indian and will be Indian. . . . The only true Peru is Indian Peru."[23]

In the opinion of Valcárcel and his numerous socialist associates, exploitation of the Indian by decadent and pseudo-Peruvian elements, with which the Catholic church was identified, could be terminated

only by revolutionary violence. Consequently, these socialist Indio-
philes frankly advocated the forceful elimination of the institutions
and even of much of the human resources of white and mestizo
Peru.[24]

In part because of the bitter extremism of their adversaries, Catholic spokesmen of fascism for a time turned their backs to the Indian,
thereby repudiating a long tradition of church-encouraged paternalistic protection of the native. Even those churchmen who remained
steadfast in their desire to aid the Indian refrained from advocating
a system of reform based upon social pluralism. Peru's problems, they
felt, could only be solved by providing a tutelary, master-ward relationship through which a traditional upper class would care for the
natives, who were felt to be incapable yet for years and generations to
come of equal participation with groups already fully initiated in the
workings of westernized society.

Catholics in Peru were less assertive than Chilean Catholics in
attacking the social and political philosophy of fascism, and they did
little to prepare the way for the rise of a Christian-oriented movement advocating social pluralism and democracy. Still, the church's
consistent tendency, at least until the mid-1940's, to identify itself
with many features of fascist ideology did not redound so seriously to
the disadvantage of Catholicism as did the church's long-sustained
association with fascism in Argentina. The values reviled by Argentina's Catholic fascists were defended by a large and articulate element in society, an element that was politically sophisticated and able
effectively to strike back against its critics. In Peru the element in the
population that could most logically have been expected to react with
anger toward the position assumed by the church on the issue of
identity was the Indian mass of the sierra. But the Indians had not
yet been politicized. Unaware of what was transpiring in society, they
were oblivious to the racial-cultural prejudices involved in the association of Catholicism with fascism and hispanism. And the active elements in Peruvian society by and large felt rather grateful to the
church for having helped protect them against the imminent danger
posed by Indiophile socialists.

By the mid-1940's the extremism of socialist Indianism and fascist-
tinged hispanism was happily subsiding, as a majority of reputable
intellectuals began to share a consensus view that the true national destiny of Peru lay in mestizaje. No longer faced with the attempt of its

foes to use the Indians to destroy it, the church resumed its concern for the protection of the Indians, becoming thereby once more a national institution rather than the servant of a particular interest group.

With the matter no longer presented in terms requiring their liquidation and the total suppression of their way of life, Peru's westernized populace was to some degree ready to face up to the Indian problem and to proceed, even as the church had begun to do once more toward the gradual integration of the native in the national existence. In this changing intellectual milieu, the church reflected the thinking of a majority of the already politicized Peruvians, as it had in the 1930's when it had spearheaded resistance to the Indiophile movements. By the 1960's with a new spirit of moderation wide spread, the church and civilian elements were prepared to co-operate in resolving the identity problem in Peru, not by insisting on the unilateral exaltation of one ethnic and cultural element, but by proceeding toward *mestizaje* and preparing the Indian to participate meaningfully in a racially and culturally united republic.

Neither in Chile nor in Peru in the mid-1960's is the Catholic church seriously handicapped by association with a minority, extremist movement. Unlike the Argentinian situation after the fall of Perón, Catholicism in Chile and Peru seems to be in a position to exercise some influence as a new generation of political leaders dedicates itself to national modernization.

THE CATHOLIC CHURCH IN CHILE AND PERU
SINCE THE EARLY 1960's

In Chile and Peru, as indeed throughout Latin America and the world, intellectuals have long debated whether reform can best be brought about by the imposition of a new system from above or by seeking to alter the values, to expand the horizons, and to encourage the full realization of the potential of the individuals who comprise the broad base of society. At all times and in all places there have been those who have opted for the instantaneous approach to reform. Reformers of this type have ignored an important element of political development. It is the development in previously silent and anonymous individuals of skills and sophistication in decision-making processes vitally affecting their own personal destiny and sometimes that of the nation.

Many church leaders of Chile and Peru seem to favor the instantaneous approach to reform.[25] Without stressing the need to develop the productive and political skills of the individuals who make up the lower classes, they suggest that the imposition of a new system, the essential feature of which is the redistribution of wealth, can quickly solve social problems, end sacrifice, and banish privation. They appear to be heedless of the argument recently advanced by Mexican novelist Carlos Fuentes:

> . . . economic development . . . and . . . social change through decree are doomed to fail without an awakened cultural consciousness that changes men so that men may change things. Only a cultural mutation can assure that our solutions will grow from the core to the surface instead of being applied from the outside on the basis of this or that prestigious model. Only a cultural mutation will be able to affect the vertical stance of power that today reduces the social participation of individuals, groups, and masses to mere gestures.[26]

The role of the church in working toward reform and modernization is complex and varied. Happily, by no means all Catholic spokesmen have been beguiled into supporting promises of a quick realization of a utopian society through the redistribution of wealth. Many prominent church figures have, in fact, begun to make important contributions to the political development of individuals at the base of society. It is this aspect of church activity that is new, exciting, and promising in Chile and Peru.

Working through various organizations, Bishop Manuel Larraín of Talca in south-central Chile had for a number of years sought to enhance the technical knowledge and political sophistication of rural laborers so that they might form effective and autonomous bargaining groups within society. The approach of many other clergymen to the problems of agrarian reform has similarly indicated awareness of the values of political development.[27]

Related endeavors have for some time been underway in Peru. In the archdiocese of Cuzco the church, under the leadership of Archbishop Carlos María Jurgens, has divested itself of much land, selling it at approximately half its market value to rural laborers with low-interest, ten-year credit provisions.[28] Furthermore, an Instituto de Educación Rural, in which Father Iván Pardo has provided inspiring leadership, has trained hundreds of young men and women of humble rural origin to play an important part in agrarian reform. Already the Instituto has performed significant work along the coast as well as in the sierra and *selva* (the semi-jungle interior east of the Andes).

Especially in the sierra, with its large Indian population, Peruvian clergymen have co-operated with United States Maryknoll priest Daniel McClellan in establishing credit and consumer cooperatives. In the past it had always been assumed that the Indian possessed no money and was therefore hopelessly outside the market economy. Father McClellan and his associates have proved conclusively that once the Indian's confidence has been won he can, after all, produce money to deposit in cooperatives. As a result, throughout the sierra, the Indians have begun in the mid-twentieth century to gain access for the first time to credit facilities and to find the means of acquiring, often at below-market cost, the goods vitally necessary for the raising of living standards. All the while they have learned how to control the associations through which these procedures are carried out. Largely owing to the activities of the clergy, the credit cooperative movement in Peru at the beginning of 1964 was established on a larger scale than in any other Latin American country.[29]

By mid-1964 a year-old radio school in Puno was reaching thousands of Indian inhabitants of the region. Established by Maryknoll priests with the strong backing of the Peruvian hierarchy, the radio school broadcasts in Spanish and in Indian dialects of Quechua and Aymara, offering its listeners lessons in reading and writing, general culture, hygiene and sanitation, and modern farming methods. Listeners interested in advanced agricultural methods and implements described on the programs can visit a model farm maintained on the outskirts of Puno and, if impressed by what they see, purchase on credit, through a church-initiated cooperative, tools, seeds, livestock, and virtually anything else required to improve their farms and homes.

In other ways as well clergymen have shown their concern for political development and have contributed to the formulation of a valuable ideological basis for modernization. Peruvian Jesuit Romeo Luna Victoria, Chilean Jesuit Renato Poblete and the Belgian Jesuit Roger E. Vekemans, who has spent many fruitful years in Chile, have been in the vanguard of those who realize that modernization can be attained only through the cultural mutation of the individual, not through experimentation with new systems imposed from above.[30]

The new approaches of some Chilean and Peruvian churchmen

have received powerful impetus from many of the policies adopted by
the Second Vatican Council. Perhaps of greatest moment in this
respect is the tendency of the revitalized church to stress the role of
the individual conscience in the attainment of salvation. This concept
is already producing revisions of attitudes in many Latin American
Catholic circles. In the past, the church tended to assure the masses
of salvation through the paternalistic solicitude and supernatural
powers of a priestly class and to attach very little importance to the
natural virtue and initiative of the individual. Here, then, is an important field in which theological modernization has had an important
relationship to the attainment of social, political, and economic modernization through self-improvement of the masses.

    In other fields, theological modernization is beginning to be reflected
in fresh viewpoints about temporal development. One example of
this is the changing attitudes of the church toward foreign capital.

    Throughout the first half of the century, traditionalist Catholic
spokesmen generally were ambivalent in their response to foreign
investment. They feared it because they were apprehensive that in
its wake might come the materialistic cultural influences of such
countries as the United States. On the other hand they welcomed it
as the means of bringing about a painless economic development in
the course of which a native bourgeois sector might, with luck and
proper guidance, avoid being contaminated by having to develop its
own acquisitive, capitalistic, "Protestant and Jewish" traits. Early in
the twentieth century Francisco Antonio Encina of Chile and Joaquín
Capelo of Peru were among the several prominent intellectuals of
their countries who warned that the prevalence of this second
approach to foreign capital could lead to the permanent economic
inferiority of their countrymen and make of their lands the colonies
of foreign imperialists.[31]

    As of the 1960's a large number of churchmen seem to have reached
agreement with Encina and Capelo. They are resolutely seeking to
impart economic expertise and production-oriented virtues to men of
the once ignored lower classes so that they can then contribute to their
countries' drives toward development. No longer do most churchmen
appear to assume that material appetites and the economic skills
necessary to satisfy them endanger the souls of the masses.

    Few of Chile's churchmen today would agree with the assertions
advanced in 1932 by an eminent Conservative party member and

presidential nominee: ". . . the suffering and the mean circumstances which beset the poor and which the sociologists say are wrong, we Christians say are proper. . . . For in our concept as Christians, poverty is the estate most rich in the means through which man realizes his eternal destiny."[32] Nor would many Peruvian clergymen express agreement with the 1937 avowal of the then Archbishop of Lima, Pedro Pascual Farfán: "Poverty is the most certain road to eternal felicity. Only the state that succeeds in making the poor appreciate the spiritual treasures of poverty can solve its social problems."[33] In both countries today's church leaders want both reasonable material comfort and political participation for the masses. They are not prepared to condone either economic or political inferiority. They appear to concur with the thesis of Seymour Martin Lipset in the book *Political Man* (1960) that instability in emerging nations results from poverty and above all from glaring inequality.

At the present moment its response to the population problem may be the most glaring weakness of the church in its attempt to contribute to modernization and economic as well as political development in Chile and Peru and throughout the underdeveloped world.

If in Chile and Peru the people, especially the poor, are not given and encouraged by all influence-wielding media to use effective means to curtail family size, then it seems there can be no tangible, material, outwardly visible reform in the foreseeable future. The only possible reform will be inward, as people learn in resignation to suffer and endure in conditions that are basically inhuman.

Recent surveys conducted in Chile and Peru reveal that nearly 60 per cent of upper-class and more than 40 per cent of middle-class women already employ effective means of family limitation.[34] It is no longer the Latin American male, with his notorious *machismo* complex impelling him to heedless propagation, who will decide the future demographic trends in Latin America. New methods of birth control are taking this decision out of the hands of Latin American men and entrusting it instead to the women. Possibly none of the feminist movements in the annals of history has produced so profound an effect in elevating women to a role of equality and in helping them to achieve their political development through the exercise of meaningful power in decision-making processes of vital significance.

The official stance of the church is not interfering seriously with upper-and middle-class women as they decide upon the issue of family limitation. Unfortunately, however, the position of the church does still interfere with the effective dissemination of birth-control information and means among the poor. So far as tangible, practical effects are concerned, then, the church appears to be discriminating against the poor. In fact, it may well be contributing to a situation in which, all other things being equal, the poor will become poorer as the rich become proportionately richer.

Theoretically, if the rate of population increase can be substantially reduced, the governments of Chile, Peru, and other Latin American countries can invest in development projects the huge sums of money that would otherwise have to be channeled into social programs and services. However, unless certain basic structural changes of a social, political, and economic nature take place, there is no guarantee that the resources saved as a result of population control will be productively invested. Thus population control will not automatically solve development problems; it is no panacea. Without it, though, there is little likelihood that effective strides can be taken toward modernization and development.

In Chile, the church appears tacitly to be accepting the birth-control clinics that have appeared in Santiago since 1964, perhaps in the hope that these will serve to reduce the country's shockingly high abortion rate. Moreover, few militant objections were raised when Chile, early in 1967, served as the host nation for the eighth conference of the International Planned Parenthood Federation. In Peru, on the other hand, clerical opposition to effective family planning remains more overt. The church's position was expressed a few years ago by the Cardinal-Archbishop of Lima, Juan Landázuri Ricketts:

> In the problem of demographic growth, the church confides in the providence of God Who will not permit the lack of material necessities for His creatures. . . . To those who propose radical remedies contrary to the natural law, the church insists upon the Christian solution to the problems based upon an international sense of responsibility and a spirit of solidarity.[35]

Except in the matter of birth control the clergymen of Peru, who in this respect may unhappily be adhering more closely to the papal encyclical Humanae Vitae than certain Chilean counterparts, have in recent years been as advanced in their social programs as the clerics of Chile. Archbishop Carlos María Jurgens of Cuzco, for example, has been as zealous a land reformer as the Cardinal-Archbishop of

Santiago, Raúl Silva Henríquez; José Dammert Bellido, Bishop of Cajamarca in Peru's northern sierra, has been as much the eloquent, dynamic spokesman of social justice[36] as was Chilean Bishop Manuel Larraín of Talca before an automobile accident brought a tragic end to his life; Peruvian Jesuit Romeo Luna Victoria has been as much in the forefront of reform programs as Renato Poblete and his fellow Chilean Jesuits; and Peruvian Catholics have produced a mass of literature advocating substantial change and modernization that matches in quality if not yet quite in quantity similar works published in Chile.[37]

By and large, churchmen tend to be as much in the vanguard of change in Peru as in Chile. Sometimes their pronouncements are less bold than those of Chilean clergymen, and it may be true that the vanguard has advanced less far in Peru than in Chile. But this is a result of the *de facto* backwardness at the present moment, according to Western criteria at least, of the Indians who constitute nearly 40 per cent of the Peruvian populace, as well as of the glaring lack of technically-trained specialists, which makes social change more complex and difficult than in more racially integrated and better-educated Chile.

Whether in the long run the Catholic church in Chile and Peru will achieve notable and lasting results in its role of social reformer remains to be seen. For the moment it is significant that some churchmen in these countries are taking the lead in encouraging individual political development. Moreover, they have entered into a mutually advantageous interaction with lay political figures. And this interplay resembles the give-and-take of equals more than it does a tutelary kind of relationship. The church in these two republics may emerge from this process of change stronger than at any time in the twentieth century, although its strength will not lie in an ability to exercise direct temporal power. Rather, strength will flow from the church's acceptance of a role as one of many autonomous and semi-autonomous groups working co-operatively for the spiritual and political development of individuals and for the economic modernization of Latin America.

Perhaps in time the church in Argentina will accept such a role. It may then be able to take a constructive part in the development of that troubled land and to facilitate rather than impede the emergence of broadly-shared national values.

5: TIME, PERSONS, DOCTRINE: THE MODERNIZATION OF THE CHURCH IN CHILE

Henry A. Landsberger

In the first part of this chapter, we shall analyze the onset of change in the church. We shall also make some speculative generalizations concerning the persons who have stimulated and protected the process of *aggiornamento*. We hope thereby to complement Vallier's very thorough analysis of the stages and conditions of change. We shall deal with the "when" and "who," while Vallier dealt with the "what," "how," and "why" of change. Illustrations will be taken from several countries, in part as described by the contributors to this volume, so that this chapter highlights some of the major conclusions immanent in the book.

In the second part of this chapter, we shall deal with the position of the hierarchy of one country, Chile, relative to the social doctrine of the church. We hope thereby to complement chapters to follow, those by Msgr. McGrath and Abbé Houtart, who deal with doctrinal and structural problems in Latin America as a whole. Pike describes what has occurred in the evolution of lay political thought in Chile; we shall focus on the evolution of the social ideas of the church hierarchy.

THE PROCESS OF CHANGE: TIME AND PERSONS

Concerning the timing of change in the Latin American church, perhaps the most important point to be made is that it began, at least in some nations far earlier than is generally thought. One possible indicator of the onset of change would be the recognition that the new industrial working classes were assailed by special evils needing new solutions. In Chile we find traces of such recognition in the 1880's, i.e., even before Pope Leo XIII issued the first social encyclical, *Rerum Novarum*.

Compared with most of Latin America, Chile, throughout the nineteenth century, possessed an outstandingly vigorous system of Catholic charity,[1] in the form of hospitals and schools, although at that time these served mostly the middle and upper classes. But a different kind of charity had also appeared: The "Society of Workers of St. Joseph," founded in 1883, and the so-called "*patronatos*," the first of which was established in 1890. They were, on the one hand, mutual aid societies in which, as the term implies, workers helped workers. But they were also educational institutions in which workers were no longer the object of charity on the part of interested members of the upper class, but the object of educational efforts. This education was no longer confined to matters of theological doctrine and ritual; it included the social doctrine of the church, then in the process of formulation, as well as "moral" and conventional secular education. While it appears completely paternalistic from today's vantage point, at that time it represented a very important, though subtle, step forward. For it carried the implication that, while the worker might now be a dependent, untutored, and immoral child, he possessed the potential for being educated and becoming moral. He was, therefore, basically the same kind of human being as members of the upper class themselves. The same shift in ideology had taken place in Western Europe only very little earlier.[2]

The idea of mutual aid societies and *patronatos*—like many ideas since—was imported to Chile from the Catholic south and west of Europe: Belgium, in this instance. But it was far from an isolated, barren import in Chile. For the 1890's also marked the beginning of the use of the professorial chair of social economics in the Law School of the Catholic University for purposes of social research and action.[3] This was to result some twenty years later—in the decade 1910–20— in very serious discussions in the Conservative party over the most appropriate kind of legislation concerning trade union structure and recognition for Chile.

As Morris emphasizes, the motivation behind this discussion was in part how to write a law that would enable control over the working class to be maintained,[4] but Pike, in chapter IV of this volume, has drawn attention to the fact that this was not the sole motivation. Humanitarianism, based on Christian doctrine and the social encyclicals in particular, played a role. It is in any case undeniable that in the middle of the second decade of this century, Catholic trade unions of transport workers, white-collar employees, workers in the needle trades, and railway workers were being established by two priests, Daniel Marino and the famous Guillermo Viviani, assisted by a substantial group of young laymen. Magnet makes it quite clear that the vast majority of the Catholic laity was either oblivious to the suffering of the new working class or decidedly hostile to any efforts to ameliorate it. But equally, there is no doubt that the germ of progressivism is to be found in the 1880's and 1890's, and that it grew slowly and steadily thenceforth.

The chapters by Pike and de Kadt show by way of contrast that concern with the "social problem" did not become serious in either Peru or Brazil until the late 1950's, although a very rapid reorientation has taken place in certain sectors of these churches in the years since then. The Chilean case is therefore not the rule. But neither does it stand in isolation. Although usually overlooked, there were progressive as well as conservative trends in the church in Mexico from the very beginning of this century. It would be wrong to associate the Mexican church exclusively with the counterrevolutionary activities of the Cristeros in the mid 1920's. Between 1903 and 1909, a Christian social action movement was organizing so-called "social weeks" (semanas sociales), again an institution taken over from Catholic Western Europe, as well as congresses of various kinds to discuss social and specifically rural social problems.[5] The movement was opposed to the infamous tiendas de raya (stores operated by hacienda owners on hacienda grounds, where peones were obliged to buy). It sought to establish production and consumption cooperatives for small landholders. Committees of lawyers were formed to defend Indian interests and to stimulate the expansion of education. Admittedly, more radical measures, such as land reform, were not envisaged by these Catholics, any more than they were by most groups deemed liberal at the time. There was heavy emphasis on the moral uplift of the peasant rather than on changes in the institutions under which the peasant lived. Nevertheless, a voice of protest inspired by church doctrine was heard very early in Mexico, and, inadequate though they may seem today, there were efforts to improve the lot of the oppressed.

For the academic interested in the process of institutional change, the histories of the different Latin American churches point up an interesting problem: when, if ever, can change be said to have a beginning point? And may it not be that new movements with traditional, even reactionary ideologies, have modernizing effects when they move the church into taking an explicit view of society? This point could be raised, for example, in connection with Jackson de Figueiredo's ideology in Brazil in the mid-twenties. Several of the fascist or fascistoid Catholic movements included, besides their more objectionable characteristics, elements of purification and of social dedication, as well as a critique of prevalent *laissez faire* tendencies. Such ideologies, which moved the church to concern with the total structure of society, could be interpreted, in part, as a step toward a more complete ideological change at a later stage.

Concerning the participants in the process of change, several generalizations seem to be justified. Perhaps these should be regarded as hypotheses to guide future study rather than as generalizations, and we are aware of the need for exceptions. Nevertheless, we can state that modernization movements within the church do not prosper unless and until they have the good will of a person highly placed in the hierarchy, generally a bishop or archbishop. Movements may *begin* without such sponsorship, but they do not prosper. This is inevitable in view of the strongly hierarchical nature of the church, which gives bishops very wide latitude over the activities and even the location of priests in their episcopal territory. The outstanding examples of such protectors are, of course, Bishops Dom Eugênio Sales and Dom Helder Camara in Brazil and the late Bishop Manuel Larraín of Talca in Chile. These men encouraged and permitted progressive movements to flourish, whereas the absence of such sponsorship has had tragic results in Colombia.

The support of such highly placed individuals is never, of course, as unequivocal as hoped for by the lower level progressives who so badly need it. It cannot be. The bishop must remain influential as well as progressive. Without enough general influence to protect the progressives, the bishop's progressivism would be of little use: the high-level protector must maintain firm links with his more neutral colleagues.

One of the unresolved puzzles of the process of change is how it happens that a generally small minority of progressive bishops have been able to move a much larger body of neutrals and even strongly conservative prelates. In Chile, it is known that a progressive papal nuncio played a part in the 1950's. But this was really after the main battle had been (however tenuously) won in the forties. It is also thought that the progressive bishops have been helped by their being generally impressive as persons: Widely traveled, knowledgeable, evidently moved by humanitarian concerns, and generally radiating a feeling of love and acceptance, even toward adversaries. But the influence process remains a mystery.

In addition to the need to remain close enough, in their public position at least, to the neutrals in the upper hierarchy to maintain influence, there is a second reason for the sometime cautious progressivism of the protectors. The lower-level progressives have generally begun in one or another of the Catholic Action organizations and therefore have been explicitly under episcopal control. But they usually have moved in the direction of greater independence. The hierarchy, whatever its orientation, is bound to feel some personal ambivalence during this process and hence lose some of its sympathy, even if the process is recognized to be inevitable and, indeed, beneficial and vitally necessary. Finally, sympathetic episcopal protectors are apt to appear passive at times because the almost inevitable divergences within the progressive movement make it difficult for the protector to be active without appearing partisan.

The second generalization concerning the makers of modernization is that in this sphere, as in others, university youth often spearhead the drive toward modernization. This is well brought out in the chapter by de Kadt in the case of Brazil and by Pike for Argentina and Chile.

Chile is particularly interesting in this respect. The first move to the left of the younger generation seemed to have begun already at the level of the *colegio* (high school). The generation of Msgr. Manuel Larraín and Fr. Alberto Hurtado, which made history in the forties and fifties, first became concerned about social problems and politics in the period 1916–20, as a result of the deep and affectionate relationship they formed then and sustained later with their teacher and spiritual guide, Fr. Fernando Vives, S.J., in the *Colegio de San Ignacio*. This aristocratic and, at that time, not generally progressive boarding school was run by the Jesuits, and to it the Catholic elite of Chile sent its sons.[6] The more socially involved position that the National Association of Catholic University Students (ANEC) took from 1928 onward under the aegis of its spiritual advisor, Oscar Larson; and the formation of various leagues, secretariats, and parties in the early 1930's (well before the founding of the predecessor of the Christian Democratic party in 1938) cannot be understood without going back to the second decade of the century and the inspiration which Fr. Vives, Fr. Fernández Pradel, and the Rev. Viviani gave to their then adolescent students.

This brings us to our third generalization and this concerns the lay groups who play such an important role in the transformation of the church. These frequently have, in their early years, lower-level clerical mentors who are to be distinguished from higher-level protectors. These advisors are frequently from one of the orders. Jesuits have been notable in Chile and Brazil, and in the latter country, the Dominicans have also played an important role. These priests are often more radical and, therefore, more vulnerable, than the episcopal protectors of the modernization movement. The role of these counselors—*assistentes* and *asesores*—is well brought out by de Kadt in his description of the Catholic University Youth Movement in Brazil. The most famous—but by no means unique—example is the tragic young Colombian priest Camilo Torres Restrepo. We have already mentioned the most famous names in early Chilean development: Vives, Fernández, and Hurtado; later came Vekemans, a Belgian Jesuit.

While these are the best known, there have been many others, often priests who were not members of orders, who fulfilled the same crucial role of legitimating innovative activity and reducing the spiritual stress of those engaged in it. They have also contributed through their administrative and policy formulating skills.

A fourth and final generalization is that innovators in the church, whether lay or clerical, tend to come from a social class background which is at least upper-middle class and, frequently, from the aristocracy.

This was evidently the case of Msgr. Manuel Larraín Errázuriz, the late Bishop of Talca, in Chile. But perhaps as frequent is a more complex situation. The innovators may tend to be from families whose status and fortunes are fluid. In some instances, they have been downwardly mobile. Such was the case of the family of Father Alberto Hurtado, whose parents, of well-known families, were themselves economically in relatively humble circumstances but were connected with many persons high in Santiago's political and social circles. Or the mobility may have been, as in the case of several leaders of the Chilean Christian Democratic party, in an upward direction: Some fathers have been prosperous immigrants and some married aristocratic wives.

There are exceptions to this rule of high social origin or mobility. Chile's first Cardinal, Archbishop José María Caro, came from a quite modest background and was an important, though apparently erratic, participant in the process of change.

In 1938, upon the defeat of the Conservative candidate and the electoral triumph of the Popular Front (a coalition of the Radical, Communist and Socialist parties), the new Archbishop issued a statement expressing his personal confidence in the new Radical President and criticizing the wealthy for their neglect of the working classes, especially the peasants. Since Catholics had regarded the Popular Front with great abhorrence and fear, Mgsr. Caro's stand provoked a furor among them.

While the Archbishop did not exert his full authority to protect the progressives during their bitter struggle against extinction in the early and mid-forties, once again, in the late forties and early fifties, he spoke out in their favor, particularly in connection with trade union activities. Conservatives disliked him sufficiently strongly that rumors recurred in Chile that pressure was being put on the Holy See to replace him. Support for our hypothesis comes from the attribution of his occasional failures to uphold the progressives to his modest background. It was said that he was somewhat open to flattery and pressure from the aristocracy.

It is also interesting to note that the first Chilean Archbishop to take a decisive step toward separating the Chilean church from identification with the Conservative party was the scion of an old and aristocratic family. Msgr. Crescente Errázuriz, in 1922, announced that the church "cannot be held accountable for the act of any political party, nor does it seek to influence them. It leaves them completely free and in turn demands absolute and complete independence for its own activities."[7]

Perhaps the high social origins of the innovators is merely a reflection of the fact that before modernization, all those who are active and influential participants in church affairs—whether in a progressive direction or not—come from the upper strata of society. Low mobility in society at large is likely to be reflected in each of its institutions, including the church. Nevertheless, it is worthwhile to note that in so hierarchical an institution as the church and in a relatively traditional society, the impulse toward modernization has come not only from those whose institutional position is elevated, but from those whose personal, social, and familial situation has also been well above average.

NATIONAL HIERARCHIES AND THE DEVELOPMENT OF SOCIAL DOCTRINE: THE CASE OF CHILE

In the chapters by Msgr. McGrath, Abbé Houtart, and Dr. Shaull, the reader will find the topic of doctrinal change and of current doctrinal position approached from different points of view. Msgr. McGrath focuses particularly on the events of the Second Vatican Council and its partial roots in, as well as its later effects on, the position of Catholicism in Latin America. Abbé Houtart examines in greater detail those social changes in Latin America to which the church is responding and which it in turn influences. Dr. Shaull notes the differences in response made by the most advanced sectors of the church in Brazil as compared with that of Chile.

To complement these papers which deal with Latin America as a whole, it may be of interest to focus upon doctrinal changes over time in one country, Chile.

In Chile, unlike most other Latin American countries, Leo XIII's *Rerum Novarum* ("On the condition of labor") was given at least some diffusion. The primate of Chile, Msgr. Mariano Casanova, Archbishop of Santiago, issued a special pastoral in 1891 consisting substantially of quotations from, and praise for, *Rerum Novarum*. Insofar as there was a personal note, it was conservative:

> Superficial minds easily convince themselves of the apparent injustice which they believe to have discovered in the providential fact that men equal before nature are unequal in social condition. And this false belief is beginning to engender a pernicious antagonism between rich and poor, employers and proletarians, those favored by fortune and those disinherited by her.

The "divinely effective remedy" for any social ill is taught, according to Msgr. Casanova, by the Evangelicum: That the rich "divest themselves" of some of their wealth, and that the poor "resign themselves to their fate." He inveighs strongly against strikes, and while mentioning the desire of Pope Leo XIII that there be associations of workingmen, Msgr. Casanova states only that he expects "later, when circumstances permit, to insist on the practical manner in which the desires of the Holy Father and his teachings can be utilized by means of associations."[8] The elaboration promised seems never to have been issued. Even the calling of the "First Social Catholic Congress" in 1910 by the Archbishop of Santiago, Msgr. González Eyzaguirre, did not result in further pastorals.

The next public statement did not in fact come until 1921, thirty years after the first. By this time much blood had been shed in the industrial cities of the center of Chile and in the nitrate mines of the north. Much debate had taken place within Catholic political circles over labor legislation. The Conservative party, which was the Catholic Right and indeed the only political emanation of Catholicism, was becoming increasingly concerned over possible deviations within its ranks, particularly among the young. Nevertheless, despite this sensitivity of powerful laymen, Archbishop Errázuriz issued an extremely vigorous pastoral dealing with social problems.[9] He painted a pathetic picture of the plight of both the urban and the rural worker, and attacked the rich who, "in great numbers, do not know the noble feeling of comforting the unfortunate, but instead seem to cling more passionately to their material wealth, the more of it they have."

> To make more certain that the proletarian receives the share of wealth to which he is entitled, and since individual action is generally impotent to bring efforts of great importance to a successful conclusion, the worker seeks associations which . . . facilitate the defense and the recognition of the rights of the proletarian. . . . [The] church, his natural protector, is pleased to favor the formation of associations of workers which put them in a position where they can defend themselves, help each other, and protect themselves against the cruelty of heartless employers.

This statement was, in many ways, more vigorous in its attack on the upper classes and more explicit in its defense of the right to organize, not only than *Rerum Novarum*, but also than *Quadragesimo Anno*, which would be issued ten years later, and other Chilean pronouncements for some time to come. Interestingly enough, it was a spontaneous act in the sense that it was not an exegesis of any papal pronouncement. But Archbishop Errázuriz was ahead of his time and resigned two years later.

Eleven years later, in 1931—this time indeed in response to an initiative from the Holy See, Pius XI's *Quadragesimo Anno*—the first collective pastoral was issued by the Chilean episcopate, under the title "The true and only solution of the social question."[10] This consisted very substantially of lengthy quotations from the new papal encyclical.[11] But in the Chilean context this represented a stance of some ideological independence from the Conservative party. For the pastoral repeated and defended the controversial claims of Leo XIII and Pius XI that the church had every right to intervene in social questions. Nor did the Chilean bishops tone down the encyclical's condemnations of private greed; of the *laissez faire* doctrine; of nineteenth-century liberalism; and of the theory that the only function of the state is that of protector of individual rights and interest. Naturally, the pastoral also summarized Pope Pius' lengthy attack on communism and socialism as well as his detailed defense of private property. But with respect to the latter, the bishops also referred to the state's limited right to expropriate property under certain circumstances.

The section in the Chilean pastoral devoted to trade unions was, however, considerably more brief and appears more negative in tone than *Quadragesimo Anno*. While accepting in principle the right to form associations,[12] the pastoral went on to lament the plethora of existing workers' associations and describes most of them as organizations of violence and force whose leaders are "dictators" intent on putting the suffering worker into the chains of socialist unionism. "The desire to unionize workers with no other aim than to give them arms for their defense against capitalism is extremely harmful to social peace." The pastoral looks forward, therefore, to the establishment of Catholic unions, whose primary aim is to be religious and moral.

This pronouncement seems on the whole less advanced than *Quadragesimo Anno* which it summarized. But compared with the reaction in the remainder of Latin America as well as with any previous statement by the Chilean episcopate, it is astonishing that it should have been issued at all. The papal encyclical itself was not published by the Catholic press at the time, a fact which became something of a *cause celebre* when the publisher of the chief Catholic daily paper, *El diario ilustrado*, was quoted as saying that "the church must be protected from the imprudences of the popes."

A further collective pastoral was issued in 1937 and entitled "Concerning the just wage." Once again, this consisted substantially of quotations from *Quadragesimo Anno*. Pope Pius XI had dealt with the topic of wages in some detail, and his underlying philosophy had been to refute the doctrine that the determination of wages, like that of other prices, could be left completely to the free play of market forces. He had stated that a wage had to be sufficient at least to meet "ordinary domestic needs."

Perhaps the chief reason for the issuance of the 1937 pastoral is to be found in its very last paragraphs. These announce formally the establishment of various Catholic Action Groups and the so-called Secretariat for Social-Economic Action. These were encouraged to teach the social encyclicals and other formulations of the social doctrine of the church. However modest their aims, such groups are invariably attacked by traditional lay sectors everywhere. This was the case in Chile, and de Kadt makes it clear that this was also the case in Brazil. The pastoral presumably sought to shield the fledgling organizations by putting the weight of the bishops behind their activities, as Pope Pius XI was to do three months later in his encyclical, "On atheistic Communism" (*Divini Redemptoris*).

The next relevant pastoral, issued by the Chilean episcopate in 1949 under the title "Concerning social problems"[13] begins to show several marked differences from its predecessors.

First, it no longer is limited to quotations from and paraphrases of the two basic social encyclicals, but cites widely from various papal pronouncements, even though the basic structure of the document and its headings are those of the encyclicals. For the first time, we find references to several radio addresses of Pope Pius XII and to speeches delivered by him to meetings of Catholic Action Groups. In particular, the Chilean pastoral quotes crucial sections from the famous reply of June, 1929, made by the Holy Congregation to an inquiry by Cardinal Lienart, Bishop of Lille, concerning the position of the church on trade unions.

Second, the selection of quotations seems to have been made in order to support a stance which would be slightly more, rather than slightly less radical, than Vatican documents. Concerning property, for example, it quotes approvingly a radio speech by Pius XII to the effect that no social order can be deemed just which makes it impossible for great masses of workers to enjoy their natural right to acquire property. In other words, the concept of the natural right to private property was no longer used to defend the existing owners but in defense of measures which would redistribute property. The bishops not only recommended that special steps be taken so that workers could be made property owners, but they went on to attack bitterly certain practices of which they accuse Chilean employers generally and landowners in particular: e.g., an attack upon landowners who discharge from their *fundos* workers who were born there and whose ancestors may have served the owners' families for centuries. This, in addition to sections dealing with the abuses of capitalists and the vices of the rich in general, is taken largely from the encyclicals.

Finally, there was a long section on associations and trade unions. For the first time we find here a separate subheading for "Strikes"; it begins with the statement that "just and legitimate strikes are in conformity with natural law," though it then proceeds to caution against the abuse of that right. In its discussion of unions as such, however, the sequence is reversed. The pastoral moves from a traditional to a more independent stance. The section begins with quotations from the letter to Cardinal Lienhart to which we have already referred, emphasizing the need for Christian unions parallel to socialist unions, and specifying that they dedicate themselves to fostering social peace and to upholding the faith. The pastoral then goes on to say, however, that "this does not mean that they might not claim the rights they deem just and legitimate." An entire paragraph, very vigorously phrased, is devoted to demanding that all opposition to the establishment of unions cease and that, on the contrary, everyone help in their establishment.

We regard these—the defense of trade unions; the specific attacks on the practices of Chilean employers; and the tone of impatience with the continued resistance to and attacks upon Catholic Action groups—as major breaks with the past. There is a note of great urgency with which Catholics of power and wealth are asked to change their ways and, most significant, there is now explicit recognition of the need to change institutions, a need which at one point is given the same importance as the personal, moral-religious reform for which the church had previously exclusively called and which it had at that time deemed sufficient.

In 1950 followed a further sharp statement that active participation in the solution of social problems was an indisputable obligation of all Catholics. It dealt particularly curtly with two favorite Conservative arguments (without, of course, naming names!): (1) that the encyclicals were to be taken only as general guidelines which might or might not apply to the specific situation prevailing in any one country (and they did not, they said, apply in Chile); (2) that those who did not agree with the Conservative party (e.g., the National Falange, later to be the Christian Democratic party) were virtually placing themselves outside the church by their disagreement.

Later in the same year, Fr. Hurtado received from the Episcopal Conference official recognition of his efforts to establish *Acción Sindical Chilena*—ASICH, an institution to advise and educate Catholic trade unionists. Father Hurtado died in 1952. Two years later, at the outbreak of a strike of vineyard workers led by young Catholic intellectuals who had been influenced by Fr. Hurtado, both the Archbishop of Santiago, Cardenal Caro, and the Bishop of Talca, the late Msgr. Manuel Larraín, came publicly to the workers' defense, the former visiting President Ibañez on their behalf. Both men were bitterly attacked for their partisanship by powerful Catholic laymen of the right, and they replied vigorously and publicly.[14]

The last two collective pastorals with which we shall deal were both issued almost a decade later, in 1962. They set the tone for the critical election of 1964, won by the Christian Democratic party. The first, issued in March, 1962, dealt with the problem of the peasant.[15] The other, issued in September of that year, addressed itself once again to the social problem in general.[16] Both are so different from their predecessors that they can be said to mark the beginning of a new epoch and thus, for this discussion, mark a fitting terminal point.

First, they address themselves explicitly and almost exclusively to the problems of Chile rather than to problems of the modern world, a level appropriate to the encyclicals but somewhat evasive in a specific national context. Their structure and headings bear little resemblance to that of the papal encyclicals. Indeed, the more general of the two pastorals, "Man's social and political duty today," although it appeared more than a year after Pope John's *Mater et Magistra*, contained only five quotations from it and only one from each of *Rerum Novarum* and *Quadragesimo Anno*. While there are considerably more references to *Mater et Magistra* in the other and earlier pastoral, "The church and the problem of the Chilean peasant," this might well have been due to the fact that the encyclical had an entire chapter devoted to the problem of agriculture.

"*El deber social y politica*," for example, opens with a concise

summary of Chile's socio-economic situation, using as references articles in academic journals, student dissertations, publications of the
University of Chile's Institute of Economics, and the census and
other national statistics. These sources are marshalled in order to
describe the maldistribution of wealth and income in Chile; deficiencies in housing which make orderly family life impossible; deficiencies
in nutrition and agricultural production; the high level of unemploy-
ment; and the immense problem of school dropouts.

The pastoral dealing with peasants is much more specific and cutting.
It accuses rich landowners of many violations of Chilean law, including failure to pay minimum wages, provide housing of legal minimum
standards, pay family allowances, grant paid vacations, and more.

The bishops advocate, in the more general pastoral, "reforms of the
social structure" and "institutional changes such as an authentic agrarian reform, reform of the enterprise, reform of the system of taxation,
administrative reforms, and others." In the *campesino* pastoral they
state with deliberateness: "It seems that the time has come to make
legitimate the expropriation of those agricultural properties which
might produce more and which can be divided . . . for it is the function of the state to provide rural property to all those who solicit it,
paying due regard to their capacity, their sense of calling, and the
guarantee of working it."

Among the most intriguing parts of the general pastoral are its
references to communism. To understand them, two points must be
borne in mind. First, from *Rerum Novarum* onward, reaching its
climax with "On atheistic Communism" (*Divini Redemptoris*, 1937),
the encyclicals had been explicit about one very powerful motive
behind the concern for the working classes: anticommunism. Popes
Leo XIII, Pius XI, and Pius XII had been quite clear that they wanted
to win back the industrial worker from the control of those sustaining communist, socialist and generally materialist and atheist philosophies—and thereby to weaken these philosophies. The errors and
sinfulness of these doctrines and their threat to the church had been
dwelt upon at length and with great intensity in all relevant papal
pronouncements.

In addition, beginning with *Quadragesimo Anno* in 1931, severe
warnings were issued to Catholics not to be misled into believing that
a reconciliation between Christianity and materialism was possible.
These statements had always been reproduced or summarized in the
Chilean pastorals.

The second background point is that the issue of communism happened to have, and was by Conservatives deliberately made to have, special relevance to the Chilean Catholic context. For the National Falange (later Christian Democratic party) had on occasion collaborated with Radical presidents[17] who had also been supported at various times by the Communist and Socialist parties. The Falange had gone even further than this in opposing a law curbing communism. The so-called "Law for the Permanent Defense of Democracy" had been passed in 1948 upon the initiative of the Radical party, after the latter broke with the Communists. From 1948 on, the Falange joined all those who campaigned for the repeal of the "LDD" (as it was commonly known) and it was repealed in 1958. More generally, important sectors of the Falange had made it quite clear from the beginning that they would vote with Marxists on certain issues and that they did not regard the parties of the left as untouchables.

Now, the Falange had come into existence in 1938 as a splinter of the Conservative party, thereby permanently weakening (and consequently infuriating) the latter. The Conservatives, well acquainted with the pertinent sections of the encyclicals, had for long used the position of the Falange concerning the Communist party in their unceasing attempts to persuade the Chilean hierarchy to condemn the new party for doctrinal error and to enjoin Catholics from supporting it. In 1947, at the time the "LDD" law was being debated, the episcopate had indeed issued what appeared to be a condemnation of the Falange, and this had almost resulted in its voluntary dissolution. It was dissuaded from disbanding only by a clarification emanating from Msgr. Manuel Larraín.

Given this history, the issue of communism was obviously an extremely touchy one for the Chilean episcopate. Its 1962 stand represented a significant change as compared with that of 1949. In the latter year, one of the headings was "A Catholic cannot collaborate with communism" (para. 49). The 1949 pastoral had also cited at length the warning contained in Pope Pius' *Divini Redemptoris* against communist proposals to collaborate even in matters completely in line with Christian doctrine.

The 1962 pastorals reversed that position completely. The *campesino* pastoral follows *Mater et Magistra* in making no reference whatsoever to communism, only to "erroneous doctrines": A tremendous change both for the Vatican and for the Chilean episcopate. The second, more general pastoral, "El deber social . . .", does devote substantial space to the errors of communism and the reasons for its spread. But in these sections, in addition to accusing communism of deviousness, it also attacks the abuses of "the liberal economy" and the "ineffectualness and weakness of democratic governments." More important are the subsequent paragraphs (22–27). Here a distinction is made between generally "collaborating with communism" on the one hand (which is condemned, even when the plan is to abandon the communists once power has been reached with their help); and, on the other hand, "loyal and necessary collaboration which Catholics may sustain with any category of persons 'in achieving objectives that of their nature are good or at least reducible to good.'"[18] "The very great problems of humanity and of each country, specifically, can be resolved only with the sincere collaboration of all, despite their ideological and even religious divergences" (para. 28).

Thus, while a more general coalition and alliance with communism are precluded, collaboration to achieve specific good objectives is permitted and even encouraged. Even though the pastoral declares that the directives of the church are to be obeyed "in this delicate matter," this is a reserve veto which goes back to the encyclicals and the wording is vague. It should in any case be balanced against the bishops' lengthy citation of an address by Archbishop Lercaro of Bologna, who inveighed against a negative kind of anticommunism and condemned those who wanted to eliminate communism only to maintain the status quo.

In both pastorals there were definitely signs of taking a middle road between left and right in general which, in the Chilean context, also meant taking a middle road between the Christian Democrats and the Conservatives. Thus, general alliances with communism were forbidden, but cooperation with all, even those holding divergent ideological views, was encouraged in order to achieve a wide range of specific ends. In the pastoral on agrarian problems, the paragraph dealing with the expropriation of privately owned land was preceded by a paragraph advocating just prices for agricultural products: long a sore point with Chilean big landowners.

But, on balance, both pastorals clearly leaned heavily toward the progressive side and were received with considerable bitterness by the Catholic right and with joy by the left. Instead of relying on resignation by the poor and charity by the rich (which had been the formula in 1891), Chilean bishops had moved to a position where the aspirations of the poor were to be met by expropriation of the rich; where the state was to play an extremely active role in promoting economic development and, of course, in obtaining right and justice for all individuals; and where a good deal of ad hoc co-operation with all, regardless of ideology, was encouraged. Instead of advocating isolation and withdrawal, Catholics were warned against "group egoism."

These positions do not indicate that the Chilean episcopate had taken a stance of extreme radicalism, nor would it be realistic to expect it to do so even assuming that would be the correct position. But we would guess that, were it possible to measure such phenomena, it would be found that the Chilean episcopate has changed its position in the realm of social doctrine at a rate far more rapid than any other group has changed its ideology or its modus operandi. Certainly, a sophisticated recognition that the survival of the church required it to change has played a part in these recent pronouncements. It did so also in the case of Archbishop Errázuriz in 1922, whose aim, in part, was to save the church by not linking it to a party opposed to the government. But throughout the world, the groups and institutions are legion who, despite the most patent need to change, fail to do so. In the case of the episcopate, most observers readily acknowledge that the change is one in heart also and not merely a political tactic.

The process of change has roots quite far back in the past. It began at least eighty years ago. It began as a study circle, highly informal, of a group of aristocratic youths in an aristocratic Jesuit high school inspired by a few devoted priests. It moved on to spontaneous action among the poor and the formation of institutions primarily devoted to education. Only later did it eventuate in the formation of a formal political party and in changes in the official stand of the highest church authorities. Its chief effect, in our opinion, has been to legitimate a dramatic shift of the main body of Catholic opinion from right of center to left of center, but not to an extremely radical position. The bishops who undertook to legitimate others, in turn needed a source of legitimacy. They found it in the encyclicals and, perhaps even more, in progressive Catholic thought and action in the area most respected by Chilean Catholics: Catholic Western Europe. With changes in doctrine, there has come an immense proliferation of institutions dedicated to putting them into practice. Whether or not this is its aim, the entire movement is in fact a rival of and a challenge to the more extreme Marxist ideologies in Chile and elsewhere. Whether it is moving far enough and fast enough is a matter to leave to historians of tomorrow.

Part III:
Doctrine and Social Change

6: CHURCH DOCTRINE IN LATIN AMERICA AFTER THE COUNCIL

Mark G. McGrath, C.S.C.

In this discussion of the effects of the Second Vatican Ecumenical Council, 1962–65, on church doctrine in Latin America (church here, of course, referring to the Roman Catholic church), we should first define the term "doctrine," then speak briefly about the Council itself, and finally investigate recent developments in Latin America.

REFLECTION ON "DOCTRINE"

For a Catholic theologian, the word "doctrine" has a precise meaning. This is important to note when speaking of church doctrine after the Council. In a Catholic theological context, the term refers primarily to revealed doctrine, i.e., to the communication through Scripture and through oral tradition of the revelation of God to his people in the Old Testament and through Christ. This communication concerns all those dealings of God with man, painting for man the whole meaning of life, its beginning, its end, its over-all purpose, its significance. It is in this historical context, called in theology the history of salvation, that all precepts and all particular doctrines have their meaning.

The church holds that Christ and his apostles revealed the final direct communication of God addressed to all man. It is not augmented. There are no new points. No new communication of this kind is expected.

It is obvious, however, that this doctrine grows. It grows in that we comprehend it more every day. In this sense, it changes. Profound truth of any order, whether scientific, philosophic, or any other, demands a certain amount of time for its hearers, individually and collectively, to work out all of its implications and applications. For believers, this is especially so in doctrines which come from a revelation of God. Thus, a whole series of moral principles are found in the Judeo-Christian tradition whose consequences are only now beginning to be worked out in many areas and which will be worked out further in the future. This happens because we think about these matters more and more. We grow in our knowledge and our understanding of them, while new situations occur which provoke us to new applications.

An example is the Christian revelation of the triune God and of the God-made man. In the first three or four centuries, these were the great doctrines, discussions about which provoked a growing understanding of many of their implications. In the immediate era, understanding of justice, liberty, and the dignity of a human person grows and the gradual elimination of slavery under its more obvious and some of its more subtle forms takes place as the principles of justice and liberty and personal dignity become more and more obvious in what they mean in the practical order. Many of our ancestors were either slaves or slaveowners. It is doubtful whether the latter found this an open contradiction to their consciences, as moral principles were then understood. Now, we could not, without doing violence to our consciences, have any part of such an institution.

Yet conditions still exist, whether of racial segregation or any other kind of social prejudice, which are carryovers of these injustices under more subtle forms. As time evolves, we should develop clearer convictions about and find more application for the guiding moral principles of liberty which runs through the whole Judeo-Christian tradition.

A particular example of the idea that revealed doctrine grows through deepened understanding is the change which has taken place in what is called the social doctrine of the Catholic church. This doctrine has been expanded in its application through increased understanding. This is not surprising for the above-mentioned reasons. Take the contrast afforded us by Pope Leo XIII, who, with his great social encyclicals, in a certain sense inaugurated the modern period, which we speak of in connection with the Council. His encyclicals considered the great social problem of his time, the social problem, which was fundamentally the conflict between capital and labor. His encyclicals had nothing to say, however, about the great international problem of today, of the contrast and the relations between the developed and the underdeveloped areas of the world, for the very obvious reason that this problem was not yet such a major one in *his* day. Yet the existence of this problem forces us to new dimensions in our social thinking. In this example, then, we see a change in church doctrine: New applications are found, expanding our understanding of what we believe from God

Another interesting aspect of this question is that the same revelation which is the essential content of Christian revelation develops in different fashions according to whether it is incarnated in one or another society. The fact that Christian revelation from its origins in Judea rapidly entered into the Greco-Roman world placed it in a mental framework that will certainly mark some of it as long as time itself. The early fathers of the church explained the meaning of revelation in a logic and metaphysics borrowed from Plato and Aristotle and the Greek traditions. Today, the meaning of revelation must be explained in our current human knowledge and in connection with our human sciences. As the center of the church moved more toward the west and was then staked in Rome, the great Roman organizational and legal tradition, the Justinian Code, became somewhat the framework for the legislation and organization of the Roman Catholic church.

From both Byzantium and Rome, from their courts, and from the previous Jewish liturgical and rubrical traditions, the church adopted most of the symbolism and most of the rites which it uses in its religious exercises. These are in a certain sense human accretions insofar as they are purely external symbols. Yet they are necessary inasmuch as they are the effort of the human mind to penetrate religious truths, to understand these truths, and to symbolize them. This is the effort of the human spirit to live religious truths in the circumstances in which men find themselves.

This fact is especially apparent in the Second Vatican Council because this Council was particularly and characteristically universal. In being so universal, many of the Western characteristics of Christianity were considered precisely as Western, and therefore not as obligatory or essential to Christians of other parts of the globe.

REFLECTION ON THE COUNCIL

There are several points about the Council which should be mentioned briefly. The first is the widespread popular assumption that the Council came into being as the result of spontaneous combustion sparked by the incandescent personality of Pope John XXIII. It is very true that Pope John was a providential figure. Yet it is also true that John, with all his greatness, did not, could not, foresee everything that this Council was to do. It is also true that there was a tremendous amount of preparation, both theoretical and practical, in the church that made the Council not only necessary but almost inevitable.

The Council was the outgrowth and result of over seventy years of intense church life, dating from Pope Leo XIII, characteristically, who opened the church again to the world, just as during the nineteenth century, particularly under Pope Gregory XVI and Pope Pius IX, it had been closed in upon itself in reaction to the historical circumstances of the Italian situation, and, to a large extent, conditions in all of Western Europe.

We know that when the First Vatican Ecumenical Council was held in 1869 and 1870, Pope Pius IX invited Protestant and other observers. Not only did they not come, but most reacted with displeasure. We also know that this First Vatican Council sought primarily to defend the church against certain abuses and errors. It was in a sense a compilation of all of the condemnations of the popes through the nineteenth century down to that time. Leo XIII came, was elected Pope, and immediately began his reign by symbolically opening the archives of the Vatican to all scholars, saying that, "The Church has no fear of truth." He began by writing encyclical letters to the world which did not deal exclusively with religious questions, but with burning questions affecting all men, presenting the church as desirous of serving men rather than dominating them.

This new attitude has grown in the church since that time over seventy years ago, down through a series of great popes, particularly the late, much-maligned Pope Pius XII, who, over many years, urged Catholics to think about the spiritual significance of every modern problem. The roots of the Council, however, were not limited to the actions of the pope, nor of the other bishops. The Council sprang from many movements and approaches to the problems of our times: Social problems, problems of the international order, cultural problems, family problems; movements, such as the Young Christian Workers, which began in Belgium and spread across the face of Europe and the world. The church's participation in today's world has been fired by many leaders, clerical and lay, who, like the great popes of this century, are the heroes and the harbingers of Vatican Council

II. The modern ecumenical movements admittedly began in other
Christian bodies and were fully embraced by the Catholic church
only in the Second Vatican Council. But now the Catholic church's
cry for unity in Christ will not be stilled, nor, we hope, will it wane.

Great theologians have developed over these last seventy years.
There is a flowering of theology in the Western world today. All of
these elements went into the preparation of the Council. This is an
important point. The Council sprang from the rich, maturing experience of the church in today's world. It was not merely a happy,
chance inspiration of Pope John; nor was it a leap of desperation by a
worried ecclesiastical body.

A second point is that it was a *world* Council. Every Council in the
past history of the church had concerned itself primarily with the
problems of a particular area and had been made up primarily of representatives from that part of the world. Even in the First Vatican
Council, the largest prior to this date, 90 per cent of the 700 bishops
were Europeans or of European origin, even if working in other parts
of the world. In the Second Council, of the 2,400 bishops present,
600 were from Latin America alone, as well as 200 from the United
States, and large numbers from Canada, Africa, and Asia. This led to
an emphasis on the problems of the world, of the entire world, along
with a preoccupation on the part of the bishops and Christians in
general for the entire world.

A third characteristic of this Council was that it was a Council of
change in a time of change. It was not directed toward any particular
error, toward any particular schism, or moral perturbation; it was a
Council of change. The church examined itself profoundly and asked
itself, in respect to her mission as given by God through Christ, what
was her way of serving this world in which we now live, this world
today? Thus, the Council crystallized itself around two documents.
The first was the Dogmatic Constitution on the Church and the second the Pastoral Constitution on the Church in the Modern World,
two documents around which all the others turn.

In this examination of itself and of the world, the church came to
realize clearly in the Council that we are living in a pluralistic society
in which it and all other Christian bodies should unite as much as
possible for a common human purpose; that we are living in a secularized society, a secular society in which human values are brought out
to their full significance, and that he who does not recognize this cuts

himself off from these values; that we are living in a society whose change is characteristically the result of scientific and technological process which, in turn, produces this great awareness of secular values; and that this whole process often tends toward the separation of secular and religious considerations, producing thereby a schism, dangerous and profound, not only between men but in the minds and the spirits of individual men.

LATIN AMERICA

We come now to the application of these developments to Latin America. Not only did Latin America receive much from the Council, it brought much to it.

There can be no doubt that the theological strength of the church today is primarily concentrated in Europe—with the most creative work being done in what is called middle Europe, from Austria across Switzerland, France, Germany, to Holland and Belgium. Nonetheless, this was a world Council. Those theologians who were the principal authors of the documents coming out of the Council had to formulate the concepts and ideas for which the bishops were looking. Three great theologians present, for example, were asked to write a paragraph for the Dogmatic Constitution on the Church dealing with poverty in the world today. They wrote a paragraph which showed that they had never "lived" poverty. The Indian, African, and Latin American bishops who had asked for this description said, "That is not it. That is not valid." Thus, these and other European theologians were forced to expand their vision to include a whole series of problems which were formerly beyond their vision but which they had now to learn and express to those bishops who came from abroad with few experts but with a vibrant sense of the problem of the church and of mankind throughout the world.

Latin America, in this sense, brought a great deal to the Council, because Latin America assumes a unique position in the church. Not only does it contain one-third of the Roman Catholic population of the world, it is also the only large area of the Catholic church which is to be found in the underdeveloped areas of the world. Were it not for Latin America, we could say that the developed nations of the world are of the Judeo-Christian tradition and the underdeveloped are of the non-Judeo-Christian traditions. Latin America finds itself, in large measure, within the bloc of the underdeveloped nations, which gives it a particularly urgent character within the church. It is here that Christians must apply their sense of justice, their sense of international aid, their sense of national obligation to development. If Christians fail here, what can Christians hope to tell the rest of the world about development?

We must retain historical perspective in our considerations of what is happening in Latin America and particularly of the role of the church in relation to social change. Experts come to work in Latin America who arrive at the scene of some small or large project of social development (whether radio schools for literacy campaigns or vocational schools or an interrelated program of cooperatives in a large or a small area) and within two weeks wring their hands over the tremendous problems of disorganization they find. They have come from a super-organized area, the United States, to an area lacking in structures, practice, and training for this kind of organization. They immediately find everything amiss and do not realize that often they are looking at some of the best aspects of Latin America. They look at the defects according to their standards and do not realize all the work which has gone into making the situation a bit better than it was.

In a similar manner, many persons arrive in Latin America and make vast, sweeping judgments about what should be done here and now, without realizing how difficult it has been to do what we have done up to now. It has been said that there exists the dual need for patience and for urgent action because often there is little time left for us to achieve what we must achieve in order to avoid catastrophe. This is our paradox in a nutshell.

Pleading, then, for this historical perspective, it should be noted that in the Catholic Inter-American Cooperation Program (CICOP) we have tried to insist constantly, particularly to North Americans, that they view Latin American problems through the perspective of Latin American history. They should not take solutions applicable to the United States, solutions which developed in the United States out of the United States temperament and experience, and apply them indiscriminately to a situation which is so different.

At the Council, Latin Americans participated in the examination of the church, which was the fundamental experience of the Council. They found that over the last sixty years the church in Latin America has been experiencing the necessity for a new expression of its life.

The church in Latin America was part of the whole feudal structure set up during the first years of conquest. It is a byword in Latin American history that the fifty years of conquest set the pattern for four centuries. The social, economic, and religious patterns then established lasted through the colonial period and the first century of the republican period. The result of recent changes* is causing the breakdown of a structure which had been, however imperfect, a stable structure, a structure in which every man had some place, a structure which was static, unchanging, not very progressive, but, nonetheless, a structure.

We now find ourselves in the midst of a process in which new structures must be born. In this process the church finds that it has a new role to perform. Some people ask, "Why has the church in Latin America taken so long to begin acting in favor of the poor?" The response to this question is that we have poor now that we did not have thirty years ago. This is true not only in terms of expansion of population, but in terms of other changes. The population of the slum areas surrounding our big cities, like the 250,000 who live in the "callampas" around the city of Santiago, Chile, and larger numbers in the "favellas" of Rio de Janeiro, are an accretion of the recent past.

In its self-analysis, the church has found many attitudes carried over from the feudal period which are less and less valid in the present era. These attitudes were examined by the entire Council. The church found that we truly live in a pluralistic society. This term is being bandied about in theological and sociological discussions and in practical applications by Catholics throughout Latin America today.

By this, it is meant that "Cristiandad," the Christian society, as conceived in the Middle Ages and existing down through three or four centuries of Latin American history, is over. A society in which church and state are almost mutually inclusive, one supporting the other and helping the other—this is over, whatever its value or its defects in the past. We now live in a society of many confessions and

* The medical revolution producing expansion of population; internal migration producing the slum areas around our cities, particularly in late years; the beginning of an industrial revolution; the influx of new ideas in the social and political order; and the creation of a mass of population, whether in slum areas or in the discontented and absentee-ownership areas of the countryside.

professions that must work together. It is a secular society, a society in which the church must move toward human values and help to promote them if it wishes them to be part of, and congruent with, a religious order, and, even more, because of the intrinsic merit of these secular values.

The future challenge of the church in Latin America lies in the area of technological and scientific progress. The challenge about which we most often speak in Latin America today is that of the reformation of the temporal order, the social problem in terms of social injustices within nations and between nations. We have some cause for hope. Yet the problem to come for those of faith in Latin America is one which is already present in the Western world. It exists in the relationship between the goals, ideals, and principles of a scientific and a technological society, its vision of life, and that of the vision of life of men of religious faith. It is not that these two groups are opposed but simply that they do not talk the same language and come together with great difficulty. This is acutely so in universities throughout Latin America. The communist conflict in the social order is reflected in the university; but the more basic problem there is the lack of dialogue between faith and technology, between Christian humanism and "scientific progress."

Another aspect of the Council vital for the Latin American church was the emphasis that the Council, by its universal declarations, gave to the serious social obligations of Christians. We have had urgent and eloquent papal encyclicals in the past; we have had urgent and eloquent sermons; we have had individual activity, and from all these efforts the Council came as a fruition. Yet there has never been language such as that found in the Pastoral Constitution on the Church in the Modern World, by all the bishops, stressing so urgently the impossibility of separating brotherhood, essential to any concept of the Christian life, from a generous dedication to the work of justice in the world. This may sound like a platitude, but it is not one when voiced by 2,400 bishops with due solemnity, when this statement is the fruit of over seventy years' efforts, and when these words are transformed quickly into measures and action throughout the world.

To those in Latin America, these writings give tremendous backing and wise guidance for all that the church has wanted to do in the social order—whether through its clerical spokesmen or through lay Christians active in the social domain. The bell has tolled for a doctrinaire laissez-faire policy among Catholics in Latin America.

One final point concerning the church and Latin America is the Council's seeking of a spirituality of progress. The key word in Latin America today is "development" or "desarrollo." This development requires an ideology. The word "ideology" is almost anathema to some. It is a bad word in the United States because it is so differently understood. By it we mean a sense of values to underlie our desire for development. It is the "why" of development. When I visit the countryside in my diocese in Veraguas, Panama, I see the poor, 90 per cent of whom are illiterate, underfed, pitiably primitive in their farming, and suffering from disease. One looks upon them and sees in their faces hunger, great patience in the midst of great suffering, great passivity. I ask myself, What is the tragedy of these people? I find my answer in these documents. Their tragedy is not only that they do not have enough to eat, not only that they do not have roofs over their heads, toilet facilities, or enough clothing, or that they are diseased. The tragedy is that they are not living fully as human beings. It is their dignity as human beings which is the heart of the problem. The external benefits of civilization should bless them, too. Yet these are only means to their progress as human beings, in human dignity. The Council's constitution bases the whole notion of progress upon the dignity of man. Progress is for men, and man is the author of progress, and man is the center of development and all that it means. This, for us, is the keynote of our entire approach to the spirituality of progress which distinguishes us so much from the Marxists and from many capitalists and from any purely technical approaches to the question of development in Latin America.

This change in doctrine in Latin America was prepared before the Council but was greatly accelerated by the Council, and it enabled the new doctrine to be implemented. There are over 600 bishops in Latin America today. The Council of Latin American Bishops (CELAM), made up of one delegate from each of the Latin American nations with its president and two vice-presidents, has twelve commissions which more or less try to co-ordinate the activities of the church throughout Latin America. Before the Vatican Council, this Council of Latin American Bishops with the existing secretariats corresponding to the present commissions, was largely composed of bishops who, in popular press releases, were the "progressive bishops" of Latin America. They were not the majority of bishops, but the majority put their confidence in them. They were considered those who most ardently looked for the kinds of applications of the church's doctrine, message, and service to the world today which the majority of bishops wanted.

The Council, as a result of the experience of listening, participating, and being in contact with the efforts of bishops throughout the world, encouraged many more bishops to courageous action in social areas. This action is not easy. The new situation in which the church finds herself today requires a tremendous amount of adaptation. In an old, rather monolithic, paternalistic, static structure, moral obligations did not change much. In a typically agrarian society, with one large landholder, his family, and his attendants or workers on the land, duties could go uninterrupted for centuries without anyone asking serious questions about obligations in social justice. When this situation is disrupted, when it is knocked to pieces, and a new society begins to form, you must expand your vision, your social dimension. All kinds of new social relations grow up.

Thus, there is now talk about agrarian reform, tax reform, fair labor practices, economic integration, and the like. A new range of problems is upon us, with others already appearing on the horizon.

The church is reacting to all of these, unevenly to be sure, because the church is made up of many persons, each with his functions, his temperament, and with a wide variety of ideas within the broad limits of the faith. In the first place, the church is not composed merely of bishops. Ninety-nine and some per cent are lay people. We bishops are a small minority, along with a small minority of priests. Moreover, in the social body of the church there is a dead weight. This naturally occurs in all traditional groups in which some have an allegiance to the past and fear the future. It is not easy to drag this whole body into a new situation, particularly when there are very few who can say with confidence that they know what that new situation holds for them or what the new expression will be.

Chile is considered today to be a nation of great social progress, where the church is giving excellent leadership in social areas. Yet, before the first world war, it was impossible to have Pope Leo XIII's social encyclicals printed in Chile. They had to be printed in Argentina and brought across because key Catholic conservative politicians prohibited their publication. This is also the church. In many areas, it is the lay persons who begin the great entry of the church into modern problems. In most areas, it is because some clergyman or some bishop has given inspiration, although lay groups translate this inspiration into action. This is also the church.

What has taken place in Chile today is the result of what was begun thirty years ago. Matters are coming to fruition in Chile and events are moving very quickly, although few would be able to predict where these events will lead. It is a period of experimentation, a period of great courage, in which many leaders push ahead, trying to be faithful to their principles, while at the same time, as the American expression has it, they play it by ear.

There are some concrete areas to which the problem of bringing a Christian vision to a new situation may be applied. There is the relationship of church and state and all that this relationship implies in Latin America today. There is the area of the church's doctrine on poverty that may be translated into terms of land reform and the social function of property under new conditions. There is the question of politics, the role of politics in the development of our society and the still all-too-deficient sense of politics as a dedication to the people rather than an expression and a means of power and wealth. Even when the middle classes rise into political power, as has happened in most Latin American countries today, its members seem to succeed to an aristocratic notion of politics as a means of personal prestige and wealth. This is, of course, a tremendous obstacle to government genuinely at the service of the people.

There is also the tremendous problem brought about by the lack of intermediate structures in our societies. Our atomized society, as it is sometimes called, contains one central authority which deals with all problems, down to the very lowest level. This central authority ruled in that other society where there were links in its paternalistic, fundamentally rural, and aristocratic structure. But those links now hardly exist. Yet, most power is concentrated in a central government without intermediate structures, with which people in the United States are so familiar, being built up. This means that in rural areas, for example, everything that must be done must be planned in the capital city. People in a particular region, district, or province not only do not have the income raised through local taxation (taxes go to the national government), money which would permit planning and execution of projects, but they also lack incentive and an awareness that this is what they should do. They, therefore, must appeal to the central authority and fall back on the old paternalistic approach. Unless these intermediate structures are built, demagogic revolutions will result because the masses are not conscious of their responsibilities nor capable of carrying them out effectively.

What is the role of the church in this complicated period of change in Latin America? Certainly, her role is fundamentally religious. It is not for the church to take upon herself the obligation of creating a new temporal order. If we were to fall into that error, we would fall into a new form of theocracy, and none of us desires that. The church has a fundamental role to exercise in Latin America, however, and unless it does exercise that role the changes which are so drastically needed for the people will be delayed too long, with growing suffering for many and desperation for not a few. By church, I mean not only bishops and priests who are a small percentage, but Catholic Christians who make up the great bulk of the church in Latin America. It is this desperation which would also launch us into extreme solutions whether to the right or left, with the consequent suppression of human liberty and many other spiritual values essential to authentic and complete human and social progress.

What must the church do at this crossroad? It must fundamentally exercise its religious function, which is that of making persons realize what it means to belong fully to a human community, what it means in terms of a sense of community, and how this understanding must be translated into the practical applications of the basic precepts of Christian community living, the love of neighbor. This love of neighbor, to be effective, has to convert itself into working for justice for all.

This mission, exercised in a religious manner through creating genuine spiritual community and causing it to overflow upon the temporal order, shows that the religious and the temporal order in the life of the individual are not so distinct as they are one. In that one life, one lives his religious values, although at the same time he can live them in close collaboration with persons who do not accept all of his religious principles. He is in a pluralistic society and realizes that all men of good will can work together, each according to his ideals. But he clearly works according to his ideals of giving himself for his neighbor as his brother in God.

When this is done, there is more required of the church. The church today has to move into the area of promotion of development.

In many cases, there is no one else to do it. In the vast areas of the hinterlands of Latin America the population is discouraged, pessimistic, and with good reason, because the bulk of the population is untrained and incapable of rising out of its poor conditions. Its farming techniques, its whole approach to the problem of life, from homes to family organization, are worse than they were three or four hundred years ago. Central governments often have done very little about this and do not appear about to do very much in the years to come. When the central governments do try to do something through various agencies, these agencies clash. One is worried about electricity, another worried about roads, another about water, and they are not co-ordinated. There is no sense of that community being a unit. There is planning from above, but it does not work out at the community level. In addition, the people are highly suspicious because most of these aids come just before an election and they expect these benefits to stop right after the election, so the agencies receive no support. Thus, even with the best of will, the government functionary often finds only frustration.

In these areas, the church may well have the obligation to "promote" social initiative. It must create this sense of community, by getting men together to ask what they can do about their problems. This is what we are trying to do in a modest way in the province of Veraguas in Panama, and this is being done in a much larger way in the northeast of Brazil and by churchmen throughout Latin America. People get together and begin to organize and send others off for training in cooperative schools and in schools of social development, and these come back and start working. We offer them a kind of moral umbrella so that they can get started, because there are frequently politicians or vested interests who try to stop social reform actions. Unless there is some kind of moral cover to insulate the action for a time from this kind of attack, it usually sputters out quickly. In its place will come, after the resentment of years, the violent movements which hope to bear everything away.

So the church may have to *promote*, often through its own social offices and projects, and to *protect*. Both these functions are in a real sense supplementary; the church fills in for other structures and defends the people. It must do so cautiously in order not to inhibit but rather encourage those civic groups who should normally carry out those tasks. Then the church, as an institution, can fall back upon her own proper, directly religious role.

When we debated the chapter on the role of the church in the world in the Pastoral Constitution on the Church in the Modern World, there were some European bishops who were anxious to state very clearly that the church was not directly responsible for the building of the temporal order. All of us can agree on this. Anyone who does not appreciate the point misunderstands the function of religion in civic society, particularly in a pluralistic society. But a group from Latin America, particularly some of the bishops on the commission, objected to so strong a statement of this point. We wanted them to understand that it was very fine to be purists in Germany, France, and the United States, where there were other institutions to help the people. But we did not wish to give the impression in a Council statement that the church, as an institution, could not and must not in any instance inaugurate programs and instil in the people the spirit of working together for justice, a spirit which is required if they are going to raise themselves up by their own bootstraps and develop organic communities. Unless they do so, all further talk of democracy and development in our nations is pretty much a waste. In passing, it can be noted that these observations were taken into consideration and embodied in the final text.

There is sometimes a popular impression that the United States is pouring great sums of money into Latin America and is being received with ingratitude. United States economic assistance to Latin America is actually a very minute sum in contrast to aid given to other areas. It becomes less, in terms of percentages, year by year in relation to gross national product. Nevertheless, in Latin America we not only need money but need worthwhile community projects in which this money, as well as volunteer money, technical assistance, can take root, prosper, and flower. This is where the church can help. The church is certainly not the sole factor in the question of community development, but it is in a real sense, in many areas of Latin America, the conscience of the people, and this conscience has to be stirred so that people will look for solutions and work for these solutions. On a local level, it is often the church that stirs men to action. Community programs are begun, which in many instances grow into regional, even national programs. In the process, they break off from their early moorings and become the civic entities that they should become.

We have spoken about church doctrine in Latin America after the Council. A doctrinal church acts upon doctrine, even in its relation to temporal affairs. There is no secret about this doctrine. At the present time, church doctrine, and the church as an institution preaching that doctrine by word and deed, can help us to discover the new demands of present-day life in order that we may improve the standards of life for our people. It is the dignity of man in society, now and hereafter, that this doctrine principally espouses.

7: THE ROMAN CATHOLIC CHURCH AND SOCIAL CHANGE IN LATIN AMERICA

Abbé François Houtart

Before entering on a discussion of the role played by the church of Rome as an institution for social change in Latin America, it will perhaps be well to describe briefly why and how I envisage the church as a sociological institution. Sociological analysis of the church is completely legitimate, even from a theological point of view. Indeed, to so conceive the church would seem in close correspondence with the new definition of the Roman Catholic church given by the constitution *Lumen Gentium* of Vatican II. The definition in *Lumen Gentium* describes the church of Rome as "the people of God"— an approach both essentially sociological and at the same time profoundly theological.

In addition to defining the church as "the people of God" and describing it as an assembly of people who believe in Jesus Christ, *Lumen Gentium* also pictures the hierarchy, the priesthood, and, indeed, the whole structure of the church as being of service to God's people. Although this is not the only definition contained in *Lumen Gentium*, its relative importance is immediately evidenced by the fact that a whole chapter is devoted to discussing the church as "the people of God," whereas only a few paragraphs are given to considering the church as the mystical body of Christ and similar theological concepts. Such a view approaches a sociological perspective more closely than it does the juridical description of the church as pyramidal, broadening out from the single figure of the pope at the top down through bishops and priests to the mass of lay people at the base, which is perhaps more classical.

Any consideration of the Roman Catholic church in Latin America as an institution presents multiple problems. We could, for example, study the church as an institution affected by social changes. Or we could seek to determine how the church acts as an agent of social change. Or again, we might study how social change affects the definition of roles within the church. What, for example, is the import of social change on the definition of priest, of layman, or upon the role of the sisters, or of the deacons?

It would be possible also to consider the different methods of action employed by the church or the different systems of norms, beliefs, social control, socialization, even of communication employed within the church, asking how the many facets of church activity and function are affected by social change. Or, again, investigation might seek to determine how some changes within the church itself—changes, for example, in the system of authority or in systems of communication—eventually affect society as a whole.

Of the many different aspects of the Roman Catholic church as an institution in Latin American social change, we shall consider only three: social change in ecclesiastical roles and institutions, religious motivations in social change, and the attitudes of Christians in Latin America who are facing social change.

The main conclusion will, of course, be the expected one of the recognition that we are faced with a great diversity of attitudes and of institutional change in Latin America. Yet, in the following discussion two important points must always be kept in mind: first, that even as the great diversity which exists among the different types of society from Mexico to Argentina or Chile essentially prevents us from considering Latin America as a single whole, so, too, we cannot speak simply about the church in Latin America; second, in addition to this great diversity in Latin American Catholicism, we are living in a very deep crisis which in itself is not necessarily negative. Theologically speaking, the word "crisis" generally carries a negative suggestion; yet it is important to recognize that, sociologically speaking, crises really act very positively in a process of change; more than a negative sense is implicit in the meaning of "crisis."

ASPECTS OF SOCIAL CHANGE IN LATIN AMERICA

Let us first consider some aspects of social change in Latin America, choosing, of course, those which will carry significance in the subsequent analysis of the church. Two main aspects of social change in Latin America, the demographic and the socio-cultural, are generally familiar. The demographic is obvious: At the beginning of this century there were 63 million people living on the continent; in 1950 there were 165 million; and in 1960 about 205 million. It is expected that by the year 2,000 the total will have exceeded 600 million. If this proves to be the case, it will mean that in a single century the population in Latin America will have multiplied more than ten times. Assuredly, this aspect functions as a major factor affecting the church.

Although it is possible to project the importance of this population change in Latin America by the simple device of multiplying the number of institutions by ten—schools, churches, work possibilities, and other representative guide posts—social change in itself is much more profound. For this reason, of even greater importance than demographic expansion are the socio-cultural aspects of social change in Latin America, whose determinants lie in the social and economic history of the continent. Latin America's culture for many years was that of a Spanish or Portuguese colonial regime. At the same time many of its features were typical not only of the colonial but also of the feudal type of society characteristic of the time. Economically, the colonial regime involved a monopoly by the mother country that allowed the colonies almost no power to develop their own economy. Under this monopoly American Spanish colonies, for example, were prohibited from commerce with places other than Spain, and the colonies were not allowed to develop industry or inter-zonal commerce, so tightly and completely did the parent country hold the reins.

Feudalism was introduced into Latin America by the Spanish and Portuguese, the type of society which was prevalent in the mother countries when Latin America was being colonized. At the time of the discovery of America the whole southern part of Spain was owned by some thirty families; even today large holdings still exist in many areas of both Spain and, especially, Portugal. When the Spanish or Portuguese came to Latin America, they imposed upon the colonies the social structure with which they were familiar, and from this has developed the kind of society which we find in Latin America today. A simplified representation of a complicated situation will suffice. Society in Latin America was divided into two main classes. The elite class monopolized the social, political, economic, and cultural life and activity, and exercised a certain responsibility for the other class, which was a marginal one—economically, culturally, and politically— and comprised, of course, the majority of the people.

When the Spanish colonies in Latin America became independent, political change was achieved. Social change, however, did not accompany it, and the established social structure was not modified. Unlike the French, English, or Russian revolutions, the Latin American revolutions were against the mother country and the oppressive colonial regime. It has been estimated that at the end of the eighteenth century approximately 80 per cent of the revenues from the Spanish colonies was spent for their administration. Obviously, those who held the real economic power in the colonies were interested in ridding themselves of the heavy colonial-political regime. Only in Brazil was the situation different. Because of the revolution in Portugal, the king of Portugal established himself in Brazil, where until 1889 the empire survived, thus prolonging the existing regime politically as well as socially.

At the present time Latin America faces a period of profound change. In the nineteenth and the early part of the twentieth centuries, a liberal political system derived from the French or American constitutions existed side by side with an essentially feudal social structure. Such conditions could endure only in a region in which a country's political life was contained in one, two, or three cities, while in the rest of the nation people continued to live in the manner which had prevailed for centuries. Now, however, things are changing. First of all, in the urban areas new elites are emerging and are challenging, sometimes violently, the traditional leaders. This situation prevails especially in those countries where industrial development has introduced extensive changes, as, for example, Argentina, some parts of Chile, São Paulo, and some parts of Mexico and Colombia.

A second contributing factor is the emergence of some kind of intermediary class between the traditional elite and the rural and urban masses. I dare not call it a "middle class," because sociologically this concept is too well defined. This intermediary class is encountering very great economic and social obstacles; consequently, its members are very ready to adopt some kind of radicalism, whether from the left or the right.

Finally, in urban areas there are large marginal groups made up of people living in slum areas—"callampas," "favellas," "villas de miseria." These groups are composed of people from rural sections who are migrating in greatly increasing numbers to the cities. In the last quarter of a century approximately 20 per cent of the rural population has migrated to metropolitan areas.

It should be noted, moreover, that social change is not confined to urban centers. Rural social structure likewise is undergoing a transformation which corresponds closely with that taking place in metropolitan centers. Indeed, the change taking place in rural areas is perhaps even more explosive and revolutionary because of the traditionally rigid character of the social structure of many rural areas. In many countries large property holdings characteristic of medieval or feudal times still exist, and there is no evidence that they are disappearing.

Two new elements are basic to social change in rural areas: demographic pressure and rising social consciousness on the part of the rural masses. Of the first, the situation in Colombia affords an illustration. In Colombia in 1954 there were approximately 500,000 peasant families who held no property of their own but lived on the large holdings of other. Usually these peasant families lived outside the economic cycle because they were not paid in money for their labor. There were also about 500,000 peasant families who owned some property, mainly "minifundia," or holdings which are too small to provide a living for a family. In addition to these two types of peasant families there were the 29,000 families who owned 65 per cent of the entire country.

Further examination of the statistics reveals that in Colombia only 8 per cent of the properties containing 2,000 hectares (4,000 acres) or more are cultivated or turned to good account. As a result, although the country itself has tremendous agricultural potentialities—Colombia could provide food for two, three, or even five times the entire population of Latin America—some peasants suffer from hunger. The situation is serious from another point of view: Colombia must set aside $100 million a year for the purchase of foreign food. This situation results principally from the rigidity of the social structure; it is, moreover, not peculiar to Colombia. In Northeastern Brazil, for example, problems of hunger and misery, infant mortality—in some areas 50 per cent of the children die before they are a year old—and a short life expectancy (the average age of the peasants is thirty-two years, less than in India) cannot be even largely attributed to the extreme dryness of the area. Rather, they are due in much greater measure to the immobility of the social structure and to the impossibility of change in the structure of land ownership.

Throughout Latin America a decline in the rate of infant mortality has contributed markedly to increasing demographic pressure. Fewer children are dying; yet although they now have perhaps even twice as many children to care for as before, the revenue of the peasant families is not increasing. Since geographical mobility seems to be the only answer to the rigid and immobile social structure, what, then, can they do except leave the rural areas and go to the big cities? And this procedure in turn provokes the tremendous problem of marginal population in urban areas.

Rising social consciousness on the part of the masses, the second element basic to social change in rural areas, has been given impetus largely through new and improved means of communication. In many rural areas the advent of the automobile, bus, and truck, by facilitating geographical intercommunication, has created a remarkable change. For the first time people have come into contact with urban areas and with another kind of civilization. But also—and perhaps even more—communication's mass media have enabled rural masses to know that their situation does not resemble what is found elsewhere in the world. Sometimes, but not always, their present situation is no worse than it has ever been. The great and essential difference at the present time, however, is that, having means for comparison, they now *can know* their situation for what it really is.

Under such circumstances increasing pressure from both population growth and social consciousness is leading to an explosion unless the rigid social structure undergoes a very rapid change.

THE CHURCH IN SOCIAL CHANGE

It is at once apparent that such explosive circumstances must affect all institutions in society. The church could not be the only institution in society not affected by such problems.

In this discussion, in respect to religious institutions, we are concerned primarily with the Roman Catholic church, since about 95 per cent of the population in Latin America is baptized in the church of Rome. At the present time the percentage of Protestants in Latin America is approximately 3.5, and although Protestantism is demonstrating a high rate of increase, it nonetheless still comprises a very

small minority except in a few countries. In Chile, for example, Protestants make up about 11 per cent of the population. The history of
the Roman Catholic church in Latin America has been varied. From
a high degree of integration in society during the colonial period it
has passed through very profound struggles and even persecution in
the nineteenth and early twentieth centuries until now it has come
to a position of social awareness and the assumption of a certain
leadership in a time of social change.

EFFECT ON INSTITUTIONS AND ROLES

Let us first consider the effect which social change is having both
upon the ecclesiastical institutions themselves and upon the roles of
the several categories of workers within the institution. In this reference ecclesiastical institutions should be looked upon as signifying all
the divisions of responsibility within the church, e.g., the diocese, the
parishes, the religious congregations, Catholic Action movements.
The roles similarly refer to spheres of activity, such as that of the
priest, the religious, the lay person, and so forth. If looked at first
from an analytical point of view, statistics (1965) show that in Latin
America there is approximately one priest for every 5,700 inhabitants;
one for 3,600 in Colombia, 3,400 in Ecuador, 3,400 in Chile, but, for
example, one for up to 12,400 in Honduras and 7,700 in Brazil. The
figure 5,700, however, should be considered as relative. In France, for
example, although there is said to be a scarcity of priests, there is one
priest for 900 people; in the United States, also, there is one priest
for 900 Roman Catholics; and in Belgium, one priest for every 600
Roman Catholics.

In a way, the situation in Latin America is a very abnormal one for
the Roman Catholic church. Speaking precisely, it would be very
difficult to name the optimal number of people per priest; in general,
however, it is thought that an average of approximately 1,000 persons
per priest is more or less desirable for the organization of pastoral
work. Because of the excessive number of parishioners in combination
with many other contributing factors—such as distance, for example
—in Latin America all the older institutions of the church are completely challenged. In addition, the sacramental life of the people is
consequently very poor, because, until now, the distribution of sacraments has been the prerogative of the priest.

Let us consider, first, the consequential effect of such a large number of people upon the institution of the parish. Canon law, for example, defines the parish as the primary group for the religious life of the people, that group in which people normally meet and worship together with their own priest and of which the members know both the priest and one another. From the sociological point of view the parish is often defined as a primary group, although such terminology can, of course, be very ambiguous in reference to a large urban parish. How does the situation in Latin America fit in? As a whole, even with allowance for the great differences which exist in Latin America, there is an average of about 15,200 souls per parish. In rural areas there are on the average from 10,000 to 35,000 people per parish; there are, for example, 10,000 in Colombia, and 35,000 in the Dominican Republic. In Northeastern Brazil, on the other hand, parishes include on the average 40,000 to 50,000 persons, and in this region sometimes a single priest is charged with the care of two or three parishes! Hence, from the sociological as well as from the pastoral point of view the parochial institution is completely frustrated by these factors.

In respect to physical size also the situation is comparably disturbing, since the rural parishes in Latin America comprise an average of from 240 to 2,400 square miles. Even in urban parishes, where distance is not so challenging a factor, the parishes tend to average a great number of people. In Bogotá, for example, in the late 1950's or early 1960's there was an average of 15,000 persons per parish, a situation which was considered commendable for a large city in Latin America. On the other hand, in São Paulo the average is 24,000; in Montevideo, approximately 25,000; in Buenos Aires, 27,000; in Santiago, 35,000; in Mexico City, 45,000; and in Havana, 60,000. In urban parishes there are generally two priests; sometimes, but rarely, three. Such conditions must of necessity completely distort the whole concept of the parish, a situation derived, of course, from the lack of priests.

The sociological meaning of the institution called "parish" is therefore completely changed. How much it is changed can be illustrated by the example of a parish which I remember in Rio de Janeiro. In this parish there were about 40,000 people and one priest. Moreover, the priest was seventy-two years old and spent all his time in the church administering blessings, baptisms, or marriages, or in the sacristy giving papers. What is the meaning of pastoral care? In the same parish there were about 500 centers of spiritism.* Herein were the real centers of the religious life of the people; the parish was an administrative structure like a post office.

The second problem concerns sacramental life. Analysis of this aspect calls for a certain prudence, and, at the same time, a clear recognition of the fact that the solution to pastoral work in Latin America calls for something more than merely extending the administration of the sacraments. A cursory analysis shows, however, that in Peru and in Venezuela only about from 3 to 5 per cent of the rural population had a weekly mass on Sunday, whereas from 95 to 98 per cent did not have even the possibility of a weekly mass. Rather, the opportunity would come at intervals of two weeks, or once a month, even once every six months, or perhaps once a year. Sometimes I am led to think that Jesus Christ did not initiate the sacraments of the Eucharist and of penance for the people of Latin America, for they simply do not have the opportunities to receive them. I also remember that in Brazil a few years ago a Eucharistic crusade, which had as its object the promotion of regular communion among children, abandoned its campaigning for frequent communions when it was finally realized that it was not possible to give communion to all the children because there were no priests to administer it! I recall also an experience I had at a place in Colombia where attendance at mass on Sunday is very high. I was asked to say mass in a parish in which ten masses were celebrated each Sunday. Each priest was assigned three masses to celebrate; I was to say the eight o'clock mass, which was the children's mass. The morning I celebrated there were about 4,000 children in the church; I was alone and was charged not only with saying mass but also with distributing communion. This I gave out as rapidly as I could because I had to complete the mass in order that people could come in for the nine o'clock mass. In all I distributed about 150 communions, mostly to adults. When I spoke to the priest later about the situation, he said, "Well, Father, we beg the children not to go to communion on Sunday."

Such then is a quick review of the situation. Immediately it elicits

---

* Spiritism is a syncretic movement mixing elements of the Christian and African religions that is one of the most important popular cultural and religious phenomena of Brazil.

the question: Why does this situation exist? How did it come into being? Sometimes when faced with the situation which prevails in Latin America, Europeans or North Americans are scandalized: Is this really a Catholic continent? How can that be possible?

In seeking an answer to such questions we must first consider historical circumstances. Before independence there were sometimes so many priests in Latin America that bishops in Quito or Mexico City, for example, because they did not know what to do with all the priests they had, begged Spanish bishops to accept priests in Spain. The coming of independence, however, brought with it a crisis for the church, especially in Spanish areas because the church was Spanish. Brazil was the exception. Because they were themselves Spanish, almost all bishops had to leave Latin America at the time of independence. Some countries in fact were without a bishop for from ten to twenty years. In many cases it is really miraculous that a national church did not develop within some of these countries.

Furthermore, because many of the movements which led to independence were inspired by the French Revolution and so were characterized by not only an anticlerical but also an antireligious feeling, after independence many political regimes developed distinctly antireligious and anticlerical policies. Argentina, for example, secularized all religious orders and congregations. In some countries, such as Guatemala, it has been impossible until very recently for the church. to develop any kind of institution. Brazil, on the other hand, has been characterized by another kind of phenomenon. In Brazil, since Dom Pedro and the political regime of the nineteenth century were quite antireligious, "regalism" was predominant by virtue of the fact that the church was controlled by the political power. Until the end of the nineteenth century no Brazilian citizen was allowed to enter a religious order. In Brazil, therefore, all religious communities suffered a complete decline. Not until after the end of the empire and the beginning of the republic was a reorganization of religious life begun.

The additional fact that almost all Latin American countries have undergone deep crises has likewise assisted in preventing the church from developing its own institutions. Only two years ago in Guatemala, for example, did it become possible to build a major seminary for the first time since independence. Likewise, for twenty-five years after independence the major seminary in Buenos Aires remained closed. Such factors have acted to impair the development of many of the church's institutions.

Furthermore, Latin America's reputation as a Catholic continent has acted also to hinder the church's development in many respects. It is well known that at the time of the great immigrations about 14 million Europeans emigrated to Latin America and about 30 to 35 million to North America. The majority of those who went to Latin America came from Spain or Italy and were Roman Catholics. Because they were going to a Catholic continent, however, emigrants to Latin America, unlike those going to the United States, were unaccompanied by priests. North America's reputed Protestantism created in Europe a feeling of the necessity to send priests along with their people. On the other hand, almost no priests came with immigrants to Latin America, especially with those immigrants who came to Argentina, Uruguay, and parts of Chile. In the southern part of Brazil, on the other hand, when German, Polish, and Italian immigrants came to settle in the rural areas, some priests came with them. These regions, incidentally, are now the areas of Brazil from which presently come the greatest number of candidates for the priesthood.

The explosion of population which began about the time the struggle between the state and the church was coming to an end likewise serves as a factor contributing to the relative shortage of priests. The rate of increase in the number of priests can in no way keep abreast of, to say nothing of outpace, the rate of population increase.

Historically, the church-pastoral approach was built within the framework of a feudal society. Such a society decreed that the pastoral role of the church should be especially oriented toward the education of the upper class of society, since (the belief was) this elite class really held the responsibility for society as a whole. Educating the elite was looked upon as essentially a service to all classes of society; educating the masses could be considered a matter of small concern.

In respect to the masses the concern of pastoral action was the exercise of some kind of social control. Even when the priest came only once every six months or a year, such an approach was both feasible and efficient, since society was highly stable, the patriarchal family was typical, and the religious tradition was transmitted along with the social and cultural. Society was not, apparently, changing, and the social values functioned essentially as a means for transmitting the religious values. Under such circumstances the organization of some minimal kind of social control from the religious point of view sufficed to keep the population in the faith; we cannot say in a very perfect state of faith, but unquestionably in a certain faith.

THE INSTITUTIONAL REACTION OF THE CHURCH

What actions were required to alleviate such a situation? The first to be initiated was the multiplication of dioceses in Latin America. During the whole span of the nineteenth century only sixty-nine new dioceses were created in Latin America. During the first half of the twentieth century, in the fifty years between 1900 and 1950, 190 new dioceses were created; in the ten years between 1950 and 1960, 148 more. As a result of this acceleration of the rate at which new ecclesiastical units (diocesan or other types) were established, there are now 547 diocesan or other ecclesiastical units and more than 600 bishops.

A second step consisted of the multiplication of parishes, primarily in urban areas and only to a small extent in rural sections, because of the shortage in supply of available priests. In 1965 the average parish throughout Latin America contained 15,200 people. The exceedingly rapid growth of the cities, however, has made it almost impossible to create new parishes fast enough to keep pace with the need, and indeed in dioceses characterized by large numbers of people the size of the average parish grew from 14,000 to 15,200 people in the twenty years between 1945 and 1965.

The third remedial step relates to the number of priests, and this has increased markedly. In 1945 there were 24,380 priests in Latin America; in 1960 there were 37,600; and in 1965, 42,400—an increase of nearly 18,000 in twenty years. It must be confessed, however, that at least 50 per cent of this increase came from outside Latin America, from Europe and from North America, in response to a call by the Holy See asking other churches to help the Latin American church.

And what of the future? From time to time it has seemed, by means of the external help and also because of the increase in callings to the priesthood in Latin America, that the situation would be improved. Simple calculations relating estimates of population made by the United Nations to forecasts regarding the number of priests in Latin America bring us to a contrary conclusion, however. Probably, because of the population explosion, the next few years will see a greater increase in the number of people per priest. So, it is expected that in 1970 there will be 5,500 persons per priest; in 1975, about 5,700; and in 2000 (insofar as it is possible to estimate) at least 7,400.

It is evident, therefore that the church as an institution must recognize, first, that pastoral work must be organized on a completely different basis and, second, that the definition of roles has to be changed. Reorganization of both pastoral work and spheres of activity might, for example, feasibly include the extension of the pastoral and sacramental function to nuns. Compared with the number of priests, the number of sisters in Latin America is increasing very rapidly, from 58,600 in 1945 to 109,700 in 1965. Indeed, experiments relating to a broadening of the sisters' functions are already being made. For example, in Brazil, in the diocese of Natal, a parish was given into the care of four sisters. The nuns direct the common prayer of the people and perform all the activities normally entrusted to a parish priest, except those of hearing confession and celebrating the mass. In other words, they are baptizing, comforting the dying in their last moments, and, in general, are taking the parish in hand. And before the liturgical renewal a few years ago the parishioners were saying that they much preferred the "mass" of the sisters to that of the priests because they could understand at least something about it!

Other experiments currently in progress include the entrusting to laymen of some pastoral responsibilities and also the direction of the organization of Sunday worship. Likewise the possibility of using married men as deacons is already a fact in several countries.

RELIGIOUS MOTIVATIONS

The second aspect of the effects of social change on the Latin American Catholic church as an institution relates to the problem of religious motivations. Why is someone religious? What are the motivations for religious participation? Through analyses of Latin America, and of many other places as well, it is clear that there are four different types of religious attitudes or motivations. The first, which might be described as the religious attitude for the satisfaction of natural aspirations, is characterized by the fact that the religious rite is looked upon as answering to natural needs. People perform religious actions in order to obtain good health or an economic or other kind of success, or to bring about the triumph of their group or class or country, or to gain the liberation of man from cosmic forces. This attitude is very prevalent in the rural areas of Latin America. As a religious motivation, this attitude has in itself a certain automatic force that is devoid of any kind of moral exigency or of any thought for the personal attitude of man. Rather, the religious rite is turned toward direct results, especially toward such results as cannot be obtained by personal efforts, and is itself conceived of as working in a mysterious way.

In Latin America this religious attitude might feasibly be described as a kind of *popular Catholicism* and is, of course, very profoundly affected both by social change and by the spread of technology. A telling illustration is found in the story of the Colombian peasant who when he asked the priest to come and bless his fields said, "You know, Father, this year I had a hard time deciding whether to ask you to come or to use fertilizer." When the priest said, "Why did you come to me? Why did you not go to your own parish priest?" the peasant answered, "Well, if you must know, last year I went to him and the result was disastrous!" Clearly, the peasant of the story was hesitating between the efficacy of the rite and that of fertilizer or technology. Clearly, also, religious motivation which springs primarily from the satisfaction of natural aspirations (an attitude which is not peculiar to Latin Americans but rather is found in all rural religions, whether mixed with Christianity or not) cannot maintain itself very long, for one or two or three generations at most, in an environment of social change provoked and fostered by the birth and development of a technological civilization.

The second type of religious motivation is that of obedience to the religious norms of the natural group, or what is usually defined as a *cultural form* of Christianity or Catholicism. It is an accepted fact that Catholicism is identified with the culture of Latin America. One is Catholic because he is born in Latin America and generally feels a kind of obligation or sense of being faithful to the culture. The statement "We are all Catholics" is sometimes heard, as if it were unthinkable that anyone would be a Moslem or a Buddhist! This attitude apparently represents some kind of cultural norm of belonging to a religion and is found very commonly among the urban population, also.

And what has happened to this attitude in an environment of social change? It would appear that although the fact of belonging to the religious group is still affirmed, the content of this membership is very rapidly lost. The tendency is for one to say that he is a Catholic because he has been born in Latin America and cannot imagine being anything else. But the avowal of being a Catholic does not necessarily imply belonging to the church of Christ. So, in the process of social change, such as that now affecting many parts of the Latin American continent, the situation obtains in which the motivation to be a Catholic derives more and more from the cultural and less and less from the religious fact.

The remaining types of religious motivation derive from real conviction. A man is religious because he is searching for religious salvation, and in so doing he tries to make the religious norms part of himself and to determine what religion is asking of him. This process, however, may reflect two very different approaches to religion. The first entails a kind of *individualized salvation through religion.* A man is religious because he wants his own salvation, and he obeys religious norms because it is necessary for him to do so to achieve this salvation. In general, this religious attitude is quite negative, in that it leads to avoidance of sin in order to avoid hell and to seeking the sacramental life in order to avoid sin or in order to be forgiven for sinning.

Generally, too, this attitude is very selfish. Belonging to the church as a group has no importance and does not play a great role. The church is there simply to function as a distribution agency for the pardoning of sins or the giving of the sacraments through which one obtains personal salvation.

Although, again, this kind of religious motivation is not confined to Latin America, nonetheless it is the characteristic attitude of many of the traditional elite who have had and still often have quite a profound religious life. This religious life is, however, almost completely disassociated from any kind of social ethos. I personally have known representative cases of people of high religiosity and piety (in the sense of personal prayer) who were yet completely unaware of social responsibility.

The second kind of religious attitude is characterized by a search for salvation and a genuine assimilation of religious norms, and it envisages religion as a spiritual transformation to be achieved within the church. Consequently, belonging to the church is important. Religion is not a force effective against a nature from which man must constantly seek protection. Rather, this last religious attitude looks upon evil not as an external force which must be avoided, but as something which is internal to every man. Therefore, persons experiencing this kind of motivation feel solidarity with all men because all men are sinners. Also, unlike the preceding attitude, this one resists the temptation to divide the world into two parts, the good and the bad.

In addition, persons inspired by this kind of religious motivation

look upon the sacraments not as merely the means for obtaining salvation but, since they are in general a gesture by Christ who wants to
cure us, as really having the power to influence the whole life, including its social aspect. For such persons, therefore, participation in a
community, in a church, is not indifferent. The church is not just a
device which automatically distributes sacraments or some other kind
of religious goods; rather, by sharing the participation offered through
the church, salvation can be realized. In this attitude also can be seen
the importance of social commitment to a program of social, economic, and cultural life, because therein lies the realization of the
religious life of man.

This motivation is typical of Latin America's *new Christian elite*.
This elite comprises those who both engage in social renewal, in many
cases undertaking leadership in trade unions or in other aspects of
political or economic life, and who also make demands of the church
as an institution, since they recognize that the one cannot proceed
without the other and that renewal through social commitment
entails a new religious outlook.

Such, then, are the ways in which social change is affecting the
various types of religious motivation. Obviously, the last religious
attitude represents that of Christians really engaged in the process of
social change, whereas the more elemental or natural religion discussed in connection with the first type of motivation is progressively
disappearing. Since the other two attitudes are also diminishing, the
field is being opened either to religious indifference or, especially in
the marginal areas of the large cities, to sects or syncretisms.

ATTITUDES IN THE CHURCH TOWARD SOCIAL CHANGE

Although a typology is always a difficult and dangerous thing, let us
distinguish the attitudes in the church toward social change. There
are four of these also.

The first attitude can be defined more or less by the following
equation: The existing social system is fundamentally good not only
in principle but also in application. The role of Catholicism in Latin
America is therefore to support that system both in doctrine and in
practice. This position is extreme and is held only by a minority.

This minority is made up of laymen as well as by some priests and
bishops. These lay people are generally members of the traditional

oligarchy, and their attitude is to be expected, both because it reflects a defense of their privileges and monopolies and because they expect support of this social situation from the church. Some of the new leaders in the industrial or capitalist world are also embracing this attitude, as are some administrators, because in the context of Latin American political life their situation has been very difficult. For a long time the administrative and political regimes have practically been servants of the existing oligarchy. In practice, much of the administration has been made up of people who are clients of the oligarchy, so it is only to be expected that they should also share its cultural values.

A part of the army also feels this way, but only a part, because in recent years in many countries the army has passed beyond its traditional role of supporting the oligarchy or the traditional elites and is conducting itself in a much more socially oriented manner.

A part of the intermediary class may also endorse this position, for especially in certain countries, Colombia or Peru, for example, where social structures are extremely rigid, this class has experienced difficulties in defining itself and takes the higher class, the traditional elite, as a reference group. Indeed, even though the intermediary class has to oppose the traditional aristocracy, because this group presents the main obstacle to its development, members of the intermediary class tend to look to the higher class for guiding principles and values in the absence of an alternative. But I say "a part" and in so saying designate that small minority in the intermediary group among whom there have originated some of the religiously motivated reactionary movements—we could call them "integralist"—which have and are springing up, for example, "El Muro" in Mexico or the "Youth of Christ the King" in Brazil. These movements are found not only in Latin America but all over the world, and it is interesting to consider the names which they have chosen for themselves. The "wall" or the "bulwark" is typical, and the choice seems sometimes to be spontaneous, sometimes to be inspired by other groups, especially French or Spanish.

In Latin America these minority groups are strongly opposed to the decisions of Vatican II, for example, concerning liturgical renewal, and also are strongly anti-Communist. Some members of the clergy and hierarchy also take much the same position. A typical expression of this point of view may be found in a book entitled *Land Reform: A*

Matter of Conscience, which was written by two bishops and published in Brazil three years ago. Although purporting to be about land reform, in point of fact the book defends the divine right of the land-owners and the right of possession of private property as fundamental and natural. Typical, too, is the fact that the two authors were leaders of the minority position during Vatican II. The book has enjoyed quite a success in Brazil, where its thesis has been used by the existing oligarchy as a basis for justifying its position.

The second attitude found within the Roman Catholic church toward social change may be defined as follows: The existing social system is good in principle but like all things human is not perfect and can be made better. How do advocates of this position look upon the role of Catholicism in Latin America in relation to the existing social system? In two different ways: some say simply "Religion has nothing to do with that. We do not have to concern ourselves with temporal problems." Others suggest that the role of religion is that of acting as a corrective to the defects of the social system by organizing the distribution of food, setting up of orphanages, establishing houses for young delinquents, and so on. This attitude is, of course, extensive among Catholics in Latin America since it accepts and even promotes what is essentially a kind of status quo. Fear of the possible consequences which a social change might entail appears frequently to be the source of this attitude, especially among the clergy but among laymen as well.

Who are the people who advocate this position? Not the masses, especially not the rural masses who live in a kind of fatalism because they think that change is not possible. As a whole, the people who represent this point of view comprise important parts of the intermediary class, including members of the administration and those engaged in commerce and industry, parts of the army, and quite a few priests and bishops, also. And among the priests endorsing this point of view there are two types. Some priests do not perceive that there is a problem of social change and simply go on in the traditional manner with their pastoral work, itself mostly ritualistic and based on social control. These priests do not care about social change, mainly because they are not aware that it is taking place. Other priests, although they are more conscious of social problems and indeed insist upon the necessity of correcting the defects of the social regime, nonetheless oppose strongly the concept of a social revolution.

The third attitude within the Roman Catholic church toward social change in Latin America recognizes that the present social system no longer corresponds to the demands of development and hence of social justice and feels that, consequently, it must be changed by rapid and decisive action. In effecting this action they feel that by inspiring the motivations of Christians engaged in social, economic, and cultural action, by giving a doctrinal orientation to the changes made, and even by sometimes taking direct action, the church may play a very important role as an institution in the social field.

Where do we find this attitude? First of all, among lay people, many of whom as Christians have accepted a social responsibility in the political field, as in Chile's Christian Democracy, in trade unionism (Christian trade unions or others), as well as in many of the apostolic movements.

It is noteworthy that this point of view contains the most dynamic elements. Typically, the lay people in this group accept the results of the Council and also are generally quite open to ecumenical contact. Among the priests and bishops who share this attitude it is necessary to make some distinctions. Some, while accepting the necessity for social action, do so without challenging seriously the church itself in its institutions, without seeing that real involvement in this situation of social change necessarily entails redefining the role of the priest, the relationship between priest and layman, the function of different organizations and activities within the church, including the liturgy and the worship, and even the role of theology.

Others among the clergy, in order to ensure a continuation of existing relationships (priest to layman, for example) are utilizing the new social and cultural means found in radio schools, cooperatives, trade unions, or similar forms of social activity as new instruments of power for the church. When the clergy of this persuasion realized that the traditional avenues of power were no longer effective, quite naturally and without rationalizing their actions they set about organizing new sources of power in order to ensure continuity of religious control. Beyond question, priests representing this point of view believe that they are serving the people; yet, unquestionably also, the motives through which they act are somewhat mixed.

The third group among these priests and bishops is made up of those clergy who, recognizing that the present social system no longer corresponds to needs, accept the change and the fact that with it, since by implication the church owes service to the poor and to the needs of development, should go a change of attitude within the church. This point of view implies a change in the relations both between the church and the world and also within the institution of the church, between clergy and laity. They even realize that a new type of worship may be called for, since people profoundly involved in social change may feel the need for a kind of liturgy and worship different from that offered by tradition. They require, as it were, a new kind of spirituality, not, as someone once defined devotionalism and pietism in Latin America, a "spirituality of underdevelopment." Priests of this persuasion realize that what is needed is an incarnated spirituality capable of uniting social responsibility and the religious life.

Such a position inspires all sorts of exemplary actions; for example, that of some bishops who distributed all the lands they held within their dioceses to the peasants; or, again, like those bishops in North-eastern Brazil who undertook, at least in the beginning, the responsibility of organizing the rural trade unions or cooperatives or similar social movements, recognizing that the church was the only institution capable of accomplishing such an endeavor without being destroyed by the social structure. People such as these, priests or laymen, dare to use the term "social revolution."

Last, the fourth attitude within the church respecting social change is the extreme that holds that the existing social system is fundamentally wrong and that only a violent revolution can change it. Adherents of this point of view assert that the proof of their position can be found in facts and that Christians must take part in this violent revolution, even if such action involves working with the Communists. For the most part this point of view represents only a minority consisting of some young laymen, mostly university students who have made the Cuban revolution a model of action and to a certain extent have idealized its results. A few priests also endorse this attitude, as, for example, did Camilo Torres in Colombia, a very honest man and a very dedicated priest who even went so far as to ask the church to reduce him to lay status so that he might be able actually to fight in the social revolution.*

* Torres was killed while fighting with guerilla forces in February, 1966, two months after his laicization was granted.

Clearly, then, social change in Latin America is of concern to the Roman Catholic church as an institution, especially since in the past ten years the church itself, as well as some of its priests, bishops, and laity, has begun to participate in the change.

CONCLUSION

What is happening in the Latin American church is an extremely interesting and moving human phenomenon, and, as such, it is worthwhile both to study and to experience. Also interesting is the way in which many people from widely differing ideological backgrounds have reacted to the spectacle. Two quite opposite examples must suffice to exemplify how many people feel. When Hubert Humphrey was still a senator, he asked that a collective pastoral letter written in 1962 by the bishops of Chile, criticizing Chilean society and listing such necessary social reforms as land and fiscal reform, be included in the Congressional Record as an example of an analysis and of a program for social change in Latin America.

The second illustration is that of a West European Marxist. He told me that the Marxists look upon the involvement of Christians in the social revolution of Latin America, and in particular on the attitude of the Roman Catholic church, as a profound challenge. It is causing them to ask whether this does not clearly mean the end of what they call "religious alienation," or the belief that religion serves to alienate people from action.

Certainly, it would seem from these two examples that the social change taking place in Latin America, both from the human and from the religious points of view, constitutes one of the most interesting phenomena of our time. It cannot leave any Americans indifferent. Indeed, it challenges all men, especially, of course, all Christians.

8: THE CHURCH AND REVOLUTIONARY CHANGE: CONTRASTING PERSPECTIVES*

Richard Shaull

It is hardly necessary to emphasize the fact that Latin America is passing through a period of profound crisis, in which explosive revolutionary forces are at work. Unfortunately, there are some people in this country, especially in official circles, who interpret the present state of relative calm as a sign that the worst upheavals are past and that a new stability is within reach. In recent decades, people of many different groups and classes in practically every country in Latin America have been going through a process of awakening and discovery. They have come to a new awareness of their existence and destiny as a people and have a new sense of their responsibility for the development of their own nation. And they have discovered the tragic character of their existence. For centuries, they have been dependent peoples, responding to initiative and forces from outside. Their national life is dominated by the structures of the old order which stand in the way of economic development and maintain the great masses of men and women in a permanent state of poverty and ignorance, of exploitation and exclusion from national life.

In this situation, a new generation is arising which is dedicated to two goals of a revolutionary nature. They propose to bring about a change in their economic and political relationships to the rest of the world, especially the United States, which will permit them to be the masters of their own national destiny. And they are committed to

* The original article appeared in German in *Evangelische Theologie*, Heft 12/1967: "Zur 'Theologie der Revolution.'" Chr. Kaiser Verlag, München.

the creation of a new social order, in which more rapid economic growth will be combined with more equitable distribution of its benefits and the participation of the dispossessed masses in the life of community and nation. When students, workers, or peasants, whose life in the past has been so integrated into the established structures, become involved in this struggle, they go through a rapid process of radicalization, for they soon see the inadequacy and injustices of the old order and recognize that only fundamental changes in the total structure will solve the problem. But they also discover that the traditional forces have tremendous power and can effectively block all attempts to bring about change; in fact, the stronger the forces of renewal, the more violent the reaction of the old order. It is this which makes the present situation so desperate and so explosive. And as the precarious stability which has been achieved at this moment in a number of countries is of this type, it must be seen for what it is: The calm before another storm.

Faced by this sudden change in the situation in which they have traditionally functioned, the churches in Latin America are at a great disadvantage. Roman Catholicism, from the colonial period onward, has been almost totally identified with the old order and has tended to provide religious legitimation of it. Catholic social doctrine has grown out of the church's response to developments in Western Europe; it is thus rather irrelevant to the problems of the developing nations and tends to support very gradual change rather than a revolutionary transformation of society. The traditional stress of the church upon authority, as well as its strong paternalism, make it most difficult for the hierarchy to understand and be sympathetic to the new mood. To support the forces of change means to run the risk of great losses in possessions, position, and prestige, an act of renunciation that is hardly to be expected. In recent years, the hierarchy has, on a number of occasions, broken with reactionary dictators. But when confronted by the necessity of a clear choice between revolutionary change and the old order, it may well follow the path which it took in Cuba.

Protestantism has not been bound in the same way to the traditional culture and social order and was thus free to relate creatively to the liberal forces of renewal in a previous period. But it too is at a disadvantage in the face of the new revolutionary pressures. Its middle-class, Anglo-Saxon heritage is now a factor of alienation. Protestant churches and their national leaders have finally won a degree of acceptance in the established order and are not inclined to risk losing this position in a new society which they do not understand. And the traditional Protestant pietism in Latin America has not prepared this generation for a creative theological response to the new social issues which have arisen. The Pentecostals are free from this burden of an Anglo-Saxon heritage and are fully inside the proletarian situation, but their attitude toward "the world" stands in the way of any clear Christian witness in society.

Given this background, the surprising thing is the degree of involvement of Christians, both clergy and laity, Catholic and Protestant, in the present revolutionary struggle. In 1962, the Chilean hierarchy published a pastoral letter in which it came out firmly in support of social change. In a number of other countries, a few of the most outstanding bishops have taken a similar position. Many priests, especially of the younger generation, are engaged in study of social problems, as well as in programs of lay education and action in the political sphere. In the last few years, the Protestant Commission on Church and Society has extended its work to almost all parts of the continent and formed small nuclei of people who are much involved in what is happening in their countries. It has a core of leaders working constantly on these problems, publishes a great deal of material for study, and recently brought together 100 key laymen and ministers from all of Latin America for a study conference on these issues. Most important of all is the proliferation of movements, from those which are more or less confessional in character to those with no distinctive Christian label or ideology, which are in the forefront of the revolutionary struggle. In fact, in a number of places, these groups now have the initiative and there are good reasons to believe that their influence will increase in the future.

In retrospect, it is possible to see a number of factors which have contributed to this development. The rapid decline in the vitality and influence of the liberal political parties of the center created a vacuum that had to be filled. Contrary to the expectations or fears of many, Marxism has thus far not been very successful in taking advantage of the crisis. This is partly due to the ideological and bureaucratic rigidity of the Communist parties; and partly to the fact that Catholicism and Pentecostalism, rather than Marxism, have the decisive hold over the urban proletariat as well as the peasants. But, ultimately, what has happened is that certain elements of the Christian heritage, not necessarily those incorporated in the traditional social teaching of the churches, have been at work in the Christian conscience and have now come to play a decisive role in the shaping of thought and action.

It is this last point which interests us in the present study, and we propose to explore it by examining two specific movements which have taken shape in two very different moments in the revolutionary struggle in Latin America and represent quite diverse perspectives. I refer to the Christian Democrats in Chile and to the New Christian Left, specifically in Brazil. As my own theological perspectives force me to take very seriously the concrete character of man's existence within a dynamic historical process, I find myself obliged to look at these moments in the light of this process and in the full recognition of my own involvement in it at a specific point, that is, in relation to the latter movement. I shall, therefore, attempt primarily to describe the significance of the shift which is now occurring in Christian social thought and action as expressed by the movement from the first to the second of these options. There are two reasons for my proceeding in this way. First, while many studies have appeared recently of the New Left in this country, I know of practically nothing which analyzes the New Christian Left in Latin America. As these forces are in a very strategic position there, due to the existence of a total revolutionary situation in many nations, and as they represent such a decisive change in the attitude of Christians, especially Catholics, toward social change, I think that the time has come when some attention must be focused on them. Second, I am convinced that, in the type of world in which we are now living, sociological analysis of political movements must be accompanied by the type of dialogue which is possible only if those who participate in such movements reflect on where they are going and expose themselves to confrontation with others outside their situation. You, of course, will have to judge, whether in this case, anything is accomplished aside from the defense, by the writer, of his own particular bias.

My thesis here is that Christian Democracy in its present form and what I have called the New Christian Left represent two different types of responses to different historical situations. In a sense, they belong to two periods in the Latin American social process and in the changing life of the church. Twenty years ago, the most revolutionary

Christian students in Chile were attracted to Christian Democracy; today, many representatives of the new generation of revolutionary students in Latin America tend to look elsewhere. Christian Democracy is a dynamic movement, open to and affected by new social forces and new historical challenges. It may, in the years ahead, respond to them in much the same way that the new movements are now doing. I do not pretend here to predict the future. But on the basis of the material thus far published by those in positions of leadership in Chile, I believe that the contrast is valid at the present time and will help us to understand some of the new developments now taking place on the continent south of us.

CHRISTIAN DEMOCRACY

Those of us who are old enough to have lived in the Latin America of twenty-five years ago find it almost impossible to believe that such tremendous changes have occurred in so short a time. In fact, about the only way we can describe the situation at that time is in terms of what had not happened. All the crises we now face were then taking shape, and a few movements appeared which should have made this clear, but we could not see their significance. There was a certain stability in the political order and a great deal of confidence in the ability of established political parties to solve the more urgent problems. No one was much aware of the complex of issues relating to national development, much less of the structural obstacles to it in the old society. There was much discussion of economic and political systems, but usually in abstract and schematic terms; we did not dream then of the revolution which would occur in the concreteness of dynamic historical existence. Protestants by and large were unconcerned about their social responsibility, while Catholics lived in that age before the renewal of Vatican II or the new lines of social thought of *Mater et Magistra* and *Pacem in Terris*.

But certain things were happening and some people were aware of them. The economic crisis in the U.S.A. and Europe shook the stability of the old colonial order and made it possible for a number of people to discover that all was not well and to look deeper for the causes of this crisis. The appeal of Marxism was growing in some circles and its threat could no longer be ignored. In the Catholic milieu, a certain ferment was at work, especially as the impact of

Maritain and other European intellectuals was felt. On most parts of the continent, this did not produce any striking results of a revolutionary character. In Brazil, for example, those most influenced by Maritain were part of a group identified by the title of its journal, *Order*, which has tended to become more reactionary as *its* order has been more threatened.

In Chile, something extraordinary happened. A number of young Catholics came together to reflect upon the situation in which they found themselves and to work out their vision of a new society. Out of this was born a political movement which developed its own strategy for revolution in Chile and has worked intensely at it. A number of factors in the Chilean situation undoubtedly contributed to the development of this unique Catholic movement but at the heart of it was the conviction and dedication of a small nucleus of young men and women who believed that revolutionary change was necessary in Chilean society and that they were called to bring it about. In later years, the assistance of the Jesuits of the Centro Belarmino contributed greatly to their eventual victory.

The Christian Democratic blueprint for a new Chilean society is presented most clearly in the publications of the Centro Belarmino,[1] in Santiago, and in the many books and articles which President Frei himself has written over three decades. Elsewhere, I have attempted to analyze the political ideology and program of the former;[2] here I would like to focus briefly on Frei.[3] All of his writings are dominated by the power of an ideal new order, which represents a very subtle mingling of a vision of a new Christian society as spelled out by Jacques Maritain—a democracy, shaped by theocentric humanism, in which economic development, social justice and individual self-fulfillment are gradually being achieved—and the progressive incarnation of this ideal in the Christian West. Chile, a "civilized nation" which shares this same heritage, must find her destiny along this road rather than that of Marxism or of the new nations of Asia and Africa. In *La Verdad Tiene Su Hora*, he writes:

> These nations, which form the democratic peoples of the West, whose culture is also ours, and whose reactions we have followed, repeating them at a distance not by chance but because of roots which go to the common sources which sustain us, have had to face, in recent years, problems similar to our own: social conflicts and tensions, together with crises and limitations in the economic

order, a dissatisfied proletariat in open struggle, within a climate of political pressure, not to mention the tremendous weight of the external threat. To a certain extent, it is as if we saw, on a larger stage and with more capable actors, the presentation of our own drama and the development of ideas and sentiments which later arrive at these distant shores in successive waves. [P. 87.]

Frei's ideal is that of the full flowering of democracy, in the socio-economic as well as the political sphere. Politically, this means discovering how to make the present structures function efficiently, at the same time that all the major groups and classes in the nation are provided with means for effective participation in the process of decision-making. It also involves the creation of a third sphere—between the state and the individual—of intermediate groups of various types which will offer a richer community life and new opportunities for participation. Economically, the key is to be found in central planning, led by the state with the co-operation of the major groups in society, which will determine the best use of available resources for national development. The basic assumption here seems to be that in the new order it will be possible to work out this type of harmonious relationship between the various communities, interests, and orders in society which will lead to co-operation for the common good without the necessity of excessive state intervention. Central to this is the concept of a new type of commercial and industrial organization, which will not be dominated by the profit motive. It will rather represent a community of effort in which labor and capital will work together, in which management will see its task as that of serving both of these groups, and the individual enterprise will be related to other enterprises and other interest groups in harmonious concern for the interests of all.

It is obvious that, for this to happen, fundamental changes will be required in Latin America. It will be necessary to break the old, established order, incorporate the masses into national life, and carry out basic reforms in land ownership, the tax structure, the social security system and the government bureaucracy. But the Western democracies have worked out patterns of harmonious interaction between government, industry, and labor, and created a society in which the masses have increasing opportunities of participation in political life and are in a constant process of economic and psychological ascent. The problems of Latin America are in many ways more acute and require solutions that are adapted to the concrete local situation, but the main lines for the future are clear, and Latin America can move in this direction along "the democratic path of progressive evolution." It can carry out a revolution with freedom.

The Frei government has now been in power for a number of years, and already the impact of utopia as an explosive force in the present is clearly evident. When one arrives in Chile, after stopping off in Brazil, Uruguay, and Argentina, the contrast is tremendous. In Chile, something significant is happening. The nation is on the move. A revolutionary land reform program has been worked out and now is in the process of being put into effect. Government initiative in planning for the use of national resources, as well as in constant stimulation of development, is evident. Significant strides have been made in meeting the problems of housing, education, and transportation, and efforts are being made to develop intermediate groups of various types.[4]

In the face of all this, you may well ask: How is it possible for a younger generation of Catholics and Protestants in Latin America to be less than enthusiastic about this option? The answer to this, I believe, is not that they are imprisoned in some new ideology or that they are unsympathetic to the revolutionary goals of the Christian Democrats. It is rather that this younger generation has been living through a new period, in which they have come to see their national reality in a new light, are aware of different issues and new dimensions, and have come to different conclusions about how these problems can be met. And as they are not convinced that the Christian Democrats have lived through this process or faced its implications, they have serious doubts about the ability of such a movement to understand the issues as now raised or provide adequate answers to them. What this means can only become clear if we turn our attention to the new elements which have emerged in the revolutionary struggle in Latin America in recent years and in the experience of these young people. To look at this shift in perspective, we might describe what has happened in terms of a series of discoveries which have rather far-reaching implications. I do not mean to imply that these discoveries represent a perception of the whole truth in the situation nor that they are entirely new. But I would contend that they indicate an awareness of certain dimensions of Latin American reality that has never occurred in such intensity with any previous generation of Christians there.

THE NEW WORLD OF THE NEW GENERATION

As part of the process of secularization, modern man has become increasingly aware of the radically historical character of his existence. It is only in recent years, however, that a new generation of Latin American youth have felt the full implications of this as they have discovered that they are part of a concrete process in which historical events and their effects on people are the important thing. In Latin America, this has meant the discovery that one belongs to a people and a nation which has a particular history and which must discover its selfhood as it works out its own future. It has also meant a growing awareness of national reality, with all its crises and tensions, and of the profound misery and suffering of masses of people.

For those who have come to this awareness, the idea of an eternal order of truth which can be rationally perceived and synthesized, or of an ideal order of society into which social reality should be fitted, makes no sense. In fact, all of these total rational systems hinder our grasp of the real situation and easily become meaningless slogans.[5] What is called for is the freedom to know reality in its richness and complexity and find ways of making sense out of it and defining goals for action. If this means the loss of easy security, the necessity of living and working with provisional understanding and awareness of ambiguity, it also offers an opportunity to perceive that the future is open and can be shaped and that constantly revised understanding of the precise nature of dynamic reality is the first and most important step toward effective transformation of it.

This has meant a complete breakdown of confidence in all Christian blueprints for a new society; it has also called for a redefinition of the terms of the Marxist-Christian encounter. For if the Christian must now admit that he has no prefabricated system to put over against Marxism, he also discovers that a large number of younger Marxists now have profound doubts about the validity of any total Marxist world view or social system. This opens up new possibilities for dialogue with the Marxists and perhaps for new types of co-operation with those who are thus "secularized"; it also calls for a new creativity and vitality in Christian thought to meet this challenge.

As they have become involved in efforts to transform their society, these Christian young people have discovered new dimensions of the struggle for national development. Originally concerned only about achieving certain limited and specific changes, they have now been forced to recognize that the major block to development is a total configuration of economic and political forces, national and international, all of which are closely interrelated; a complex of institutions which are instruments of the old society, coupled with and determining attitudes and perspectives which support the old order. Where this is the case, what is called for is a decisive break with the past and the establishment of a new order. Only as a total reorientation of that society occurs, and new institutions develop which contribute to a new attitude and to the construction of a new society, can there be any real hope for the future. It is this thesis which the Brazilian expert on development, Professor Candido Mendes de Almeida, has developed in a recent book, *Nacionalismo e Desenvolvimento*,[6] a work which provides objective justification for the attitude of the new generation.

This discovery leads to a further one: That those institutions, especially in the political sphere, which might serve as the instruments for social change, are themselves bound up with the status quo. Under pressures from outside, their leaders try to meet new challenges but are unable to understand what is happening or respond creatively. When their existence is threatened, they become even more bound to the old order. To the degree that the younger generation is aware of this situation, it reflects a profound crisis of confidence in the establishment and becomes engaged in a search for new instruments of social transformation. In other words, to work for national development where the structures of the old society are still dominant requires revolution. The founders of the Catholic oriented Popular Action in Brazil described their movement as "the expression of a generation that translated into revolutionary action, the position which it assumed as a response to the challenge of national reality."

Involvement in a revolutionary struggle has led young people to the discovery of "the people" and their relation to and responsibility toward them. For many, this has been a traumatic experience. In the past, most students from the upper classes had very little contact with the poor and even less concern about them; while those in the lower and middle classes could get ahead only as they left their families behind and concentrated on their individual careers. All this has now been radically changed. As Catholic and Protestant young people were first drawn into contact with the poor through social service and literacy projects, they were shocked by sudden recognition not only of the incredible misery, insecurity, and suffering which they found everywhere, but also by the inertia and lack of hope which dominated the lives of the masses.

It is out of this that a perspective on the priorities in national development has emerged, especially in Brazil, associated with the words *conscientização, promoção, animação,* etc. These terms express the conviction that a fundamental step in the process of national development must be the awakening of the masses to an awareness of their situation and their vocation in changing it. For only such new awareness will make it possible for the masses to discover their self-identity, break out of their former inertia, and find the possibility of a more human existence. And in a society where the power structures are controlled by the old order, the organization of peasants, slum dwellers, and industrial workers, and their united efforts to bring about social change, becomes one of the most essential elements in the process. If national development in the underdeveloped world, especially in its early stages, depends upon the emergence of a new dynamic elite committed to progress, it may well be that it will come from this union of students and intellectuals with those from the lower classes who arrive at this new state of awareness. It is here that we should look, in the underdeveloped world, for the counterparts to the Calvinist capitalists of the west.

There is one further element which has played a decisive role in the formation of the New Christian Left: the recent changes which have taken place in the social teachings of both the Catholic and Protestant churches. In the past, when Christian young people became aware of the problems of their society and took a revolutionary position, they felt so ill at ease in the church and were so aware of its identification with the old order, that they rebelled against it, abandoned it, and often ended up in the Marxist camp. At the present time, when the problem is much more acute and this new consciousness is so much more widespread, something quite different has happened. The same bitterness about the church is evident, but it is accompanied by a new sense of loyalty to the Christian heritage and by efforts to relate it to contemporary problems. This shift is the result of changes that have taken place in the social thought of the church itself. As a result of Vatican II, Catholics in Latin America are now aware of a new vitality of theological reflection on the world and society which goes far beyond the rigid and sterile concepts of a former scholasticism. New thought about the church's relationships to the world and the repudiation of a former "triumphalism" speak in an appealing way to young people who are very much involved in the realities of the world and have rebelled against all forms of paternalism. *Mater et Magistra* and more especially *Pacem in Terris* have moved beyond traditional categories to more concrete dealing with historical reality and to new understanding of the role of the state in the early stages of economic development. In Protestant circles, especially those related to the Latin American Commission on Church and Society, there has been a rather extraordinary growth of theological reflection in the very midst of the revolutionary struggle coupled with analysis of the social, economic, and political situation, which has led to a new sense of confidence among Protestants thus involved, broken down the traditional neurotic fear of or attraction to Marxism, and opened the way for creative dialogue with Roman Catholics. In fact, those Catholics and Protestants who have gone through this same process of awakening and discovery in society and in the church, now find that, although they come to the situation from different perspectives, they are essentially united in their political orientation and commitment and that their joint theological reflection can be helpful to both groups in their struggle to relate their faith to the problems now confronting them.

In this context new movements are emerging which are still in the early stages of organization and development. But given the accelerated pace of the revolutionary process, their expansion and growing influence in the struggle may well surprise us. One recent example has been provided by the ill-fated venture of Father Camilo Torres in Colombia.[7] Descendant of a wealthy and aristocratic family, Father Torres suddenly rose to prominence because of his insistence upon the need for rapid changes in the basic structures of Colombian society. Within a few months he found himself leading a rapidly expanding movement, uniting practically all those groups seeking to bring about such changes. But he soon became convinced that the powerful forces of the old order would not allow such changes to be brought about by democratic means, and in desperation decided to join the guerilla forces of national liberation. He has now become the first martyr of this New Latin American Left. It is still too early to assess the significance of his brief struggle and death, but it is quite likely that the impact will be felt far beyond the borders of Colombia.

In Brazil, in a brief period of three years (1961–64), *Ação Popular* was organized and developed so rapidly that it took control of the student movement from the Communists and became a major force in the social awakening of the masses and in their organization as an effective political force. A witness to their vitality is the fact that, since the April, 1964, military coup, this group and others associated with the Catholic left has been the main object of suppression, persecution and torture—in the name of anti-communism.

DIVERGENT PERSPECTIVES AND EMPHASES

It is natural that, out of the context we have just described, attitudes and movements should emerge which are quite different from Christian Democracy. I realize that it is always dangerous to attempt a comparison of movements of this type, for it is easy to exaggerate the differences between them, to be too critical of those with which one disagrees and too favorably inclined to the others, and to overlook the fact that in each camp there are a number of divergent points of view. In fact, in the Christian Democratic party in Chile, there is also a New Left which is perhaps closer to the position of the new movements described here than to the dominant position in the Christian Democratic tradition. Recognizing all this, it may still be of some value to attempt to spell out, more concretely, the nature of the contrasts which are becoming increasingly evident, especially in those countries of Latin America where Christian Democracy, although perhaps in a state of ferment, has not succeeded in incorporating a significant number of those representing the newer Catholic mentality.

In the writings of Eduardo Frei, as well as in the publications of the Centro Belarimino, Christian Democracy is portrayed as an attempt to carry out a *Christian* revolution and establish a *New Christendom*.[8] Coupled with this is an emphasis upon an *a priori* definition of the shape of the new society, derived logically from certain fundamental principles of social organization. For the New Christian Left, all this is out of line both with the newer theological developments in the church and contemporary understanding of the social order. Their concern is not to Christianize the revolution but to be so involved in it as to help to humanize it. They do not have a prefabricated economic and political system but rather hope to be participating in a dynamic historical process with the type of awareness and sense of direction which will make it possible to find the most authentic and adequate solutions to specific problems along each step of the way.

For those accustomed to think in terms of traditional social doctrine, this shift is incomprehensible. In an article about the recent Latin American Conference on Church and Society (Protestant) held in Chile, a Christian Democratic reporter for *Ercilla* (January 26, 1966) has this to say:

> Unlike Catholics, Protestants have discarded the possibility of Christianizing society or its structures. Thus, they have not elaborated a Christian philosophy nor . . . a Christian social doctrine.
>
> When a Protestant feels the call to the political or social struggle, he cannot deduce from his theology the consequent principles on which to act. For this reason the Protestant of the Left is inclined to seek refuge in already-existing political parties which recognize a concrete political philosophy and a definite battle strategy.

The ironic thing here is that it was precisely the failure of this "Christian social doctrine" which led a new generation of Catholics to turn toward what this writer condemns as Protestant. In doing so, they have not sold out to other political ideologies, but rather have found a way to meet and challenge them creatively.

For them the old approach broke down a long time ago—when they first understood that their ideal solutions could not be related to the changing situation in which they were struggling and stood in the way of their observation of the reality around them. They found themselves mouthing great but meaningless slogans, which left them less and less able to deal with the concrete social, political, and economic problems arising in their country. And they discovered that often those who were most influenced by these social doctrines were least open to re-examining their thought and program in the light of changing circumstances and little inclined to the type of renewal that can come only through serious dialogue with opposing perspectives inside and outside the movement.

Over against the dissatisfaction with this perspective, a new type of Christian social thought is taking shape, which is most clearly indicated by Popular Action[9] in Brazil. As this movement has developed, it has placed increasing emphasis upon constant observation, study, and research which focuses on the concrete social, cultural, economic, and political developments in Brazil. But it is also concerned about serious reflection on the nature of man and his fulfilment and on the meaning of the historical process, both of which concerns come primarily from Christian faith. It is out of the constant dialogue between this observation of the empirical and continued philosophical reflection that a new type of ideology takes shape. It is an ideology which is relative and provisional and thus open to constant revision on the road to the future. The specifically Christian contribution at this point may well be that of sustaining this type of ideological flexibility and openness and challenging other movements, especially Marxism, to do the same. It is perhaps not merely coincidental that, while in Chile, Marxism continues to be quite doctrinaire, a group of outstanding young Communists in Brazil are insisting upon the need for constant dialogue with Christian groups in order to move toward new ideological openness and creativity.

In Chile, the Christian Democrats place great emphasis on *revolution* and are committed to a program of major changes in society. The New Christian Left is not yet convinced that Christian Democracy will be able to fulfil its promises and is searching for new perspectives on and alternative roads to revolutionary change.

We mentioned earlier that Christian Democracy took shape at a time when progressive Latin Americans were not yet fully aware of the basic structural differences between the advanced and the developing nations, nor aware of the need for a radical and comprehensive change in the external relations as well as the internal structures of colonial society in order for rapid development to take place. When this is not understood, it is quite likely that limited and accidental changes will be made, which may leave the over-all structure of relationships undisturbed. There are a number of signs in Chile which already point in this direction or are at least sufficient to raise grave doubts among Christians in other parts of the continent:

— Stress upon planning and technological advance (the "metaphorical" revolution of Father Vekemans[10]), without adequate emphasis upon the need for comprehensive structural change.

— Insufficient attention to the degree of state initiative which may be necessary for an underdeveloped country to arrive as quickly as possible at the "take-off" stage.

— The continued dominance of the myth of Western Christendom and of Chile's place in it, which leads to a certain enthusiasm for patterns of economic, political, and social life which have developed in Western Europe and the United States[11] and are already in need of renewal there. Such an attitude makes it difficult to see the need for greater independence if the nation is to find its own authentic road to development.

— An exaggerated emphasis upon such slogans as "revolution in liberty," reform by "democratic means of progressive evolution," etc., which may make it very difficult for the government to challenge the real power of the old order, carry through on its promises if and when such methods are not effective, or deal with the dynamics of its own social revolution, if once launched.

Whether or not these suspicions are correct, the fact of the matter is that many young Catholics and Protestants are convinced that a more realistic program must be found for getting and using power to re-order society. Central here is the conviction that the state must take greater initiative and play a greater role in development at this stage. Thus, as the Christian Left has moved further away from ideological Marxism, it has become more socialistic and now sees some form of socialism as an essential element in the struggle to overcome economic backwardness and create a more just society. There is very little interest here in socialism as a total world view and system. The emphasis is rather on "new experiments in socialism" and pragmatic decisions about when and where the use of state initiative in the economic order is essential at different stages in the process of development. Rather than an effort to impose an ideology in the traditional sense, this position is a reaction against the highly ideological character of the insistence upon capitalism for the underdeveloped nations. Some sort of socialism appears simply as the logical way to use most effectively the limited resources available to stimulate economic growth and achieve a certain degree of justice in the distribution of goods.

It is interesting that one of the first voices raised in this regard was that of Dom Helder Camara, Archbishop of Recife in Northeastern Brazil. In an address at the inauguration of a new seminary early in 1965, he declared that one of the objectives of this institution should be the study of new forms of socialism most appropriate for that particular situation of underdevelopment. In various Protestant and Catholic groups an effort is now being made to work through this question from a variety of angles. Some indication of what this involves may be given by a brief reference to an unpublished document which was circulated recently by Popular Action.

> The union of socialism and democracy means . . . that authentic humanistic construction of socialism is not possible without the simultaneous implantation of a real socialist democracy. This real democracy is necessary not only in the economic sphere but also in the specifically political and cultural sphere as well. Without economic democracy, social ownership of the means of production and state planning run the grave risk of becoming instruments of forms of bureaucratic and technocratic domination over the economic life of man. For this reason, without forgetting the necessity for greater centralization in the initial phases of the construction of socialism, it is important to have the objective and make the effort to create, as rapidly as possible, political, economic, organic and cultural conditions which will lead to progressive democratization of planning and also of management. Without political democracy, on the other hand, the entire effort of socialist construction is threatened by forms of bureaucratic, political and ideological domination which, alienating man, would deny the very historical significance of socialism as humanism.

The Christian Democrats speak a great deal about the end of paternalism and the need to organize the masses so that they can take the initiative in working for revolutionary change. The New Christian Left, having discovered, as a result of its identification with the masses in recent years, that this can come only from an almost total change in attitude toward the masses and toward the social order, cannot quite believe that Christian Democracy is capable of this task.

In the Catholic milieu, the fundamental problem here is found in the church's traditional paternalism in relation to society, which has a solid theological foundation. Father Vekemans states this very sharply when he declares: "The Catholic church verifies in itself the same verticality it attributes to itself; it receives the attribution of the entire transcendency, and therefore of all the verticality of the divine authority."[12] This is "valid and legitimate in the ethical and religious realm" in which "the critical spirit cannot be allowed to enter."[13] Vekemans then affirms that the transfer of this attitude to the profane sphere had disastrous results and must be broken by a cultural mutation provoked from outside. For the New Left what is called for is rather a revolution in the Christian understanding of society as well as of the church's role in it.

In Brazil, this theological revolution has been taking place at the same time that those most identified with the masses have discovered for the first time how thoroughly the old paternalism has permeated their society and influenced the perspective even of revolutionary movements, with their emphasis upon the role of the elite in the revolutionary process. At the same time, Christian sensitivity to the meaning of *personal* existence has led to a deeper understanding of selfhood and maturity and to a new awareness of what is involved in breaking the dehumanizing order of the past and setting the masses free to achieve selfhood as they become protagonists in the struggle to transform their society.

In a brilliant study of the work of Popular Action in Brazil,[14] Candido Mendes de Almeida describes what happened as Catholic youth became involved in this process and worked out methods by which this goal could be achieved. He portrays the gradual deepening of understanding among these young people as they discovered the nature of the task they had undertaken and came to see that what was called for was not merely the creation of opportunities for involvement of the masses in community and political life but a radical reorientation of their attitude toward nature and society. In the whole area of popular culture, and especially in the literacy work carried on by the *Movimento de Educação de Base*, this was accomplished as illiterate peasants were led to reflect on their situation in relation to nature and society through dialogue about it made possible by the use of key concepts in their vocabulary. Thus a process was set in motion by which growing self-awareness, coupled with awareness of the concrete social situation and the possibility of changing it, led to action in the organization of peasant unions and community movements. Participation in such a struggle led, in turn, to new discoveries of selfhood and a new perception of the nature of social revolution, which eventually became an explosive force.

It is this which led Mendes to conclude that the Brazilian experience focused attention on a new element in the struggle for national emancipation, which can be of very great significance for the future of the developing nations. In a situation in which the forces working for a total change in the old order are so limited, this could be a major factor in revolutionary strategy. To be sure, it opens the way to chaos, anarchy, and violence. But, as was clear in Brazil, it can also develop a new sense of solidarity, take advantage of the basic unity of the primitive world view, and become a major force in social integration—in those areas where the social order is healthy enough to permit this type of social change during the process of modernization and development.

It is relatively easy to look at Christian Democracy from the vantage point provided by more recent developments; we have no similar perspective from which to judge the New Christian Left. The important thing is that it has emerged and that it can offer an alternative to Marxism as an instrument of social revolution as well as a new foundation for building a new social order in the underdeveloped world. As yet, we have no way of knowing whether or not it will succeed at either of these two points. What is most evident is the fact that it faces formidable obstacles. For those very movements which offer an alternative to Marxism are now being denounced and persecuted as Communist. And at the moment when this new basis for social change has developed, all the roads to such change by normal democratic means seem to be effectively blocked. Wherever military governments preserve the status quo with the support of North American economic and military power, the younger generation of revolutionaries will be pushed either toward giving up in despair or espousing violence as the only way to bring about fundamental changes. This is the situation which will test most severely the resources of insight, wisdom, and courage of the New Christian Left in Latin America.

Part IV:
Specialized Sectors
and Internal Structures

9: THE LEGAL STATUS OF THE CHURCH IN LATIN AMERICA: SOME RECENT DEVELOPMENTS

John J. Kennedy

Within the last decade scholarly interest in the Catholic church in Latin America has undergone a considerable shift in emphasis. Interest was once largely directed toward questions concerning the legal status of the church in relation to the body politic. At the present time the concern seems to center on the social action and influence of the church. For many observers the juridical niceties marking the dichotomy between church and state are less meaningful than they were when the Latin American nations had a more static social organization. These shifts in interest and approach correspond, roughly, to signs of change on the part of the church itself. The Second Vatican Council is widely interpreted as signaling the abandonment by the church of a "siege mentality" that characterized ecclesiastical attitudes for nearly two centuries. Within Latin America much of the church leadership has shown a sympathetic awareness of the forces of revolutionary change, and a considerable part of the leadership has sought to move the church, together with its moral and material resources, into the mainstream of contemporary social dynamics. In brief, a church which not long ago rejected modernism today seems disposed to accept and even to embrace modernization.

The acceptance is obviously not complete in every corner of the globe, and certainly it is not complete throughout Latin America. Nevertheless, a trend is visible and as the trend grows it seems to dim the importance of the old church-state issues that produced so much civil-ecclesiastical friction in the nineteenth century and in the early decades of the twentieth. The big question that the new situation poses is whether these issues, so largely formulated in nineteenth-century terms, are alive even today or whether their submergence in the more pressing current concerns of both church and society has not meant their quiet, and perhaps unmourned, demise.

This question cannot be answered, however, merely by referring to the spirit of change within the Roman Catholic church. No less important is the position of the several states that have been involved in the matter. The church-state problem could not have come into existence if there had not been political as well as religious elements in the problem. For this reason it is an oversimplification to expect that the future of church-state relations in Latin America depends upon the church alone, however far-reaching its tendencies to change may be at this point in history.

This paper undertakes to examine some of the political and religious elements that have most consistently characterized the problem; to consider some recent changes in detail; and to offer some speculation about what these may suggest for the future. This examination will place major emphasis on the Spanish-speaking countries with a regalistic tradition in their public law. The tradition itself was characteristically asserted in a legal formulation and its perpetuation provided the most continuous confrontation of the factors making for civil-ecclesiastical tensions and conflict. We may note that the two non-Spanish speaking nations, Brazil and Haiti, have not experienced complete absence of tension and conflict. But despite nineteenth-century similarities between Brazil and the Spanish countries in the exercise of the patronage, Brazil and Haiti are special cases requiring a separate treatment that largely eliminates them from the discussion that follows.

ORIGINS OF THE PROBLEM

It is not necessary here to go into descriptive detail about the stormy history of church-state relations in the nineteenth century.[1] At the same time, in order to appreciate the dimensions of the twentieth-century problem it is necessary to have some understanding of why this history has had so many stormy episodes. The root of the problem goes back to the Spanish regalism of the colonial epoch. The crown exercised basic control over the church in a way that left, for many practical purposes of public policy, little real distinction between church and state. Though the exercise was bolstered by specific papal endorsements, the general practice of the crown was comprehensive enough to suggest a broader power than one resting exclusively on papal concessions.[2] Independence at the beginning of the nineteenth century eliminated the crown but not the church. While there were some variations in the attitudes of the successor states, their general tendency was to claim for themselves the *regalia* of the Spanish monarch. At issue were the following:

1. The appointment of bishops, canons, and other officers of the church
2. The creation of dioceses and other ecclesiastical jurisdictions
3. The control of the monastic communities
4. Communication between the Holy See and the church within the respective national territories.[3]

In brief, what the new governments sought under (1) was a primary role in the selection and appointment of bishops through the so-called right of "presentation," and under (2) a similar role in determining the territorial jurisdiction of the church. With regard to (3) there were several considerations, among them the status of the property of the communities, the admission of religious communities to the national territory, and the qualifications of persons joining the monastic communities. In connection with (4) a rather comprehensive privilege was claimed, namely that governmental approval of papal briefs, bulls, and other canonical documents was necessary prior to their divulgation within the national territory and prior to their taking effect in the governance of the local church. This was an attempt to perpetuate the *placet* or *pase* that had been the privilege of the monarch.

Rome resisted on all these points and for many reasons, at least two of which are pertinent here. One was that while the church had appeared a willing partner in the practical obliteration of a church-state distinction in the colonial period, the idea of a fundamental distinction had never been entirely abandoned, and church authorities at Rome—fresh from their difficulties in the Napoleonic period—were not ready to acquiesce in the transfer of control from one political power to another without giving challenge. Moreover, churchmen argued that the patronage privileges had rested in the person of the monarch, not in his government, and that the personal privilege could not be inherited by the institutions that had supplanted the monarch's rule.

A second reason relates to the political and diplomatic status of the church and the Papal States in the immediate post-independence period. This was the period in Europe of Metternich, of the Holy Alliance, and of the reaction against the French Revolution and its aftermath. Papal politics and diplomacy were greatly involved with a general European policy that rejected any basis for recognition of the new Spanish-American states and regarded them as still legitimate realms of the Spanish king. The papacy's adherence to the general European line led it into a position of opposition to the independence of the new nations. Modern Catholic apologists have sought to demonstrate that the central administration of the church was an unwilling party to this policy and the victim not only of the Metternich pattern but also of the particular pressure exerted at Rome by the restored Spanish monarchy of Fernando VII.[4] For present purposes, however, this defense has little importance. The early papal attitude established the "foreignness" of the universal church vis-à-vis the new nations and made Rome appear the challenger both of the patriotism of the men who had won independence and of the responsibility of the governments that were trying to manage the new states. Within a relatively short time Rome extricated itself from this line, and the Muzzi mission to Chile in 1824–25 provided concrete evidence of a change of attitude. The change did not come in time, however, to blot out entirely the foreign image of the church, or perhaps more accurately, of the Roman headquarters of the church.

Therefore, the political leaders of the first decades of national existence could argue that in pressing the patronal claims they were defending the legitimate national interest. To relax the claim would have opened the path to an infringement on national sovereignty. Local church governance was inherently too vital a part of the national life to deny the responsible authorities of the state a role in the selection of those who were to govern the church and in the determination of the latters' relations with the extranational authorities of the church. Moreover, if the Spanish crown had exercised these controls, how in logic could the new governments do less? To do less would suggest that the new states had not succeeded to the full sovereignty that the crown had formerly exercised. Even the appearance of a diminution of sovereignty carried a threat to their precarious status in international law.

The same politicians and statesmen could also argue that they could not be accused of any hostility to Catholicism as a religion. They arranged for its material support from public revenues. They gave it a favored or even exclusive position against other religions. They made adherence to its creed a test of qualification for public office. From the church side there was a disposition to accept these favors as legitimate concessions to the true religion but as insufficient to compensate for the recognition of the patronal claims that were simultaneously being pressed. Not that the church was committed to a total exclusion of the states from the exercise of the patronage. Churchmen pointed to the possibility of establishing the patronage through concordats, under which church-state relations might not be vastly different from those prevailing under the Spanish crown, while making the situation more acceptable in principle to the church. Patronage would then be established through mutual consent, in the reaching of which the church would be a free negotiating party in contrast to the subordinate character it would have to acknowledge if it accepted the unilateral assertion of patronage privileges by the new political authorities. Though political leaders acknowledged the possibility of arrangement by concordat, the prevailing view was that even to undertake this kind of negotiation would raise questions of competence equivalent to an impairment of sovereignty.

Later in the nineteenth century the problem was, so to speak, frozen into the political complex through the incorporation of patronage into several of the national constitutions. With neither side able to accept openly the position of the other, some practical accommodation had to be found. One way was through a *modus vivendi*, on the basis of which specific actions could be accomplished without questioning the claims of either party. This device and related practices, however, did not solve the basic problem.

At approximately the same time, however, some new elements entered the picture. New forces arose to challenge the church in a different way. The challengers were not interested in finding a basis for the functioning of an official church in harmony with the civil power. Instead they questioned whether any church had the political right to any kind of official existence. Their attitudes ranged from favoring the suppression of the church as an anachronism, to the cutting loose of the church from the state and allowing it to take its chances as a voluntary association on an equal footing with other voluntary bodies. On the whole, churchmen saw a much greater peril in these attitudes than they had seen in the earlier regalism of the new republics and, in general, church resistance was stronger toward these new forces. This is not the place to examine all the intricate questions concerning the disestablishment of the church or the separation of church and state as this began to be achieved in the later nineteenth century and continued into the twentieth. Two observations are, however, in order.

One is that when separation was decided upon it had to be introduced into a political system where the earlier regalism had already created a most complicated and difficult situation. Moreover, the model to which most of those favoring separation looked, chiefly the United States, had developed in a situation largely free of this kind of complication and with the further political advantage of a genuine diversity of creeds that was not duplicated on the Latin American scene. Separation then did not generally reproduce the equivalent of the United States situation. The second is that while separation in certain Latin American countries, for example, Chile, has had some success in eliminating or at least reducing the church question as a political factor, separation in itself has not proven to be a complete guarantee that the religious question would be removed from the political arena, as nearly a century of Mexican history has demonstrated.

THE VARIOUS NATIONAL SOLUTIONS

Nevertheless, the tendency to separation of church and state did continue, and by the middle of the present century well over a majority of the Latin American states had abandoned, suppressed, or modified official ties with the church. The results were not identical in all countries because of the variety of legal means employed. As of 1950, however, it would be possible to summarize church-state relations in the Spanish-American countries in accordance with the following categories.

1. The pattern of relations preferred by the church, that established by concordat, although much defended by Catholic apologists

and at least formally left open by several governments as an eventual possibility, had its only enduring example in Colombia,[5] which dates from 1887.

2. Mexico, too, filled a unique category. While public law had long abandoned the customary patronage interests, the Constitution of 1917 placed severe restrictions on the church.[6] After the civil discord arising over the enforcement of these restrictions in the 1920's, an attempt was made to put an end to the strife. While the government did not relax the letter of the law, accommodation between the two parties made peace possible. Since that time the church has learned to live within the restrictions and even to find on occasion some compensatory advantages in them. For example, the denial of juridical personality to the church and the prohibition on ownership of property leave title to the cathedrals and other churches in the nation under the administration of the government. At the same time, to the extent that the state maintains these edifices and provides for their upkeep and repair, the state is providing the church and its followers with places of worship. In general, the church's attitude in recent decades seems to have been one of acceptance but not approval,[7] while from the state side there appears to exist little or no disposition to revise the fundamental laws.

3. In another group of countries the separation of church and state had been achieved without anything like the dramatic clashes that occurred in Mexico. In some of these countries constitutional provisions extended guarantees and favors that could only be regarded as advantageous to the church. Examples could be found in Chile's exemption of all churches and their dependencies from taxation[8] and in a similar provision of the Uruguayan Constitution.[9] Uruguay also, in contrast to Mexico, placed ownership of church buildings in the church itself rather than in the nation. Panama, without a state religion, nevertheless extended special recognition to the Catholic church and opened the public schools to religious instruction.[10] While these provisions dealt only with minutiae, they probably helped to contribute to the general church-state harmony in this group of countries.

4. Less advantageous to the church but in practice not notably burdensome were the restrictions placed on clerical conduct and functions in certain other countries. For example, Honduras prohibited the existence of monastic communities,[11] while Ecuador denied clergy (of any church) eligibility to serve in the national legislature.[12] Colom-

bia, already more fundamentally classified above, maintained even broader restrictions against clergy in public office.[13]

5. In a final group of countries the public law maintained the regalistic tradition that had been asserted in the early years of independence. Whether the law recognized an official religion or not—there were some variations and ambiguities on the point—the arrangement kept the church and state in a close, if not always comfortable relation. These countries were Argentina,[14] Bolivia,[15] Costa Rica,[16] Paraguay,[17] Peru,[18] and Venezuela.[19]

The foregoing categorization is obviously somewhat rough but is sufficient to show, as of 1950, the degrees of variation in church-state patterns. It also shows a fundamental difference between the fifth category and the preceding four in combination. Under the latter, the state had not uniformly relinquished all controls, but the church-state problem no longer existed in its original form. That form, however, continued under the fifth category.

The principal features of the Argentine pattern may be used to illustrate how a regalism surviving into the twentieth century operated at the time. Two constitutional provisions allegedly offered advantages to the church, one declaring federal support for the Catholic church, the other requiring the president and vice-president to be members of that church. The first was ambiguous, the second relatively meaningless.

Other provisions governed the filling of episcopal offices. They required the president of the republic to select the candidate from a list of three persons voted by the federal senate. In practice, the presidential selection was usually handled through the Ministry of Foreign Affairs and Worship which in turn dealt with the Buenos Aires Nunciature to assure, so far as possible, the presentation of candidates not unacceptable at Rome. Success usually marked these unpublicized negotiations, but occasionally they broke down, sometimes drastically so.[20] The Holy See then announced the appointment without reference to the prior negotiations and entirely as though it were initiating the appointment on its own. Certain further legal formalities then had to be met before the bishop-designate could take office. Despite the elaborateness of the face-saving devices on both sides, the practical effect of the arrangement was to keep the political authorities constantly involved in the selection of the chief ministers of the church.

Another constitutional provision required the president, the supreme court or the congress (as the particular case might determine) to pass on the bulls, briefs, and rescripts from Rome before they could take effect in Argentina. As noted earlier this privilege of the *placet* had been of importance in the nineteenth century. By the middle of the twentieth it had little real significance, but ecclesiastics looked upon it as a potential obstacle to freedom of communication within the universal church.

For the church to escape from this general situation—never very much to its liking—there appeared originally to be two possibilities. One was through a concordat, which, in spite of a great deal of discussion and public pronouncement, never was a real possibility. The other was through disestablishment of the church, freeing it of these controls. Liberally inclined Catholics of the later nineteenth century gave some evidence of willingness to take the risk of disestablishment. At about the same time, however, the Argentine congress enacted legislation pertaining to marriage and education which these Catholics regarded as hostile to religious doctrine. The result was that they were frightened away and decided that the continued acceptance of the status quo involved less danger than did opening up the whole church question. Such at least seems to have been the evolution in the thinking of the most important of the Catholic liberals of the period, José Manuel Estrada.[21]

A situation roughly parallel to that in Argentina prevailed in the countries of the regalistic tradition. Each had its own unique characteristics, but the common prominent feature was a theoretical deadlock. As of 1950, there was little or nothing to suggest that any solution other than face-saving accommodation was possible.

RECENT CHANGES

It is then somewhat surprising that the last few years have seen the beginning of the resolution of the deadlock and that in terms of church-state relations this development currently offers the most important evidence of genuine change in the situation. Undoubtedly, the spirit of the Second Vatican Council helped to promote the possibility of change. In this connection mention should be made of the hope for a "voluntary resignation" of patronal rights that is stated in *Christus Dominus*, the conciliar decree dealing with the bishops' office.[22] Even before the voting of this decree, however, in October,

1965, there were moves on the part of governments toward opening negotiations on the patronage. Two agreements resulting from these negotiations are to be considered. They are the 1966 Argentine accord with the Holy See and the earlier Venezuelan convention of 1964.

A skeleton history of the recent Argentine experience runs as follows.[23] In 1965, the Minister of Foreign Affairs and Worship undertook conversations with the Nuncio at Buenos Aires to explore the possibility of reaching an agreement that would "free" the church of "patronal interpositions." By September of that year negotiations progressed to the point where President Arturo Illía could assure Pope Paul VI that the Argentine government was disposed to arrange an agreement with the Holy See. The assurances were extended in a letter which the Foreign Minister delivered to the Pope in New York on the occasion of the latter's U.N. visit. The Pope's reply emphasized the Holy See's disposition to "examine concretely whatever your government may wish to propose" that may lead to a pact acceptable to both parties and of "genuine utility" to the Argentine nation. At the same time the government officially informed the national hierarchy through the Cardinal Archbishop of Buenos Aires of the status of the negotiations. In January, 1966, Foreign Minister Zavala Ortiz made a television address in which he informed the Argentine public that negotiations were under way. On June 6, 1966, an agreed text was initialed at Buenos Aires by the Foreign Minister and the Nuncio, and preparations were made for a solemn ceremony of signing on June 30 (the Feast of St. Paul, the Pope's official nameday). The scheduled ceremony could not, of course, take place because by that date the Illía government had been overthrown and replaced by the revolutionary regime headed by General Juan Carlos Onganía.

Rumor, in no way officially confirmed, has it that the new government wanted to proceed with the signature of the agreement but that the Holy See hesitated to conclude the agreement with a government that had come to power through the overthrow of its predecessor. Apparently this hesitancy was overcome, and the following explanation of why it was overcome, while reasonable, is entirely without confirmation. The explanation is that since the agreement had been entirely negotiated by a constitutional government there should be no hesitancy about dealing with a revolutionary regime that was only trying to carry out the work completed by its constitutional predecessor. In any event, signing did take place on October

10, 1966, and ratifications were exchanged on January 28, 1967.[24] Needless to say, the Argentine ratification was given without the approval of congress since the latter body had been suppressed.

To turn to the Venezuelan case, its chronology can be summarized in the following way. As far back as 1947 the questions of "regularization" of the church in Venezuela was raised publicly. In the 1958 elections, following the overthrow of the Pérez Jiménez dictatorship, the "Minimum Program" accepted by all the presidential candidates included a pledge to seek "regularization of the relations between church and state."[25]

President Betancourt's government subsequently undertook negotiations to that end. Agreement between the government and the Holy See was achieved during his term of office, and the formal signing of the instrument occurred just prior to the inauguration of Dr. Raúl Leoni. The date of signing was March 6, 1964. On March 10, the Foreign Minister transmitted the text to congress for approval prior to ratification. On June 26, 1964, congressional approval was given, and the exchange of ratifications took place on October 24, 1964.[26]

The text of the agreement with Venezuela is similar in many respects to the somewhat shorter document signed by Argentina, just as the two countries have in the past had many parallel experiences in their respective church-state histories. The following examination of the two texts may help to indicate how the church-state situation in each country differs from what it was prior to the agreements.

With regard to the central issue of patronage, namely the intervention of the state in the appointment of bishops, there undoubtedly is a formal change. Where the constitutions of the two republics claim government control, this is relaxed through the new conventions. Article III of the Argentine agreement recognizes the "competence of the Holy See" in the appointment of bishops. The corresponding Article VI in the Venezuelan accord implies, but does not state so clearly, a similar recognition. Both the cited articles, however, place the initiative with the Holy See, although they require the latter to inform the government in confidence and in secrecy of the name of any person under consideration for episcopal appointment. This prenotification gives the government thirty days in which to raise objections to the proposed appointment, and in the Venezuelan case special circumstances may extend the period to sixty days. Both instruments limit episcopal appointments to citizens of the country, and a declaration of the Venezuelan Foreign Minister of March 6, 1964, interprets this provision (Article VII) as limiting appointment to native-born citizens only.

These stipulations do not leave the church with absolute freedom in the selection of its governing personnel. It can also be said that the procedures established do not greatly differ from what in recent times has been the *de facto* arrangement between Rome and these two governments (as well as certain others). As the Venezuelan Foreign Minister pointed out in his letter of transmittal to the congress, a "tacit accord" between the two parties has long regulated church appointments simply because it was impossible to apply in full the clumsy procedures of the "anachronous and ineffective" patronal legislation. Two years later his Argentine counterpart characterized the previously existing Argentine controls as "artificial, nominal and mortifying." The pre-notification principle then, as established in these treaties, largely conforms to what had long been standard, if informal, practice.

It would be a mistake, however, to conclude that the formalization of the practice leaves church-state relations exactly where they have been for the last few decades. On the contrary, the agreements appear to introduce a genuine innovation[27] into the church-state formula. This is because they do away with the theoretical and legalistic impasse that has prevailed in these countries for over a century. They provide an escape from this impasse and they offer advantages to both parties. The church gains the clear right of initiative in ecclesiastical appointments. The state obtains what it has long sought from Rome without previous success, a recognition of the legitimacy of the political interest in these appointments. Strictly according to the letter, it appears that Venezuela obtained greater concessions than did Argentina, although the practical consequences of the difference remain to be determined. Article XVII of the Venezuelan agreement specifically recognizes the force of Article 130 of the national constitution, which is the basis for the exercise of the patronage. The Argentine instrument in the preamble contains only a general reference to the national constitution without any later mention of the specific provisions of the constitution according to which patronal rights have been claimed.

Article VI of the Venezuelan agreement also specifies that in the event that the government registers "objections of general political character" to an episcopal candidate, then the "Holy See will indicate the name of another candidate." This appears to leave the government with an absolute veto. The Argentine agreement seems to be more open in that Article VI, dealing with "observations or objections" that the government may make, merely obligates the two parties to seek the "appropriate forms for reaching an agreement."

There are also some differences between the two treaties regarding the advantages won by the church. Common to the two texts are the guarantees of the "full and free exercise" of the "spiritual power" of the church and the "free and public exercise" of the Catholic religion, (Article I of both agreements). In addition to the initiative in the appointment of bishops, the two treaties also leave the initiative with the church in the creation of new archdioceses and dioceses. Again, there must be a confidential pre-notification to the government with an opportunity for the latter to register objections. In other respects, however, there are some differences of detail worth noting.

Article XI of the Venezuelan agreement provides for financial support by the government of the "bishops, vicars general, and ecclesiastical chapters," as well as for the construction and upkeep of religious edifices. The Argentine text is silent on this point. In public discussion of the agreement the Argentine Foreign Minister did suggest that while the government had been contributing modest amounts to the church, financial support was not a major consideration.[28] Linked to Article XI of the Venezuelan text are two other articles, VIII and IX, which apply to the appointment of canons in the cathedral chapters and to other recipients of ecclesiastical benefices. There are no corresponding articles in the Argentine text.

The Venezuelan agreement also recognizes more explicitly than does the Argentine the legal and juridical aspects of the church and its administration. It recognizes the "international juridical personality of the Holy See and the Vatican City" and pledges the continuation of an exchange of an ambassador and a Papal Nuncio, the latter to be dean of the diplomatic corps at Caracas (Article III). The status of juridical persons before the civil law is also accorded to the Venezuelan church, its dioceses, and certain other units (Article IV).

On two other points the church also appears to have made gains, but perhaps of a significance that may be more nominal than real. The first of these concerns freedom of communication within the church. As noted earlier, patronal legislation placed restrictions on communications. They made papal bulls, apostolic briefs, and other documents subject to the approval of the national authorities before they could be made public within the national territory. Rome never recognized these provisions, but in the nineteenth century, when they had more practical importance than they have had in the twentieth, the church tended to avoid any direct challenge. The new agreements tidy up this situation in that they accord the Holy See an unrestricted right of communication with the national churches and recognize a similar right on the part of bishops with the local churches and their members (Article IV, Argentina; Article II, Venezuela). While most observers in recent times have regarded the traditional restrictions in this field as pretty much a dead letter, there is no doubt that the church will look upon their elimination as the removal of sources of potential difficulties.

The second point concerns the admission of the religious orders and monastic communities into the national territory. Here again the traditional restrictions of the state have diminished (Article V, Argentina; Article XIII, Venezuela). The texts establish in the national hierarchies the initiative in the matter, but leave the government with certain legal and administrative controls. There were some important conflicts in the past in several Latin American countries over the admission of religious orders, but the new measure of freedom that these two instruments give to the church is probably more important today for the elimination of difficulties *in posse* than *in esse*.

This brief review of the general features of the two treaties may lead one to say that on the surface at least they do not appear to be very revolutionary or innovating instruments. They regularize and legalize what has generally been *de facto* accommodation. They eliminate some dead letters. They remove the sources of potential conflicts as much as they settle actual cases. Compared to the grand revolutionary sweep of the pronouncements of the Second Vatican Council they appear to have a pedestrian quality that somehow is discordant with the over-all tone of the church today. An evaluation along these lines would, however, do the agreements considerably less than justice. An amicable settlement of issues long in contention that is reached freely and in the absence of threats and pressures is always a gain both for the parties directly concerned and for the world as a whole. It would probably be more accurate to compare the two agreements with cases involving the peaceful settlement of a long-standing dispute over territorial limits between neighboring states. Even though the dispute may have involved only occasional dramatic clashes and may have gone on in a general absence of border strife, everyone would agree that it is better to have it settled than to allow it to continue. This is approximately what these agreements between the Holy See and the two republics have accomplished. In this sense at least they have an immediate importance.

THE POSSIBILITY OF OTHER CHANGES

Apart from their relevance to the respective national situations these new arrangements with Venezuela and Argentina may also indicate the possibility of change in other countries. From the church side it seems likely that the Holy See, relying upon the policy declaration in chapter ii, 20, of the decree *Christus Dominus*, will continue to work for the reduction or elimination of state controls. A certain measure of success in two major countries could pave the way to similar achievements in others. While immediate church concern can be expected to concentrate on those nations which still retain the patronage through the national constitution, the cited clause of the decree appears to be broad enough to suggest changes in the concordatory arrangement as well.

From the political side it must be assumed that statesmen will continue to be concerned about safeguarding constitutional traditions and concepts of national sovereignty. To an outsider this concern may seem to be so formalistic as to be meaningless. But it is always easier for outsiders to dismiss the force of historical precedents than it is for those who have to live with them. Government statements and public debate at the time of the conclusion of the new agreements indicate that it was politically important to demonstrate that sovereignty and national tradition had been respected in the negotiations. Both governments found a suitable formulation of respect and protection which could easily serve as a guide to other nations facing the same problem.

Another political problem is related to the guarantees of the church that these countries extended as a kind of compensation for maintenance of state controls. These supposedly have had a particular importance in holding the good will of church leaders and the more militant sectors of Catholic laity. The real significance of these guarantees has long been open to question, but public pronouncements in these recent cases gave considerable attention to them. Defenders of the new arrangements insisted most steadfastly that the effect was to "free" the church and that this freedom was more advantageous to the church than any other possible arrangement. Moreover, the texts of the agreements seem to be basically in accord with Vatican II's declaration on religious liberty, *Dignitatis Humanae*.

Turning from the countries retaining patronage to those that have abandoned it, one is tempted to speculate that the long-range effect of the new treaties will be, if they are accepted as precedents, to equalize more or less the church-state situation throughout Latin America and establish a uniform pattern of relations. The common elements in the pattern would be the disappearance of state controls and the elimination of privileged status for the Catholic church. The church could then function freely subject only to the requirements of the civil law as the latter may apply to all persons, natural and juridical. Meanwhile, the political process would be "freed" of the religious question.

Such speculation, however, is rather utopian. A more realistic view must take into account that the institutional religious question has had a long political involvement in Latin America and the involvement has not been limited to the countries of the regalistic tradition. Undoubtedly, there is at present a general tendency to seek harmony between the civil and the ecclesiastical parties. The tendency of itself, however, is not enough to dispose of the problem. Within each country any solution that has been achieved has resulted from careful attention to the particular tradition of the country. The Venezuelan and Argentine agreements suggest that progress toward harmony must come on a piece-meal basis. This makes a future Latin American uniformity unlikely.

If the agreements have a general significance for Latin America, it is not limited to the particular precedents they create. They provide concrete evidence that change can be achieved even in cases where until recently all the factors involved denied any such possibility. More importantly, however, for students of church-state relations in Latin America the agreements suggest that the real possibilities for change rest not merely on the sweeping declaration of a much-heralded movement of *aggiornamento* but also are dependent upon patiently undertaken and undramatically paced negotiations at a workaday level. It is largely at this level that any further changes can be expected to emerge.

10: HISTORY, STRUCTURE, AND PRESENT ACTIVITIES OF CELAM

Cecilio de Lora Soria, S.M.

INTRODUCTION

When in 1955 at the First Latin American Episcopal Conference the diocesan bishops of Latin America set up the *Consejo Episcopal Latinoamericano* (the Latin American Episcopal Council, or CELAM), their action was looked upon as noteworthy both by virtue of being more or less unparalleled and also because of the reasoning behind it.

In establishing CELAM the Latin American bishops were motivated by a desire to create a body which would be concerned first and foremost with the role of the Roman Catholic church in Latin America. Fundamental to CELAM's founding is the recognition that continental churches are faced with many situations and problems which particularly concern the entire continent and so call for a continental treatment and consideration from a locally oriented point of view. Through awareness on the part of the Latin American bishops of the existence of such needs and acceptance of the church's obligation to do something about meeting them, CELAM came into being. Its accomplishments and continuing activities in the twelve years since have served to demonstrate the knowledge and wisdom which prompted its founding.

Before discussing the history, organization, and meaning of CELAM, let us first review some of the general terms which pertain both to the structure of the church and to the different levels at which authority is exercised within it. In such a review we are, of course, looking at the church not from the "mystic" perspective, which considers it as the "mystery" of the presence of God among men, but as an institution.

Within this institution the powers and authority that are particularly episcopal are clearly set forth in the Decree on the Bishops' Pastoral Office in the Church. Thus, the Decree states that in this church which was founded by Christ with the Apostle Peter, to whom as his successor "Christ entrusted the feeding of His sheep and lambs. . . . he [the Roman Pontiff, as the successor of the Apostle Peter] enjoys supreme, full, immediate, and universal authority over the care of souls" (No. 2). The care of all other bishops is then defined: "For their part, the bishops too have been appointed by the Holy Spirit, and are successors of the apostles as pastors of souls. Together with the Supreme Pontiff and under his authority, they have been sent to continue throughout the ages the work of Christ, the eternal pastor." In this way the bishops, even when they exercise their authority and their care chiefly in that diocese or portion of the church that has been confided to them are "Sharing in solicitude for all the churches, . . . in communion with and under the authority of the Supreme Pontiff. All are united in a college or body with respect to teaching the universal Church of God" (No. 3).

Although episcopal communion with and dependence upon the bishop of Rome is clearly emphasized, it should be pointed out that each of the bishops, as a member of the episcopal college and successor of the Apostles, is not only responsible for his own diocese but also must share in the responsibility of the Universal Church (No. 6).

In addition, the Decree clearly allows the bishops of dioceses within a country to unite in episcopal conferences as instituted and promoted by Vatican II (Nos. 37, 38). Within the conditions prescribed by Vatican II, these episcopal conferences also have normative power within the national territory in which they operate. In prophetic anticipation of such authority, in 1955 the First Latin American Episcopal Conference was convened at Rio de Janeiro, and the bishops adopted a series of agreements that were later accepted and implemented on a national level.

THE ORIGINS OF CELAM

The First Latin American Episcopal Conference met in Rio de Janeiro, Brazil, from July 25 to August 4, 1955. It was the first experience of this kind on the continent. Indeed, at that time only the Colombian Episcopal Conference had a permanent executive branch, or permanent secretariat.

The most significant result of this first conference was the creation of CELAM, which was, subsequently, approved by Pius XII on November 2, 1955. Bogotá was later designated as the site of the general secretariat of CELAM. Bishop Julian Mendoza, then Father Mendoza, the permanent secretary of the Colombian episcopacy, prepared the first meeting of CELAM, which was to be held in Bogotá in November, 1956.

AIMS AND ORGANIZATION OF CELAM

From the beginning the following functions have been the concern of the Latin American Episcopal Council: (1) to study matters of interest to the church in Latin America, (2) to co-ordinate activities, (3) to promote and assist Catholic initiatives, and (4) to prepare other conferences of the Latin American episcopate when these should be convoked by the Holy See. All these aims continue to be maintained in CELAM's statutes. Structurally, too, CELAM's organization reflects its continental character. It is made up of members from each of the Latin American episcopal conferences. Each national episcopal conference elects one delegate and one alternate, according to its own statutes, for a period of time to be determined by itself.

CELAM itself, acting as a body, elects a president and two vice-presidents from among its members. The president's term of office is two years, and he may be re-elected once. In the year 1967 the president of CELAM was Avelar Brandão Vilela, Archbishop of Teresina, Brazil, who was elected in October, 1966, to succeed Bishop Manuel Larrain, whose untimely death occurred in Chile in 1966. Pablo Muñóz Vega, Auxiliary Bishop of Quito, was first vice-president, and Marcos McGrath, Bishop of Santiago de Veraguas, Panama, was second vice-president (see Appendix: CELAM's Presidency).

In the beginning the general secretariat was so established that it operated through five sub-secretariats which were directed by priests from different Latin American countries. The work of each sub-secretariat was designated as follows: (1) preservation and propagation of the faith, (2) diocesan clergy and religious institutes, (3) education and youth, (4) apostolate of the laity, and (5) social action and social assistance.

The general secretariat and the other organs of CELAM are financed by quotas assigned to each of the episcopal conferences. Donations are also received from various international organizations.

At its first meeting in 1956 CELAM agreed to create a committee on finances, to be headed by a bishop. Archbishop Tulio Botero Salazar of Medellín, Colombia, directs the general treasury; Monsignor Alfonso Schmidt is the general treasurer.

DEPARTMENTS AND SPECIALIZED INSTITUTIONS

At its sixth annual meeting CELAM decided to revise its organization and to establish specialized departments for the different fields of its apostolate. The departments may function anywhere in Latin America, and they may also be attached to already existing organizations, even if these organizations are headed by national or local directors. In this way, and because each department has an episcopal commission, the responsibility for the activities of CELAM is shared by a greater number of bishops. This fact is a tremendous asset and contributes to making the activity of CELAM more successful. At the moment CELAM has twelve departments: the departments of over-all pastoral planning; of liturgy; of the Latin American committee on the faith; of the missions; of vocations; of seminaries; of university pastoral action; of education; of secular apostolate; of social action; of public opinion; and of ecumenism.

The work of each may be briefly described as follows:

The function of the Department of Over-all Pastoral Planning (*pastorale d'ensemble*) is to promote co-ordinated plans by which all the forces at the disposition of the church may be reasonably organized. This organization and promotion presupposes basic studies in the field of religious sociology to facilitate the knowledge and understanding of problems at the ground level. Efforts are coordinated as much as possible through an assessment of available forces and their economical use.

The Department of Liturgy seeks to encourage renewal of rituals, vernacular translations, adoption of reforms, and so forth, in accordance with conditions recommended by Vatican II.

The Department of the Latin American Committee on the Faith, or CLAF, is concerned principally with catechetics and the adapting of content to modern teaching methods. It is concerned also with making known to all Catholics the Word of God as revealed in the Bible, or, as it is called, the Bible pastorate. Until now ecumenism has also been a concern of this department, but the importance of relations between Christians and the recognition of this importance by Vatican II has led to the decision to establish a department specializing in this field.

The Department of Missions has a double objective: first, concern for the current problems of mission territories as such, where work with primitive societies consists mainly in initial evangelization or the first communion of the Christian faith; and, second, awakening in all Catholics a feeling of personal responsibility for missionary work.

The fundamental work of the Department of Vocations consists in studying the Catholic vocation in its various dimensions—theological, sociological, and psychological. Essentially, therefore, it is concerned with investigating the scope of responsible Christians in the progress of the church, specifically of those working within the church as priests or religious men or women, according to the particular inclination of the individual and the supernatural call of God. Given the scarcity of these vocations and the growing needs of Latin America, this department has the important task of co-ordinating all efforts being made at national levels to awaken consciousness throughout the continent of the church's needs.

Closely allied to the Department of Vocations is the Department of Seminaries, which specializes in problems presented by the adaptation, to the needs of the modern world, of the schools in which future priests are prepared, here again in accordance with the teachings of Vatican II. It is important that existing seminaries work together in such a way that they consolidate on regional levels, not only to avoid duplicating effort but also to deepen the training of candidates.

The Department of University Pastoral Action is confronted with one of the gravest problems in Latin America: the religious crisis in universities during a time of rapid and deep social transformation. This social change affects political and economic structures and also Latin American cultural values and the Christian way of life handed down through many generations. How best can the true Christian life be presented to the questioning university student? How can the work of the church be organized both in her own universities and those of the state? These are some of the problems that this department attempts to resolve.

Related to it is the Department of Education. This department tries to reconsider the mission of the church in promoting culture and in adapting the present school system to the new social and ideological demands of the continent. This is of great importance, since it forms the link between the church and the international organisms working in Latin America on the same problems.

The Department of Secular Apostolate tries to co-ordinate the several organizations through which lay people, as Catholics, try to bring to life in their own environment the thinking of the church and to incarnate in her life the pre-occupations that animate these moments of transformation for all the members of the people of God. This department is also of great importance, for since Vatican II lay people have been fulfilling more and more roles which for various reasons have until now been overlooked.

The Department of Social Action looks for ways of promoting active and efficient participation by Catholics in the process of integration and development taking place in Latin America. Understanding that a life authentically Christian is not possible without human development as a base, this department also works for an evangelical foundation for the socio-economic transformation that is urgent in our land.

The Department of Public Opinion, or of Means of Social Communication, tries to keep the presence of the church alive in all channels of communication by collaborating in the formation of a genuine image not only of Catholic thinking but also of the ideals of development and integration in Latin America.

Finally, the recently organized Department of Ecumenism strives to relate CELAM's activities to those of the non-Catholic Christian confessions according to the spirit of CELAM's present orientation.

According to the statutes each department is composed of five main groups: an episcopal commission, an executive organ, a co-ordinating council, groups of experts, and other instruments or organizations. The episcopal commission is the policy-making organ. It consists of a president named by CELAM after consultation with the episcopal conference concerned, and after hearing the opinion of the president of the department. These members compose the commission, not as representatives of their own episcopal conference or nation, but rather as having special experience, competence, or influence in the field. As far as possible they also represent the different geographical areas of Latin America. The president and the members of each of these commissions have a term of office of two years. The executive organ, which functions as its name implies, is headed by an executive secretary and the necessary technical staff. The co-ordinating council acts as liaison with Catholic institutions that have interest and responsibility in the same field of apostolic activity; for example, the Department of Public Opinion has a co-ordinating council which acts as liaison with the Latin American Union of Catholic Press (ULAPC), the Latin American Secretariats of Radio and Television (UNDA), and Cinema (OCIC). Groups of experts are consultative bodies of study and work. For example, there is a group of experts in the Department of Liturgy which studies the application of the conciliar directives and takes care of the necessary translations. This group works in cooperation with Spain in the joint commission for all the Spanish-speaking countries. The groups of experts may be permanent, as is the case with the liturgy group, or temporary. Other instruments or organizations include any which may be set up as needed for fulfillment of a specific function; for example, among these instruments and organizations are found the institutes under the departments. Till now there have been the two Latin American Institutes of Catechetics (ICLA) in Santiago, Chile, and in Manizales, Colombia, which are under the CLAF; the Latin American Institute of Doctrine and Social Studies (ILADES) in Santiago, Chile, which depends upon the Department of Social Action; and the Latin American Pastoral Institute (IPLA), which had been created by CELAM before the departments were established. This institute has a traveling team which gives courses on *pastoral d'ensemble*. IPLA has its location in Quito, Ecuador, under the Department of Pastoral Action. Finally, the Institute of Liturgy is located in Medellín, Colombia.

In 1965 an important agreement was reached between CELAM and the Latin American Confederation of Religious (CLAR) regarding the co-ordinating of activities and the consequent prevention of duplication of work; for example, the Department of Vocations of CELAM integrates its activities with those of CLAR in the same field.

ANNUAL MEETINGS OF CELAM

At each of its annual meetings CELAM has concerned itself with one specific topic related to pastoral work in Latin America. The subsecretariats kept in touch with the national organizations mostly by letter, since financially it is impossible to enter into a wider field of activity.

Let us now consider the most important of the aspects discussed in the annual meetings of CELAM from 1956 to the present.

The first meeting of CELAM took place in Bogotá in 1956. Its aim was to organize internally the council and its general board. A comparative analysis was made, the conclusions of the General Episcopal Conference of Latin America in Rio de Janeiro were studied and an effort made toward making them more concrete, the statutes of CELAM were approved, and its economic maintenance by the Latin American countries which constitute CELAM was organized.

The second meeting also took place in Colombia at Fomeque in 1957, during which four themes were studied: the collaboration of religious with CELAM, national episcopal secretariats, co-ordination of the lay apostolate, and the "Major Project" of UNESCO.

At the third meeting, which was held in Rome in 1958, the following subjects were discussed: preservation and defense of faith, catechetics, Caritas, bilingual ritual, regulations of the general board, and the provisional project relating to the statutes of the Latin American Organization of Seminaries (OSLAM) and of the Latin American Conference of Religious (CLAR). This meeting served as a framework for the official presentation of the Pontifical Committee for Latin America (CAL).

During the fourth meeting, which took place again at Fomeque, Colombia, in 1959, apostolic action by the church in regard to the problem of Communist infiltration in Latin America in social, educational, and public opinion sectors was planned. The Latin American Committee of the Faith (CLAF) was also discussed.

The fifth meeting was held in Buenos Aires in 1960 and was dedicated to the study of pastoral problems from the parish, diocesan, and rural and urban points of view. The Pastoral Institute (IPLA) was created, and it was also decided to form the first Catechetical Institute (ICLA), with Father James McNiff as first director.

During the sixth meeting, held in Mexico in 1961, the family and family pastoral problems were treated.

The seventh meeting, in Rome in 1963, was dedicated to the reform of CELAM and its statutes, since the centralized work begun in 1956 was meeting neither the needs nor the exigencies of the church. To correct these faults, reform of the statutes was begun by decentralizing its services and by creating specialized departments. These special departments carried out their work in the different countries under the direction of the presidency and in co-ordination with the general secretariat. In this way the first six departments were created: liturgy, education, vocations, seminaries, public opinion, and university pastoral action. Furthermore, in this meeting, vocational pastoral action in Latin America was treated as a principal theme.

The eighth and ninth meetings, which were held in Rome during Vatican II in 1964–65, were also concerned with the relationship of the departments with the general secretariat and also among themselves. Approved during the eighth meeting, the study continued to be deepened in the ninth, during which the new statutes of CELAM were also decided upon and approved. In these two meetings some themes of the council and various liturgical matters were also discussed.

At the tenth meeting, which took place in October, 1966, in Mar del Plata, Argentina, the main theme was "The Presence of the Church in the Development and Integration of Latin America."

At the eleventh meeting, which was held in Lima, Peru, in November, 1967, attention was centered on preparing for the Second Latin American Episcopal Conference, which was to convene the following year. This great meeting did, in fact, open in August, 1968, in Medellín, Colombia. We will refer to it later on.

LATIN AMERICAN CONFERENCES ORGANIZED BY CELAM

Through its departments CELAM has promoted various gatherings at a Latin American level, among which several are outstanding.

The First Latin American Meeting of Pastoral Planning was held in Baños, Ecuador, June 5–11, 1966. Thirty-four bishops from sixteen Latin American countries were present, along with nineteen invited experts, principally theologians and sociologists. These bishops were responsible for the work of the church in the fields of education, social action, and the secular apostolate. They were trying to find a practical means of co-ordinating in the best way possible the efforts which were being made in these fields. For this reason the Department of Over-all Pastoral Planning was responsible for the organization of this meeting.

From October 9 to 16, 1966, an extraordinary meeting of CELAM, organized by the Department of Social Action on the theme "The Active Presence of the Church in the Development and Integration of Latin America," was held in Mar del Plata, Argentina. Besides the episcopal delegates of CELAM a large number of experts in social matters, as well as the bishops responsible for these matters on the Latin American continent, also attended. The results of this meeting, after having been approved by the Holy See, were presented in January, 1967, to the Catholic Inter-American Cooperation Program (CICOP), which took place in Boston. Afterward, they were similarly presented on January 31 to Secretary General U Thant of the United Nations and to Señor José Mora, Secretary General of the Organization of American States. The accomplishments of the conference at Mar del Plata represent a notable advance in the doctrine of the church in relation to social problems. The recent encyclical of Pope Paul VI, *Populorum Progressio*, has come as a confirmation of the work realized in Mar del Plata. These results, as well as others from other meetings, have begun to appear in a collection of documents of CELAM that are rightly entitled *Conclusions of Mar del Plata*.

It should be noted also that the extraordinary assembly of Mar del Plata attempted to act in response to the apostolic exhortation of Pope Paul VI to CELAM on November 24, 1965, the tenth anniversary of its founding, at which time His Holiness exhorted the Latin American episcopacy to work together in a common effort in Latin America in respect to all plans on a continental level.

The first Latin American Congress of Vocations was organized by the corresponding department of CELAM and took place in Lima, Peru, November 21–26, 1966. Twelve bishops from ten different nations and about two hundred specialists in this field met in this congress.

Other important encounters could also be noted, including that which took place in Chaclacayo, Peru, November 17–21, 1966, for the reform of seminaries, or the two in Buga, Colombia, February 12–25, 1967, the first of which studied the "Mission of the Catholic University" in the present Latin American situation, and the second planned the program of the church in the university world of Latin America. In these last two meetings a considerable number of bishops and experts again joined in the efforts.

In addition, the foundational meeting for the making of plans for the work of the Department of Missions which took place in Ambato, Ecuador, April 24–28, 1967, advanced a whole doctrinal program and one of up-to-date missionary action according to the council's orientations. Finally, in 1967 there were also meetings in Montevideo and San José de Costa Rica on the "Means of Social Communication," in which the bishops who were serving as presidents of the episcopal commissions for social communication as well as the directors of the national centers of means of communication in Latin America participated.

A REORGANIZATION DUE TO GROWTH

With growth and development has come an increasing need for CELAM to co-ordinate its own internal activities. For this purpose a meeting took place in May, 1967, in Bogotá, under the immediate direction of CELAM's presidency. It was attended by the presidents and the executive secretaries of all departments and by the directors of the institutes, as well as by the president of the financial committee, its general secretary and general treasurer. This meeting was of great importance, since it was the first since the departments had begun to function successfully in their co-ordination, both among themselves and with the presidency and the secretariat.

THEOLOGICAL FOUNDATIONS OF CELAM

In many respects it can be said that CELAM represents a kind of prophetic intuition of the aforementioned "collegiality of the bishops." The peculiar situation in which Latin America finds itself in respect to social and religious matters exercised pressure on the bishops and made them conscious of a common responsibility.

It is true that there are great differences among the several Latin American countries. It is also true, however, that there are common cultural roots and a growing consciousness of common interests as a result of the rapid social changes which impel the several countries together toward a common goal. Given this fact, the Latin American bishops meeting in Rio de Janeiro felt the need to unite their efforts in a common attempt to deal with common problems. They hoped also to search for and to find more efficient common solutions.

When subsequently Vatican II spoke of the "collegial responsibility" of the bishops in work of the church, the Latin American bishops felt that this constituted approval of what they had done in establishing CELAM. During the regular meeting of CELAM at

Mar del Plata in October, 1966, while dealing with the relationship between CELAM and the national episcopal conferences, several bishops expressed the need for a new approach in depth. They hoped to explore the theological reasons behind the existence and the work of CELAM, as well as trends in the current situation of the Catholic church toward decentralizing Roman institutions.

DIFFICULTIES

The very novelty of this development, in doctrinal as well as in organizational aspects, is a partial explanation of the difficulties which CELAM has met from the beginning. On the one hand, there are structural difficulties. The national episcopal conferences themselves are just now being properly organized. For that reason their relationships with CELAM lack the direction that could make them more effective. At times, for example, delegates are elected for one year; at other times, for several years or even for an indefinite period. When an election is for one year, lack of continuity makes it difficult to achieve efficient co-ordination between the episcopal conferences and CELAM.

On the other hand, insufficient financial resources and the almost explosive development of CELAM's activities through its departments have combined to make the channels of communication between CELAM and the national episcopal conferences insufficient. Indeed, the last regular meeting of CELAM concerned itself with this problem. A scientific study of what is needed for an adequate communications system between CELAM's presidency and the presidency of the episcopal conferences and between the departments of CELAM and those national episcopal commissions which have the same ends is much needed. Although a bulletin reporting on activities has been published, up to the present it has proved inadequate to the amount of information to be circulated.

That there is also a difficult change of attitudes and patterns of thought involved here cannot, however, be forgotten. In many respects CELAM really represents a "metanoia" in the exercise of episcopal functions within the new perspectives which Vatican II opened for the progress of the people of God—in the doctrine of collegiality and in the dynamic approach to functions within present social and cultural conditions.

Many times such changes in thinking are not accomplished without pain, and, unfortunately, in many cases they are not accomplished at all. There are resistances, some more or less passive, others more or less conscious, which act as serious obstacles to the work of CELAM and which prevent adequate communication and understanding of this work among the lower echelons of the national churches. Sometimes the work of CELAM is looked upon as dangerous interference with the work of the national churches. At other times CELAM is identified with the sporadic actions of one of its members, and dangerous generalizations are made about the doctrinal orthodoxy of the organization.

These difficulties are recognized and fully acknowledged by the most influential members of CELAM. Indeed, they study attentively and with increasing concern and delicacy each step taken by CELAM in the effort to avoid wounding sensitivities.

PASTORAL PERSPECTIVES:
CELAM AS AN ORGAN OF SERVICE

Of CELAM's several functions, one of the most important is its activity as an organ of service and a means of communication among the episcopal conferences of Latin America.

In an environment where social change and development are of major concern it is especially important that groups working for similar objectives in different parts of the continent be able to remain informed of what is being done in other areas.

Through its many and specialized departments CELAM is particularly well suited in theory to act as a communications center, the more so since each one of its departments aims at offering specific help to the national episcopal commissions which work in the same fields of the apostolate—and through them to the episcopal conferences and the national churches. Such an objective, for example, prompts the Department of Liturgy to offer courses of high caliber for the training of those responsible in this area at the national level. CLAF has also organized courses for the training of those responsible for catechetical work at the national level, and the Department of Education has offered to arrange a meeting of Latin American experts on the problems of the Catholic university. It is hoped that after this meeting these experts will be able to provide the bishops responsible for the apostolate in the universities with a wide basis for study and pastoral planning. However, aside from CELAM's potential to act as a communication's catalyst for the church in Latin America, in practice communications still leave much to be desired.

Such services as these can be offered by CELAM and its departments on its own initiative, or they can be requested directly by the episcopal conferences or their specialized commissions. Either case represents a service and not an imposition.

CELAM AS AN ORGAN OF CONTACT

CELAM also offers opportunity for annual contacts among representatives of the national episcopal conferences. Its meetings afford opportunity for formal and informal exchange of opinions, sharing of experiences, common discussion of difficulties, and the finding of solutions which often are also common. Extraordinary meetings, such as the recent one at Mar del Plata, allow for consideration of contrasts in experience on a wide basis, since they provide an opportunity for the bishops to meet with experts from many areas, both geographical and disciplinary.

In addition to its own meetings, CELAM provides a rational and efficient connection with other international organizations, such as UNESCO, as well as with such private organizations as the Latin American Bureau, Adveniat, Misereor, and so forth. Although CELAM does not attempt to "direct" the initiatives and activities of these organizations, it does try to provide communication channels at the Latin American level.

A second general conference of the Latin American episcopate was held, following the Thirty-Ninth International Eucharistic Congress in Bogotá, Colombia. The second conference opened in Bogotá in the presence of Pope Paul VI in August, 1968, and continued for two weeks thereafter in Medellín, Colombia. CELAM took advantage of the experiences of the past and of the conclusions of Vatican II to make this second conference dynamic and apostolic. It gave a great new impetus to post-conciliar renewal on the basis of episcopal collegiality and integrated the specialized departments that had recently been created.

CELAM SUPPORTS INTEGRATION

The Latin American episcopate recognizes that the integration of Latin America is an on-going process that cannot be reversed and that integration not only is indispensable to the harmonious development of the region but also, as a milestone in the movement toward the unification of the human family, is an essential contribution to world peace.

Recognizing in this process of integration a "sign of the times," the Latin American episcopate intends to contribute, in so far as is within its power, to "the noble enterprise of the integration of the Latin American continent" (Pope Paul VI).

Impetus is given to this desire to serve the continent by the inspiring words of the Holy Father in his message to the tenth extraordinary meeting of CELAM when he said: "In the name of the Gospel, the church can contribute positively to further the ideal of integration, awakening in all Christians the conviction that the national destinies cannot be reached except within international solidarity, thus forming a supranational conscience. . . . Therefore, the church commits itself to the historical process of the integration of Latin America, thus fulfilling her twofold mission of prophecy and witness" (Group VI of the tenth extraordinary assembly of the Latin American Episcopal Council, CELAM).

In general, CELAM wants to contribute to the process of integration in two ways: by example and by doctrine. As far as example is concerned, CELAM wants to co-operate in integrating the work of the national churches to reduce duplication and make action in the different fields more fruitful. Hence, importance is given to common pastoral action, not only nationally but also as far as possible at the Latin American level, as Pope Paul VI indicated. On the other hand, CELAM wants to be the light that will give doctrinal clarity to the several aspects of the process of integration within the specific field of responsibility of the church. To this end, informal contacts have been established with organizations which work for this end, such as the Institute for Latin American Integration (INTAL) of Buenos Aires. It is noteworthy also that in this case contact with CELAM was brought about as a result of a request by experts who work in the institute.

THE MORE IMMEDIATE TASKS

The work done so far and pastoral perspectives for the future represent a series of tasks and demands which CELAM tries to undertake in so far as it is able to do so adequately.

First among these tasks is the planning of CELAM's work in accordance with its proper ends. With this aim, at its meeting in Mar del Plata in October, 1966, CELAM created the Service of Information, Documentation, Statistics, and Technical Assistance (SIDEAT). SIDEAT, as its project for creation states, recognizes that "No plan for government can be properly developed without adequate information, documentation, statistics, and technical assistance. Even though these things in themselves are not sufficient for a pastoral orientation, they are indispensable as basic instruments." Through its orientation by solid theological reflection and integration with the general secretariat of CELAM, SIDEAT can be expected to fulfill these functions. Indeed, its planning and organization have been directed by a group of sociologists, statisticians, and experts in documentation from all over Latin America.

Second among the immediate tasks confronting CELAM is, as already pointed out, the finding of new channels of communication and the revitalization of those already existing in such a way that CELAM's services and contacts can be used effectively to fulfil an efficient role in the development of the Latin American church. It is hoped that this task can be undertaken through co-ordinating the efforts of the general secretariat and SIDEAT with the most important Latin American Catholic organs of mass communications. It must be recognized, however, that the Latin American church in general and CELAM in particular still have a long way to go and must work hard if they are to meet the social needs and also satisfy the exigencies of Vatican II in the field of mass communication.

Finally (and intimately related to the task described above) there is the need for the national episcopal conferences to achieve greater sensitivity in regard to the work which CELAM is doing. If this is to be done, it is necessary, first of all, to reach a theological formulation that will clarify the pastoral consequences of the doctrine of collegiality of bishops as it applies to the integration of apostolic efforts at the regional and continental level. To this end, CELAM is encouraging research and seeking information from the most outstanding theologians of the continent. It hopes to provide opportunities for these theologians to meet periodically in order to revitalize its own action as well as that of the episcopal conferences through the means of a common theological reflection.

Along this same line, and with the approval of Pope Paul VI, the presidency of CELAM has begun to visit each of the Latin American episcopal conferences in order to present to them, as a service, the documents elaborated at the extraordinary meeting of Mar del Plata. It is hoped that such meetings or visits will provide the occasions for an open and constructive dialogue that in turn will serve both to strengthen the relationship of CELAM with the conferences and also to make the conferences themselves more fruitful.

This series of tasks culminated concretely in the work of the second general conference of the Latin America episcopate in August, 1968, which received the greatest encouragement from His Holiness in as much as the Pope himself presided at the opening session and later confirmed its conclusions. This conference, through CELAM, which so vitally exemplifies the ideal of integration, provided the starting point for more positive action on the part of the Latin American church.

APPENDIX

CELAM'S PRESIDENCY

The presidency consists of a president and two vice-presidents chosen by the members of the council for a period of two years.

First Period—Constituted in 1956

President: Most Rev. Jaime de Barros Câmara, Cardinal-Archbishop of Rio de Janeiro.

Vice-Presidents: Most Rev. Miguel Darío Miranda, Archbishop Primate of Mexico.
Most Rev. Manuel Larraín, Bishop of Talca, Chile.

Second Period—1959–60

President: Most Rev. Miguel Darío Miranda, Archbishop Primate of Mexico.

Vice-Presidents: Most Rev. Manuel Larraín, Bishop of Talca, Chile.
Dom Helder Câmara, Auxiliar Archbishop of Rio de Janeiro, Brazil.

Third Period—1961–62[1]

President: Most Rev. Miguel Darío Miranda, Archbishop Primate
                 of Mexico.
Vice-Presidents: Most Rev. Manuel Larraín, Bishop of Talca, Chile.
                 Dom Helder Câmara, Auxiliar Archbishop of Rio
                 de Janeiro, Brazil.

Fourth Period—1964–65

President: Most Rev. Manuel Larraín, Bishop of Talca, Chile.
Vice-Presidents: Dom Helder Câmara, Auxiliar Archbishop of Rio
                 de Janeiro, Brazil.
                 Most Rev. Carlos Humberto Rodríguez-Quirós,
                 Archbishop of San Jose, Costa Rica.

Fifth Period—1966–67

President: Most Rev. Manuel Larraín, Bishop of Talca, Chile.[2]
Vice-Presidents: Dom Avelar Brandão Vilela, Archbishop of Tere-
                 sina, Brazil.
                 Most Rev. Pablo Muñóz Vega, Bishop Coadjutor
                 of Quito, Ecuador.

11: JUC AND AP: THE RISE OF CATHOLIC RADICALISM IN BRAZIL[1]

Emanuel de Kadt

Seen in historical perspective, the Catholic church in Brazil has never been a particularly powerful institution. During the colonial period the secular clergy, usually ignorant and of lax morals, were for the most part scattered throughout the rural areas and were more subject to the domination of the sugar planters and other landowners, whose plantation chapels they served, than to their bishops. Some religious orders, and especially the Jesuits, in missionary activities among the Indians and educational activities in the towns, represented Catholicism as an institution that was independent of society's powerful men. The Jesuits were in fact the only well-organized and purposeful ecclesiastical force in the country, and they maintained a moral self-discipline that was not to be seen elsewhere in the Brazilian church, in addition to preserving a wide margin of independence from the civil authorities. The hierarchy itself was weak and totally subordinate to the crown, chiefly by means of the *padroado*, an arrangement which had gradually emerged as a result of concessions wrung by the Portuguese kings from the papacy in the fifteenth and sixteenth centuries. Under the *padroado*, church appointments were the subject of secular patronage rather than ecclesiastical necessity. The state's domination of the church was sealed by the "regalist" reforms of Pombal, the centralizing and despotic representative of the Enlightenment in Portugal who expelled the Jesuits in 1759.[2]

Shortly after independence (1822), the Brazilian emperor assumed the ecclesiastical prerogatives that had previously been exercised by the Portuguese kings. This situation was accepted, *de facto*, by the

Vatican. During the period of the empire, the state's control of the church was virtually complete and had the acceptance of almost the entire secular clergy, who supported the regalist order in which they were enmeshed. A prominent example of clerical involvement was Father Diogo Antônio Feijó, at one time regent of the empire. There was much flaunting of the church's independence from Rome, an independence that was formally expressed by the imperial consent that was needed before the promulgation of papal proclamations. Repeatedly, the abolition in Brazil of clerical celibacy (it was, in fact, non-existent) was put forward, and Masonic influence on the church remained great, even after the condemnation by Pius IX in 1864.

Catholic agitation for loosening the ties that bound God to Caesar in Brazil began in the early 1870's, under the "ultramontane" influence of the *Syllabus Errorum* (1864) and the proclamation of papal infallibility in 1870. An open clash over the issue of Masonry between the government and two bishops in 1873–74, which led to the bishops' condemnation and imprisonment by a civilian court, was indicative of the mounting tensions. Though the particular issue was resolved in 1875 by a new government that was willing to accept "defeat," the wider question of church-state relationships remained a matter of contention between the empire and the Vatican. The solution came at one stroke, however, shortly after the proclamation of the Republic in November, 1889: the new and positivistic leadership of the country had as little use as churchmen themselves for the *padroado* and all that went with it. In January, 1890, church and state formally separated.[3]

Thus, the church freed itself from a relationship in which it had been prevented from expressing, or even developing, its own viewpoint. The earliest efforts at independent Catholic thought were, therefore, devoted to "revitalizing" the church as an institution: to improving the status and the qualifications of the clergy after centuries of decadence that were the result of its long subordination to the interests of the state. During this largely pre-ideological phase, credit must be given to Padre Júlio Maria, whose life and writings constitute a *tour de force* in helping the church through the transition to independent status. In 1900 he still found it necessary to castigate the clergy for their inability to act in new ways. Old ways die hard. The past, which had seen priests functioning as part of the apparatus of the state, lingered on in a predilection for personal priestly involvement in politics and in a failure to establish true links between priests and the bulk of their parishioners. Under the influence of Leo XIII's *Rerum Novarum*, Padre Júlio Maria admonished the clergy to concern themselves with social and economic questions connected with the interests of the nation and the people. He told them to be "social reformers," rather than ministers to a small "aristocracy of the devout," in whose service they provided "feasts for the living and funerals for the dead." On the other hand he fulminated against the ideology of the new Republicans: over and above their laudable goal of full separation of church and state, the new men in power, he held, have secularist, anticlerical, and antireligious convictions: in effect, they want to banish God from the Brazilian state.[4]

The state, of course, had always been very much an instrument of the country's small elite, and during the latter period the empire and the early period of the republic the "ruling ideas" of this group were a confused and imported mixture of positivism, Darwinism, and other less coherent systems of thought. This general situation of intellectual disorientation continued to prevail through the beginning of the twenties. It was not until then that the hitherto isolated expressions of the specifically Brazilian culture in literature and the arts began to be presented by its advocates as a new movement. In 1922, the centenary of Brazilian independence, a "Week of Modern Art" was observed in São Paulo, an event which formally, so to speak, proclaimed the new ideas to the country.[5] This was also the year of the famous revolt of Copacabana Fort, the first open sign of dissatisfaction with the general condition of society and politics from among the younger officers, whose expressions of rebelliousness, which flared up throughout the twenties, became known as the *Tenentismo* movement.

This is not the place to analyze the cultural or political scene in Brazil during the first quarter of the twentieth century. But it is not without interest to note that the earliest distinctively Catholic ideology, which, though promulgated by one man (Jackson de Figueiredo), did reach a wider circle, was negative in character. It developed as a reaction against the still isolated, disparate, and far from coherent impulses expressed in the "Week of Modern Art" and the *Tenentes*' revolts, the first stirrings of innovation in the country after decades of political stagnation and cultural and intellectual confusion.[6] Jackson's ideology, inspired by the ideas of de Maistre and of Maurras, was very precisely a reactionary one—in fact, he took pride in the epithet. The journal he founded, A Ordem (Order), proclaimed the virtues not only of order, but of authority, morality, Catholicism, and nationalism. His nationalism looked back to a pure Catholic past, when Brazil was not yet threatened by Protestantism or by international Freemasonry, capitalism, and Judaism. Order and authority would safeguard the country against revolution, not only of the mild kind, which the Tenentes seemed to threaten, but also that which had engulfed Tsarist Russia in 1917.

Jackson had gradually been converted to Catholicism, taking the final step of confession in 1921 at the age of thirty after an interview with the Archbishop (later Cardinal) of Rio de Janeiro, D. Sebastião Leme. D. Leme was quietly involved in much that happened on the Brazilian Catholic scene from his appointment to Rio in 1921 until his death in 1942. As Archbishop of Olinda (Recife) his first pastoral letter (1916) had dealt with the problems of religious indifference in Brazil, with the agnostic, secularist, and positivist frame of mind of most Brazilian intellectuals and with the lack of doctrinal foundation in the ideas of those who called themselves Catholics.[7] Once he had reached Rio, he stimulated study groups and associations of Catholic laymen, and he was fully behind Jackson's activities in the Centro Dom. Vital, from which A Ordem was published, activities which he saw as part of the effort to Christianize the Brazilian intelligentsia. D. Leme vigorously promoted what he considered to be the interests of the Catholic church on the national political scene, but he resolutely opposed Jackson's desire to found a Catholic political party. He gave him full freedom as director of the Centro D. Vital, and it is quite possible that the views promoted by the Centro and published in A Ordem received their polemical imprint as a result of the frustration of Jackson's political ambitions.[8]

Jackson died suddenly in 1928. His successor as editor of A Ordem and as director of the Centro D. Vital was Alceu Amoroso Lima, also known by his nom de plume, Tristão de Athayde. He resolutely steered the Centro away from the all-too-open involvement in politics it had pursued under Jackson. Amoroso Lima's views on man and society were, from the start, rather different from those of his predecessor. It is true that he opposed the Revolution of 1930, the political culmination of the Tenentes movement, and that late in 1932 he became the secretary-general of the Liga Eleitoral Católica (LEC), D. Leme's answer to those who were still pressing for a Catholic political party. The LEC acted as a pressure group to ensure the acceptance of "Catholic principles" by candidates from all parties in the elections of 1933 and to see that these principles (e.g., sacredness of the family [i.e., no divorce], religious instruction in schools) were incorporated in the 1934 Constitution—which they were.[9] Alceu also flirted for a few years in the early thirties with the *Integralistas*, whose parafascist ideology had been clearly foreshadowed in Jackson. From the middle of that decade, however, he definitely turned away from reaction and became the main channel in Brazil for the ideas of Jacques Maritain, whose *Humanisme Intégral* (1937) was a landmark on the road toward what we now think of as progressive Catholic social thought.

Amoroso Lima continues, in 1969, to direct the Centro D. Vital. Under his direction, the Centro, by means of study groups and discussion circles, helped lay the groundwork for the "renewal" that came about from the late fifties on. But despite this fact, and despite Alceu's own remarkable intellectual openness and his capacity for ideological renewal, the Centro D. Vital has not attained a real position of influence among Catholics in Brazil, has not helped to disseminate a specific ideology, has not become the center of a deeply committed social movement. Its links with the diocese of Rio, since 1943 directed by Cardinal D. Jaime Câmara, a very conservative prelate, made that impossible.

The social movement from which, after many years with no clear direction, a truly radical social Catholicism emerged was Catholic Action, another organization in which Alceu Amoroso Lima has played a leading role. Catholic Action is a form of the "lay apostolate" which has been encouraged by various Popes from the beginning of the present century and which was given formal status by Pius XI in the mid twenties. By the early thirties it was well established in Europe: in Italy the emphasis was on a general mass movement, with separate branches for men and women, adults and youth; in France and Belgium greater stress was placed, from the beginning, on a "specialized" lay apostolate, a result of the success of the organization of working-class youth in JOC (*Jeunesse Ouvrière Catholique*).[10]

D. Leme closely followed the gradual development of the idea of Catholic Action. The charter and guidelines for the coordinating organization of lay Catholic organizations, which he founded in 1923, the Confederação Católica, had in fact been called Ação Católica. In 1929 he had set up a university group in his diocese, Ação Universitária Católica, and three years later a working-class movement, the Confederação Operária Católica. When from 1935 the establishment of branches of Catholic Action was formally encouraged for all dioceses in Brazil, the movement followed the Italian pattern, with which D. Leme was personally familiar. At the same time the student branch in Rio was renamed Juventude Universitária Cathólica (JUC), and the youth branch of the working-class movement, JOC: Juventude Operária Católica. A branch for secondary-school students, Juventude Estudantil Católica (JEC), was also organized in Rio.[11] Alceu Amoroso Lima was appointed the first national chairman of the over-all organization.

Catholic Action was organized on a large scale. It sponsored mass rallies and pilgrimages; its thousands of members enthusiastically wore their badges and turned out in public places for demonstrations of faith. But its impact was not very deep, and the enthusiasm did not last. The organization languished during the forties, remaining impressive only on paper. The beginnings of change came toward the end of that decade, when specialized movements—particularly among youth—were given greater prominence. The first to be officially recognized by the hierarchy on a nationwide scale was JOC in 1948. Then in July, 1950, other branches were nationally launched: JAC (Juventude Agrária Católica) for the agrarian youth; the two student branches, JEC and JUC, which had existed for various periods in several of the more important dioceses; and a kind of catchall for the residual category of "independents," JIC (Juventude Independente Católica). Each (except JUC) had a separate branch for women. Only JIC failed to establish an identity of its own, let alone an ideology or a recognizable mode of action in its hazy, vaguely middle-class "milieu." The other four would all play a part in the development of Catholic radicalism in Brazil.

Least effective of these in the early years was JAC, its weakness a result of the backward conditions in the rural areas. JOC's role depended much on local conditions and on the attitude of the assistente, the ecclesiastical adviser appointed by the diocesan bishop. Where he was a progressive, a person with an outlook not unlike that of the French worker-priests, JOC branches and their adult equivalent, ACO (Ação Católica Operária) could be quite aggressive, stimulating the urban workers into a strong defense of their existing rights and to the conquest of new ones. When the *assistentes* were chiefly concerned about preaching cooperation and understanding between the opposing sides in capitalist industrial enterprises, the impact of JOC and ACO was not very great. But JOC and ACO came to be influenced by the students' radicalism, and after the coup of 1964 they became, in the light of the existing circumstances, quite militant.

The secondary-school branch, JEC, should not be underestimated, especially for its impact on the students in religious schools. Toward the end of the period under consideration, they had developed their own socio-political activities and even ideas, but their influence, naturally, did not reach as far as that of the university students, although one must remember that many of the latter had been members, or leaders, of JEC. The truly crucial movement was of the university students, JUC. Thus, an analysis of the evolution of JUC's ideology is requisite for understanding the phenomenon as a whole.

JUC did not start as a movement with a particularly radical bent. Its motto and method were those of similar Catholic Action organizations elsewhere: see, judge, and act. It was oriented toward the spread of "good" Catholic ideas and behavior by the activity of Catholic "militants" in their own milieu. At the first national congress in 1950 the various commissions took up problems ranging from internal administrative matters to religious teaching in the university; from sex education, the family, and spiritual life to the cinema.[12] From that year onward the movement's national council met annually to discuss problems and policies and to review the achievements of the past year. These achievements usually seemed to lie mainly in the sphere of the spiritual: Easter retreats, pilgrimages, courses on Catholic culture, and the provision of religious services in the universities. But the movement failed to grow sturdy roots in its milieu. It neither reached many people, nor did it seem to have a particularly profound effect on those who participated in its activities, not even on the so-called militants. Dissatisfaction among the successive cohorts of leadership increased; at the Eighth National Council in 1958 the discussions of the vague sense of unease made way for a more concerted effort in self-criticism.

JUC, it was felt, had become a movement which discussed, especially at the level of the annual national councils, well-prepared and high-sounding texts, which came to nothing in the concrete life of the movement.[13] The terse report of the 1958 discussions, in which the *assistentes*, as usual, took active part, evinces almost a feeling of desperation about the working of the movement, which seemed unable to reach anyone but those centrally engaged in its direction.[14] The cause of JUC's ineffectiveness was seen in the "lack of life" within the movement, its excessively abstract theoretical discussions and orientation, its lack of engagement in concrete reality. This had become obvious because "Brazilian reality" was being increasingly discussed in the country at large, and especially because one or two branches of JUC were successfully carrying out practical, socially committed, projects. But it was realized in 1958 that a switch to activity with deeper roots in concrete reality and its problems would raise the issue of JUC's incapacity, as an apostolic organization formally subordinated to the hierarchy, to take specific positions on socio-political matters. In fact it was awareness of this restriction which had kept the movement on more theoretical grounds in the first place.

This report of the 1958 Council of JUC was the first significant airing of the central "existential problem" of JUC: to find a course between the Scylla of sterile abstraction and the Charybdis of concrete political commitments. Padre Almery, an *assistente*, suggested that a compass for safe sailing could be found by developing a body of thought within the movement to provide basic ideas to orient all action. A year later, at the 1959 council, his proposal emerged as the movement's *Ideal Histórico*.[15]

He read a paper at that council which was to have profound influence.[16] He began by stating that for Christian militants it is not sufficient to know that they have a task to fulfil in this world, a task involving such matters as "creating a Christian social order," "bringing salvation to the social structures," or "restoring all things to Christ." They need much more specific guidance in order to apply such undoubtedly excellent precepts to the immediate situation. Though a Christian will find the *ultimate* meaning of history in his faith, faith is not necessarily of any help in enabling him to make sense of the history of his own time and society. On the one hand, the teaching of the church and the speculations of theologians provide him with the universal principles by which to guide his action. Social scientists, on the other hand, have supplied many facts and some theories about society, but these facts and theories are usually not connected with an explicit philosophical, let alone theological, concern. Almery, therefore, concluded that "it is absolutely necessary, if we aim at an effective Christian commitment in the temporal order, to reflect amply and carefully in the light of reality . . . so that we may arrive at certain *principia media* [intermediate principles] which express what one might call a Christian historical ideal." He added, however, that knowledge and reflection by themselves are not enough for the emergence of such intermediate principles; reality must also be experienced personally, by living in it actively and with commitment.

Almery sees the *ideal histórico*, not only in intermediate principles, but as a "realizable ideal essence." It is the relative maximum of social and political perfection which is both capable of existing in reality and toward which events tend "in a specific historical climate." In sociological parlance it may be called an "ideal type," and it has affinities to a utopia, understood as an ideal construct which "helps to prepare public opinion for certain possible realities."[17] The availability of such an *ideal histórico* should, according to Almery, prevent one from arguing, in a relativistic manner, "that the iniquities of this world should be accepted with tranquillity." But there is the danger that it may lead people to "fall prey to the illusion that the Kingdom of God can be established on earth," an illusion against which Almery warns with some insistence. His fears proved to be well-founded. For although the more sophisticated intellectual and philosophical leaders of the young Catholic radicals never succumbed to blatant millenarianism, a clearly socially unrealistic, "utopic,"[18] streak developed among the secondary ideologues and publicists when they had brought together Christian principles and social analysis based on empirical data of history and society.

Social analysis had been in the wings for some time. A series of articles by the French Dominican Friar Thomas Cardonnel published in July, 1960, in O Metropolitano, the paper of the Students' Union of Guanabara state (UME), marked the watershed between the thought of two generations. For the first time a large number of students protested as *Christians* about the shape of their society. Until then Christian social thought in Brazil, including the episcopal pronouncements beginning to be concerned with social injustice, almost exclusively emphasized the need for social harmony, promoted the

idea of interclass solidarity in opposition to the Marxists' acceptance
and even furtherance of class conflict, and looked to cooperation
between all the sectors (classes) of the community as the solution of
the nation's social problems. It centered on the elusive concept of the
"common good," which was always presented as something clear-cut
in philosophical terms and obvious in practice. "The community is
the natural place where men think and want together, where they
plan and decide together in function of the common good," pro-
claims the *Manifesto Solidarista* of Pe. Fernando Bastos Ávila, S.J.,
who is a more progressive representative of this viewpoint that remained dominant till the end of the fifties.[19] How different a sound
do we hear from Cardonnel: "We can never insist enough on the
need to denounce natural harmony, class collaboration. God is not so
dishonest, so false as a certain kind of social peace, consisting in the
acquiescence of all in an unnatural injustice. Violence is not only a
fact of revolutions. It also characterizes the maintenance of a false
order."[20]

  Thus various factors combined to swing JUC into a more radical
mood. There was the growing dissatisfaction inside the movement
with its lack of success and with the failure to relate itself to the concrete problems facing its potential membership. The changing outlook of European Christian circles was reflected in Brazil, not only in
the Cardonnel articles, but also in the writings of Lebret, Mounier,
and other "advanced" Catholic thinkers, which were increasingly
available in Portuguese.[21] This coincided with a growing concern
among students—Catholic and other—with social problems. In Recife, Belo Horizonte, Natal, and other cities, they began various educational and organizational projects among the urban masses. Thus,
the discovery of "Brazilian reality" was coming about not by means
of academic study and evaluation alone, which was reflected in the
increased sociological output mainly from the Universities of São
Paulo and Belo Horizonte and from the Instituto Superior de Estudos Brasileiros (ISEB),[22] but through direct contact and the indigna-
tion that sprang from it. Finally, important changes in the context in
which JUC was operating, which will be examined at a later stage,
further contributed to the radical tone the discussion was beginning
to acquire.

JUC's national council had decided to make the search for and elaboration of an *ideal histórico* into the centerpiece of its tenth anniversary congress, to be held in July, 1960. This was no ordinary meeting—five hundred delegates as compared with the usual score or so attended. A long analysis, a kind of working draft of the project, was presented to the congress by the *equipe* from Belo Horizonte. JUC was strongly represented there among students in the Faculty of Economics and Social Science; the main outlines of their analysis of social reality will provide an indication of the way in which the radicals' ideology was developing.[23]

The basic options for Brazil are considered to be three. In the first place there is the need to overcome underdevelopment. Secondly, the freeing of the country from the "gravitational field" of capitalism, since the continued existence of capitalist structures in Brazil is an impediment to development. Finally, there is the need to break the international equilibrium generated by capitalism, which is, shamefully, based on the complementarity of the metropolitan and the colonial nations. Thus, in a negative sense, development involves disengagement from the free play of international exchanges, the rules of which are set by the economically dominant countries and the "egoistical policies of the monopolies (trusts, cartels, holdings, etc.)." In a positive sense it is seen to involve the creation of a solid infrastructure of basic industry, an efficient transport system, the elimination of regional disparities, and the enlargement of the internal market. One of the preconditions of the last requirement is agrarian reform, which is to lead to the modernization of agriculture and to the creation of cooperative and "socialized" agrarian institutions.

The economy must be planned so that its workings reflect an ordering of priorities based on the needs of the people; it is to be organized within the total perspective of the personalist ideas of Mounier, to become a "personal economy, of persons and for persons, using means which are appropriate to persons." This would mean the acceptance of the principle of the primacy of labor over capital, "the substitution of the institution of private property . . . by an effective instrument of personalization for all Brazilians, with due regard to the higher requirements of the common good." The commanding heights of the economy are to be nationalized, i.e., put under state control; in other sectors of industry worker comanagement should be instituted. The anonymous nature of capitalist property, with its great and powerful limited companies, should be eliminated; the "proletarian condition," a term used to refer to the situation in which the Brazilian masses, whose work produces the national riches, are robbed of the benefits of this production, is to be ended.

Even such a short, and necessarily inadequate, summary shows the mixing of ideas from very different sources in this first tentative posing of the social analytic side of the *ideal histórico*. Socialist ideas and Marxist slogans are mingled with barely digested pieces of personalist philosophy, whose implications for practical policy are hardly considered. Apparently, the congress debated the project with such gusto that its publication after the congress was followed in the JUC bulletin by a page of cautionary observations from the national leadership. This pointed out that the ideas were merely provisional, that the paper had been written in haste, and that intemperate language was used at times (though not intemperate ideas). Moreover, these ideas at many points went beyond the intermediate principles which ought to constitute the essence of any *ideal histórico* into the formulation of specific lines of policy, the choice of which should be left to the individual. The goings-on at the congress resulted in cries of Marxist infiltration being widely raised.

As a specialized section of Catholic Action, JUC's primary concern was meant to be its own "milieu," the university. Henceforth, JUC's activity in the universities had two main lines: participation in general student politics, specifically in the National Union of Students (UNE), and the development of support for university reform. The Latin American university reform movement, which originated in 1918 in Córdoba, Argentina, had till then completely by-passed Brazil. In May, 1960, however, a seminar on university reform held in Salvador, Bahia, in which a majority of the participants were Marxists, marked the beginning of agitation in the universities.[24] This was first directed toward the democratization of education, then took up demands for the democratization of society. Thus, university reform led, by a different path, to the same over-all social, economic, and political preoccupations we have just discussed. It aimed not only at the achievement of some power for students in the running of the universities, but also at the "de-alienation" of the whole system of education, whose archaic curricula was seen as irrelevant to national development and where gross inequalities of opportunity effectively excluded all but an insignificant number of students from the urban masses.

It did not take JUC long to realize that the centers of learning are not islands isolated from the rest of society. As early as the 1960 congress, the university milieu was seen as "comprising all the micro-structures of the university, and the macro-structures of society insofar as they influence, or are influenced by, the university micro-structures, and are closely linked to them."[25] During the next two years, however, the struggle for university reform, which JUC waged together with other, chiefly various kinds of Marxist, student organizations, got nowhere, despite strikes, demonstrations, and other forms of militancy. This only strengthened the students' conviction that changes in the university and education would result from, rather than bring about, a basic restructuring of society. This was expressed in a JUC bulletin early in 1963: "At the present time the student movement, and particularly its leadership, is becoming conscious of the fact that university reform is part of the [more general] Brazilian process, intrinsically articulated with the socio-economic and political structures. This being so we could not simply start with university reform and move on to achieve [changes in the wider society]; university reform has to become part of the Brazilian Revolution."[26] And so yet another road turns out to have led to a more general revolutionary position, a position which drove all students, Catholics and non-Catholics alike, out of their own "milieu" into the wider society.

The other means of engaging in activities in their own milieu was participation in student politics. This was more an individual than an organizational undertaking. But, of course, it was difficult to draw the line: individuals who stood for office in UNE were known to belong to certain groups, and votes were cast for candidates as associated with organizations at least as much as for personal characteristics.[27] In 1960 the UNE congress took place shortly after that of JUC, and a left-wing candidate, Oliveiros Guanais, was elected to the presidency of UNE with support from JUC and the Marxists. In 1961 an actual militant of JUC, Aldo Arantes of the Catholic University of Rio de Janeiro, was elected to the highest office in UNE. Arantes' success no doubt owed something to the furore caused by a manifesto published early that year by the students' council of his university, in which he played a prominent part. This manifesto, coming from the students of a Catholic university, shocked estab-

lished Catholic opinion. It not only denounced the alienating bourgeois university, the class nature of the state, and the vacuousness of
the constitutionally guaranteed liberties, but also presented a very
daring theology of history, which was far "in advance" of anything
commonly accepted as progressive in Brazil. This owed much to the
thought (and, in fact, to the active help) of Pe. Henrique de Lima
Vaz, S.J., a brilliant young philosopher and theologian, whose influence on the entire generation we are considering was profound during
this period.[28]

The massive entry of JUC into national student politics brought it
into closer contact than hitherto with other student groups, including
those of the secular left, with which it collaborated on an increasing
scale. In 1962 only one candidate for the UNE presidency was nomi-
nated; he had the support of all major groups, from Communists to
JUC. UNE's pronouncements on and incursions into national politics multiplied; these became headline material in the national press.
But political involvement removed the leadership from contact with
its student "bases" and tended to blur the ideological outlines of the
various groups, which, in the case of JUC, were never very clear in
the first place. Action, any kind of action, became good in itself. A
little later, in the middle of 1963, an article in a JUC bulletin dealing
with the movement's involvement in student politics would muse:
"We in JUC lost the habit of seeing and judging. Thus our action
became poor in humanizing and salvation-bringing content, often
even lacked it altogether." Another writer, in the same issue, had this
to say:

> A sudden awakening to a reality which required a response from
> Christians . . . [led to] an over-valuation of socially oriented
> activity and the reform of structures, while the structure of the
> movement itself was neglected. As the movement grew, took
> up coherent positions, came to be believed in in the student milieu,
> gradually became committed, it came to lack depth, reflection,
> and organization. The most diverse commitments were entered
> into, although they had virtually no apostolic meaning. The move-
> ment thus denied its own raison d'etre.[29]

Almost certainly, these criticisms did not reflect the views of
the majority of JUC's membership, for whom the opening, finally
achieved, to social and political reality was only to be welcomed. But
the criticisms are very similar indeed to the complaints made by the

hierarchy two years earlier. This had led to a major conflict between students and bishops, caused in the first place by the fact that JUC was obviously developing a view of the proper role of the church in the world, and of the layman in the church, which was not at all shared by the vast majority of bishops, and, second, by the bishops' disagreement with JUC's public position on socio-political matters. For although the bishops' own attitudes on these matters changed in the course of the 1950's, their pronouncements increasingly turning to questions of social structure and social justice and thus contributing to create the atmosphere in which the "radical explosion" occurred, the hierarchy's statements had never gone beyond the church's traditional social doctrine.

In July, 1961, the national council of JUC met in Natal (RN) for the first time since the tenth anniversary congress. The discussions again took up the themes that had been raised in 1960. Present, as an observer, at this meeting was the then apostolic administrator of Natal, D. Eugênio Sales. D. Eugênio is a churchman of reformist social views whose approach to ecclesiastical matters is paternalist. He is reluctant to allow freedom of movement to Catholic lay organizations. Various of the points of view expressed during that council meeting disturbed him greatly, and he raised the matter of JUC's position with the episcopal commission for Catholic Action when it met shortly afterward.[30] His strictures met with much sympathy among other members of the commission, who had been outraged by the manifesto of students in Rio's Catholic University, made public a few months before, in which JUC was believed to have had a hand. They decided to be direct and issued an extremely strong directive to JUC's national and regional directorates and their *assistentes*, roundly forbidding the movement to make radical pronouncements or to engage in what the bishops considered undesirable political activities.[31]

JUC then found itself in the crisis of legitimacy which had loomed ever since it embarked upon the uncharted seas of *ideal histórico*. The crisis had been present embryonically in the very concept of *ideal histórico*, which was, after all, made up of two ideas whose practical implications were very different. The first is the notion of "intermediate principles," which is supposed to guide the individual in his specific choices under concrete circumstances, is indeterminate and ambiguous, and is vague enough to leave much play to individual judgment of those circumstances. It shares this characteristic with much of Catholic social thought, which is thus serviceable to a wide range of opinions and policies.

But the second element of the *ideal histórico* tends to the concrete and specific, spelling out the details of an ideal, yet potentially realizable, social order. Utopian blueprints for the future have much greater specificity—and persuasiveness—than intermediate principles for guiding behavior in a general direction. They tend to support one rather than a variety of socio-political viewpoints. Utopias allow less room for choice and lead to wider areas of commitment. It was this apparent commitment of JUC, an official organ of the church with a mandate from the hierarchy, to specific social and political options for Brazil which brought down the wrath of the bishops—partly, no doubt, because the options did not coincide with those of the prelates, which were more conservative, partly as a result of pique over the trespassing on the bishops' authority.

One cannot say that the students had been unaware of this problem. It had been put to them at the 1960 congress by one of their *assistentes*, who had remarked: "The hierarchy has the task of governing the church . . . from them we must filially receive the authentic interpretation of Revelation and Tradition; to them we must submit our experience and our conclusions." And although he had pointed out that "the task of Christian initiative falls to the faithful [the laymen], who are the front-line soldiers," he had added: "When the hierarchy approves our conquests, it is as if they are canonized and inserted into the tradition of the church."[32] The laymen, however, showed little inclination meekly to submit their social and political judgments, arrived at as Christians, to priests or bishops. They had become aware, as another of their *assistentes*, Frei Romeu Dale, explained in a document which appeared shortly after the bishops' restrictive directives were issued, that "the authority of the clergy normally is limited" and that it does not belong to the hierarchy to organize the structures of society. They also resented the often very "authoritarian and distant" exercise of authority by bishops, who treated all laymen "as if they were minors." Such behavior does not go down well with a generation that has struggled hard to free itself from the weight of parental authority in Brazil's traditional patriarchal family.[33]

All this was true and important, and yet there was force in the argument, formulated by Frei Romeu, that the work of JUC could have no meaning without a vital link with the bishops. Catholic Action was a movement of the church; as part of it JUC was subordinated and owed obedience to the hierarchy. The problem was that its members had, in a sense, run away with the organization. As members of JUC, the only nationwide Catholic organization in the universities, the students had embarked together on an exciting journey of discovery. On this journey they had met others, non-Catholics, similarly engaged, and they were proud of what they had found and committed to hold on to it.[34] Too bad that the hierarchy had originally given them a mandate; it was intolerable that the bishops now wanted to control them. JUC was their organization, they had shaped it into what it now was, they made use of its structures to think and act together. In short, they were JUC.

To the *assistentes*, the problem did not present itself in such a simple light. Many of them had fully identified themselves with the new course of the movement, and they wanted as much as the membership to use the organization for the promotion of a social revolution in Brazil, to which they felt the church should give its blessing. But they were priests, after all, specifically appointed by their bishop to a position of trust, and they were torn, in a dilemma of loyalties, until precise instructions had been received from the hierarchy. They were preparing the following question for the bishops, when the latter intervened:

> Would it befit JUC, as a movement, to assume the responsibility for organized work in the political field? Or would it be better for the members who are militants in university politics to organize themselves on their own behalf, in a separate group, acting on their own responsibility, as Christians—but including others who are not from JUC, and even not Christians?[35]

The *assistentes* looked at the matter from the point of view of its appropriateness. JUC members, thinking in such terms even before the hierarchy forced them to take their politics elsewhere, had clearly begun to have doubts about the very nature of the movement. This was part of a wider reappraisal of the relationship between the hierarchy and the laymen in the church, the division of labor between them, and the extent to which their relationship should be governed by authority or cooperation, by a requirement to obtain permission at least for the outlines of action (and thought) or by freedom to develop under their own steam and on their own responsibility. *JUCistas* were also beginning to feel, as they moved from student politics to activities outside the universities, that they should broaden their base to include intellectuals, workers, and peasants. JUC was not yet willing formally to break with Catholic Action and the hierarchy, and to declare itself an independent lay movement (a step that was to be taken in mid-1966). Instead, as a result of internal necessities and the bishops' external pressure, a new movement, *Ação Popular* (AP), was born. Once this alternative vehicle for social and political action, which was joined by most of the more active members of JUC, came into being, the preoccupation of JUC itself turned more and more to reflection about the question that had originally sparked the crisis: the role of the layman in the church and the theological and philosophical analysis of his action in the world qua member of the church.[36]

Ação *Popular* had been informally started some time late in 1961, but was officially launched on June 1, 1962, as a political movement rather than a political party. Many of its initiators were drawn from among the most active JUC militants, though from the start AP attracted people from outside Catholic student circles. By now no trace was left of the lack of social engagement prevalent in the Catholic student movement at an earlier stage.[37] Hence the following paragraphs will deal with the most decisive phase for the non-Marxist radicals of the pre-coup period.

From mid-1962 to its violent repression after the coup of April, 1964 (in fact, the members of AP suffered more from persecution than did any other group in Brazil) the movement gathered substantial support outside the few universities which had been the centers of JUC radicalism. In the first instance, it seems to have found new adherents in the lesser universities and colleges, among young intellectuals and professionals, and among the older secondary-school students. Some of these never formally joined the movement; others became members of a specific AP "group," committed to the lines of action elaborated by the movement's *cúpula*, the twenty or thirty ideologues and activists at the top.

Most of these people must have come from backgrounds which were at least middle class.[38] Later, AP created something of a following among the more articulate workers and peasants, but their numbers never reached significant proportions and their commitment seems never to have gone very deep. Thus, AP remained till the coup essentially a "populist" movement of intellectuals for the people.[39] What occurred after AP's violent repression following the coup of April, 1964, is another matter altogether. Its history in the most recent years remains to be written; that history will, I believe, show that the movement has lost virtually all connections with its own roots in specifically *Christian* radical thought, a development that had its beginning even before the coup.

From the start, AP was careful to avoid the impression that it was a *Christian* movement. Mindful of the experience of JUC, it had no formal ties with the church, wanted to have nothing to do with bishops qua bishops, nor did it want to be known as a movement of Christians. Religious or theological references were self-consciously omitted from its documents; nowhere could one find a mention of its antecedents in the Catholic student movement.[40] Nevertheless, it was regarded by many at the time as a kind of para-Christian organization, because of the presence in it of so many who had earlier been active in JUC. For Candido Mendes, AP was *the* expression of the Catholic left, and, though one may quibble with this characterization on formal grounds, there can be little doubt that AP bore the imprint of radical Catholicism until the coup of April, 1964.[41]

This imprint can be found in its philosophy of history, whose link with Catholic theology is not less noticeable for being implicit. For AP the central line in history is socialization, understood as the increasing density and ubiquity of social (as opposed to individualistic) arrangements of human intercourse. While this concept was given prominence in Pope John's encyclical *Mater et Magistra* of 1961, it had been a main element of the optimistic evolutionism of Teilhard de Chardin, whose ideas had begun to influence the philosophical outlook of the future intellectual leaders of AP by the beginning of the sixties.[42] AP's *Documento Base*, elaborated toward the end of 1962 by its coordinating team, held: "The fact of socialization presides . . . over the emergence of human history, and appears as the fundamental matrix for the interpretation of its evolution."[43] Socialization, however, is not, in AP's view, a simple evolutionary process, but a dialectic one, a process in which struggle plays a part of overwhelming importance. In this, we meet the other chief source of inspiration, Hegelianism, as it came through Pe. Vaz.

Before we examine this dialectical aspect of socialization, we should note that under the influence of Pe. Vaz another important philosophical development took place. The previously central notion of *ideal histórico* was gradually replaced by that of *consciência histórica* (historical consciousness). Striving for a specific utopia thus resolved into a critical and conscious reflection about the historical process, with the present understood as a result of the past and as potentiality for the future. The conflicts, contradictions, and undesirable aspects of reality became as relevant as man's hopes or ideals. Historical consciousness emerges when man starts looking critically at his world and becomes aware of the fact that "history unfolds in an empirical time-span, which is given substance by the action of man in the form of historical initiative, action, that is, which transforms the world."[44] That transformation should bring about the *humanization* of the world, which is what modern Christianity specifically demands of man: "Man, in his freedom and in his action, must shoulder the destiny of creation . . . the greatest sin of the Christian will be today the sin of historical omission."[45]

In his discussion of the problem of dialectics in history, Vaz argued that history begins to exist only when one man communicates to another the meaning he gives to the world, a meaning more likely than not to be found in terms of the domination of man over man. In a significant near quote, he suggests that "history, till today, has always been this: one man who dominated another, or human groups which dominated other groups, in the most varied ways possible." But a dialectical "solution" in terms of domination "is not the final synthesis of history, its ultimate meaning." Through this dialectic of domination "little by little a more profound meaning to history manifests itself: the synthesis in terms of recognition, reconciliation, acceptance of man by man . . . as a person." Although domination and conciliation will always coexist in history, "the problem of the advance of history is that of the permanent overcoming, in ever wider and more universal circles, of domination by reconciliation. This shows us history as a kind of asymmetric movement, tending toward final reconciliation. That moment, for the Christian, is situated in a historical perspective: the eschatological hope of the final manifestation of God to man."[46]

Vaz had thus carefully formulated his final hope in eschatological terms, a hope outside history, a hope—as Karl Rahner would later put it—of the *absolute* future, which man may strive to bring nearer, but can never reach "in" history.[47] Vaz recognized the difficulty in this formulation for a wholly secular philosophy of history. Finding no obvious secular equivalent to the "final manifestation of God to man," he suggested hesitantly to those who could not base themselves on an explicitly Christian standpoint that this asymmetric tendency of history—the universalization of relations of conciliation—might just be simply accepted. He seems to have meant "accepted" as an article of faith without theological anchoring, rather like the Marxist credo of the classless society. And so, indeed, it happened: in the secularized context of AP the eschatological hope became an inner-worldly one. The hope beyond history was transformed into a belief in the actual possibility of utopia.

> The dialectic of History presents a hard countenance of strife: it is the multiplication of forms of domination on all planes of human reality. But only a desperate and absurd vision (which is still an extremely subtle form of domination of the other) can give History's final word to the relation which alienates, depersonalizes, negates man. More profoundly, and decisively, it is the movement of recognition, of personalization, and of solidarity which orients History. It is this movement which gives meaning to History and provides the ultimate standard for historically valid options, and the very measure of the human.[48]

Though this formulation was somewhat ambiguous about the possibility of fully realizing a non-dominant society, and about the period needed to achieve it, there is no question how this ambiguity was resolved in the movement at large. AP came to believe that it was possible to achieve a final "purification" of this world and to eliminate all that was "evil," power-seeking, dominating, individualistic, and alienating. After the revolution and after the theory and praxis of AP would have had time completely to permeate social relations, the contradictions that society has known so far would disappear, and all men would become "subjects of their own history." This "utopic" view[49] probably owed as much to Teilhard's ambiguous formulation of mankind's chances of reaching the "point omega" as to Marx's unwillingness to consider the possibility that social problems might continue to plague the world after the advent of communism.

The elimination of "evil" and "contradictions" would come about

as a result of promoting, in the most general sense, the well-being of
the Brazilian people, of Brazilian man.

> Our only obligation is toward man. Toward Brazilian man, first
> and foremost—he who is born with the shadow of premature death
> over his cradle; who lives with the specter of hunger under his
> wretched roof, his inseparable companion as he stumbles along the
> path of those who travel through life without hope or direction;
> who grows up stupid and illiterate, an outcast far from the blessings
> of culture, of creative opportunities, and of truly human roads of
> real freedom; who dies a beast's anonymous death, cast down on
> the hard ground of his misery. Thus we struggle for man with man.
> Our struggle is the struggle for all.[50]

Man and the full development of his potential were the chief motto
on AP's banner. Such full development would be possible only after
the structures of domination had been eliminated. In the present era
this would mean, essentially, the elimination of capitalism, which is
leading the world into an impasse of ever-increasing alienation and
domination, both within nations and between them. Its structures
must be replaced by others, in which each person might affirm
himself in freedom and cooperation with his fellow men. AP was
convinced that only structures of a socialist cast would make that
possible, although the ideology that was to guide their functioning
was far removed from Marxism-Leninism. AP's interpretation of history owed much to Hegel, in its stress on the dialectical movement
in history; to Marx, in its emphasis on relations of domination; to
John XXIII, in its use of the concept of socialization; and to Teilhard, in its optimistic and utopic interpretation of what is generally
possible in the future. But the basic—but vague—principles which
would guide social relations after the great transformation were derived largely from yet another source, which also accounts for the
movement's emphasis on "man" and the unfurling of his potential:
the "personalist" Christian existentialism of Emmanuel Mounier.[51]

Mounier stresses the paramount importance of person-to-person
relations, of openness to "the other," rather like the emphasis found
in the work of Jaspers, Marcel, and Buber.[52] While accepting the reality value of Sartre's description of human relations as of subject to
object, of tyrant to slave, and his view that man may "look at" his
fellow in a hostile, paralyzing way, Mounier is emphatic in denying
that man's existence is exhausted by these modes of relation. Real

communication is possible, and the individual only becomes a person insofar as he manages to transcend the limitations of his individualism through making himself "available" to others (Marcel). Man must strive, in cooperation with others, to create a society of persons, a society which will rest on "a series of original acts which have no equivalent in any part of the universe." Such acts would include efforts to put one's self into the position of others, to understand them, and to make one's self available to them. It also comprises a fundamental re-orientation of our relationships from concern with claims, demands, and struggles to a focus on generosity and gratuitousness. "The economy of the person is an economy of gifts, not one of compensation and calculation."[53]

It is from statements like these and from his sketchy ideas on economy, state, and society that the Christian radicals, insofar as they culled their views on the future from Mounier, suffered from his shortcomings. But Mounier frequently warned that the perspective of personalist philosophy could not be expected to become the world's exclusive reality. His was a "tragic optimism," one fully aware of the inevitable obstacles to generosity and love, of the tension between social structures and personal relations, of the permanent character of force in the world. "The real problem lies in the fact that while we are engaged in a struggle of force for as long as humanity will exist, we have simultaneously the vocation to struggle against the reign of force and against the installation of a state of force."[54] But most adherents of AP, nevertheless, seem to have believed that the reign of force, and other unpersonalist aspects of society, could be exorcized forever.

There is another aspect of Mounier's thought that has been of great influence on the Catholic radicals. With other existentialists, Mounier expresses deep concern for a life of "authenticity," through careful and honest choice between the options that present themselves from day to day. "Whenever I make a choice between this or that, I indirectly choose what I am to be. Through such choices I am edified."[55] By living with full consciousness, man comes to be what he is: he has no essence apart from existence. It is this aspect of existentialism that gives new importance to history and to the making of history,[56] and which further strengthens the importance attached by the Catholic radicals to consciência histórica, historical consciousness. Moreover, the emphasis on authenticity through free options gave philosophical support to a most important characteristic of the

movement: its populist horror of any action curtailing the freedom
of choice of the people or that forces them in directions that are not
genuinely their own. The contribution of the *povo* to the elaboration
and construction of the new society is essential.[57] And, although the
Catholic radicals were conscious of the need to organize the masses,
this was to occur after the masses had been made aware of the problems involved (*conscientisação*) and had chosen change. The movement resolutely opposed the *populista*'s modern techniques of "superficial" mass mobilization, and it accused Goulart as well as the
Marxists of *massificação*, i.e., manipulation, as opposed to a guidance
that would make free choice possible. But it rejected with equal determination those methods that depended on the traditional ways of
Brazilian paternalism.

Conscientisação involved, first, the presentation of certain facts
and theories, an ideology, to the people, hitherto ignorant of the
situation in which they found themselves. The ideology of AP was
rather similar in its views of past and present to those proposed in
the draft *ideal histórico* presented two years earlier by the Belo Horizonte team of JUC. But AP's views were better worked out, both
more elegant in wording and more consistent in analysis. The central
tool for the dissection of Brazilian reality became the conceptual pair
polo dominante and *polo dominado* (dominant and dominated pole),
obviously derived from the historical principle of the dialectics of
domination. The discussion owed much to the Marxist analysis of
class conflict. It also owed much to Marx in focusing on private
ownership of the means of production, distribution, and opinion
formation as the mediating principle of the system of domination.
    But it was Marxian analysis rather than Marxist. The *Esboço
Ideológico*, presented at the founding meeting of AP, contains a
description of interrelated institutional orders, of the different sectors
of the dominating pole—including landowners, "financial bourgeoisie," "industrial bourgeoisie," "international bourgeoisie"—not seen
as one class with identical interests, but rather as various groups
whose interests overlap. The *Documento Base* contains sections on
the course of world history, socialism, and philosophy, and also on
the historical background of Latin America's present situation in the
world and on the socio-economic situation in Brazil. Its attacks on the
Brazilian Communist party (PCB) are barely disguised: Communists

are taken to task for policies of "piecemeal economic improvements" and of collaboration with a "national bourgeoisie, with interests (supposedly) antagonistic to international capitalism."[58] On the former point the Communists were certainly on much stronger ground than on the latter. In that regard it is worth noting their riposte: "The gesture of the petit-bourgeois radical, who refuses to take note of the need for reforms and considers all struggle in this field as opportunism, is nothing but revolutionary infantilism."[59]

One could also criticize AP for badly underestimating the deepseated quality of prevailing patron-dependent structures and paternalistic relationships. Although the *Documento Base* briefly pointed to the difficulties to be expected in the most backward areas of the country, "where the population is dispersed and the peasantry highly conformist," the movement, unlike the Communists, really expected to see the old structures and old mentalities disappear fairly easily as a result of its activities.[60]

For AP, activity was of the greatest importance. Its activists did not merely debate the general evils of capitalism or the wickedness of the imperialists. Marxists acknowledge the "unity of theory and practice"; AP shares the principle with them, not only as a result of the common roots of their respective philosophies in Hegelian dialectic, but also as a result of the concern for "commitment" in existentialist thought. This principle has various important corollaries, not least the psychologically sound idea that learning (*conscientisação*) cannot occur unless it is accompanied by a testing of knowledge (the achievement of practical socio-political results).[61] But even under pre-revolutionary circumstances this is a slow process. Only in a few areas, notably in Pernambuco, had such testing gone so far as to lead to permanent results in *conscientisação* before the coup ended AP's praxis.

One aspect of AP's praxis was its penetration of existing organizations, state or private, "in order to give concrete expression to our ideological and political orientation."[62] During its approximately eighteen months of full-fledged activity, members or sympathizers of AP did in fact come to occupy responsible positions in the *sindicatos*, especially in the rural trade union movement, and a few held posts in the federal and state bureaucracies, notably in departments concerned with education. Infiltration was a favorite activity of all left-wing political movements in the hectic last year of the Goulart government. It was a manifestation of (very un-populist) jockeying for power at the top.

That was also to be seen in the several instances of the formation of a *frente única* (united front) among the movements of the left. These united fronts were more often than not rather unhappy experiences for AP, and the movement was far from united on the wisdom or the advisability of such cooperation. Moreover, AP was very much the junior and less politically sophisticated partner in the wheelings and dealings with the Communists. The latter often played a shrewd game, benefiting greatly from AP's support, without giving much in return, a situation that was beginning to cause serious soul-searching in AP early in 1964, after the elections for the directorate of the confederation of unions of rural workers (CONTAG) in December, 1963. On that occasion the federations of *sindicatos* whose advisors were members of AP allowed themselves to be maneuvered into an alliance with Communist-led unions. Together they opposed the more moderate, but far from "reactionary," federations that had been founded at the instigation of the church in the Northeast. A thorough postmortem was held following these events, and AP's leadership seems to have been preparing for a reorientation of relations with the Communists, perhaps even for a complete break with them.

This break, forestalled by the coup of April, 1964, could have been justified on several grounds.[63] AP resented the manipulative practices of the PCB (the Moscow-oriented Communist party), which was legally prevented from openly participating in politics. The party always tried to hide its true colors from the masses and was opportunistically playing a variety of roles depending on its ally: from anti-imperialism with the nationalistic bourgeoisie to anti-capitalism with the rest of the radical left. AP also doubted (and with good reason) the willingness of the Communists to promote radical change by whatever means necessary and suspected that the Communists were pushing them into exposed revolutionary positions. The Communists did not wish to be caught red-handed in case things went awry. At the same time the Communists were seen as intending to "use" the other radical forces in order to achieve their own aim of reaching power. They attempted to dictate policy, always claiming their rights as the oldest revolutionary force in the country, acting "as a kind of Holy Office of the Brazilian Revolution." Their attitude, in the view of AP, was based on the premise that the united front is a compromise, a "temporary alliance with error" that is permissible only because it will eventually help the party attain hegemony. The AP leadership concluded that, if the movement's praxis had to be linked with that of other political groupings, it would be necessary for each constituent part of any united front to have its own clearly defined and openly proclaimed identity. This would lead to a demarcation of interests and differences and prevent dissimulated manipulation of some by others.

Side by side with such more or less direct political involvement, AP's praxis took the form of actively promoting *conscientisação*. For this, two instruments were mainly used. In the first place there were the efforts to achieve mass literacy that were promoted by various organizations in which members of AP played prominent parts. The *Método Paulo Freire* was based on the educational philosophy of its initiator, independently arrived at, yet closely related to the views of AP, whose populist approach and socialist Christian existentialism he shared. Freire's view of the adult educational process[64] ("to help man help himself"), of its fully democratic nature (there were no schools, but *círculos de cultura*; no teachers, but coordinators; "education as the practice of freedom"), and of its intimate relation to the life situation of the student was very similar to that which came to be held in the *Movimento de Educação de Base* (MEB). MEB was formally under the aegis of the Brazilian bishops and was financed by the federal government under an agreement between the government and the Bishop's Conference. The movement always insisted that it was merely concerned with adult education in the rural areas and that, as such, it could not and would not become involved in the mechanics of action, in actual organization of the rural *povo*. The distinction proved hard to maintain, especially during 1963 and early 1964. The laymen who made up the movement's cadres, many of them members or ex-members of JEC or JUC and a good number at least sympathetic to AP, showed a remarkable degree of independence. But tensions developed with the hierarchy, not unlike those which have been described in the case of JUC. Nevertheless, those links with the hierarchy saved MEB from extinction in 1964. Since then it has been under sporadic attack and constant pressure, especially financial. The movement now mainly operates in those areas of Brazil, such as the Amazon region, which are socially and politically less explosive. But despite the difficult post-coup circumstances, MEB continues to hold

on to its populist convictions. It still attempts to bring about the
conscientisação of the peasants, though now the movement puts
greater stress on peasant cooperation, and has muted its previous
emphasis on class conflict and exploitation.[65]

The second and equally important instrument of *conscientisação*
was the more general movement for popular culture (*Movimento de
Cultura Popular*). From the start, students played an important part
in its development, and their unions initially sponsored many *Centros
Popular de Cultura* (CPC). Later, these became autonomous organizations financed with public funds. Many of them came under the
control of members of the PCB. These organizations tried to reach
the masses by plays, films, leaflets, and other cultural manifestations
that focused on the people's own problems and had a clear socio-
political content. Members of AP who dedicated themselves to
cultura popular saw it, in the words of Candido Mendes, as a "continuous process of feedback between action and awareness, one tran-
scending the other in the effective, open construction of a new
historical experience."[66] These views differed considerably from those
held by their Communist counterparts. The latter, in general much
less concerned with the philosophy of *conscientisação*, seem to have
believed that mere awareness, mere "de-alienation," would bring
about the necessary climate for a change in structures. *Cultura popular* to them was a political tool in the hands of the elite, to be used
for speeding up the course of history. Moreover, they regarded *cultura
popular* as an instrument to be forged by the political leadership, out
of the latter's interpretation of how best to utilize a particular cultural phenomenon in the political struggle.[67] Again, therefore, the
differences between the Communists and the Catholic populists
are clear; in the language of AP, they are the difference between
manipulative *massificadores* and dialogue-seeking, people-oriented
conscientisadores.

The coup of April, 1964, though it allowed most radical theorizing
to continue, banned all related praxis as subversive. It thus curtailed
an interesting populist experiment with novel features, which might
have had some chance of creating the basis of a mass-supported social
revolution in Brazil, to be carried out primarily by legal means,
though not necessarily without violence. In the five years that have
passed since the coup, most expressions of active Christian radicalism
have been forced underground, and AP has lost its specifically Chris-

tian associations, its various grouplets now holding views wholly anchored in secular radicalism—Marxist, Castroite, or Maoist. Moreover, today there is no way for a peasant who learns of his "human dignity" to test this against the social, economic, and political conditions in which he lives: in rural Brazil the status quo is maintained with an almost iron hand.

One may doubt the feasibility of the utopia that AP, as the most extreme expression of Christian-inspired radicalism, wanted to build: not only were its "personalist" structures vague, but it seemed to discount overly the realities of power, "sin," and "contradictions" which have been inherent in all known societies. But the attempt at ruthless excision by the military regime of this utopian element in the Brazilian body politic has been politically narrow-minded, anti-democratic, and in the truest sense of the word reactionary. One can only rejoice that the new rulers of the country do not appear to have been entirely successful, and that their policies toward the pre-1964 radicals have at least had the effect of helping to push Brazil's ecclesiastical establishment further away from their previous implicit support of the status quo.

NOTES

NOTES TO CHAPTER 2:

Extraction, Insulation, and Re-entry

1. Thomas F. O'Dea, *The Catholic Crisis* (Boston: Beacon Press, 1968), p. 126.

2. General theories of development would gain considerable strength, in my judgment, if they incorporated variables that take account of the church's position in and its influence on the wider society. This suggestion is particularly appropriate for theories of cultural and political development. If posited relationships among interest aggregations, party structures, legislative activities, and administrative efforts, on the one hand, or the relationships among value patterns, bases of loyalty, and modernizing roles, on the other hand, are to have any valid applicabilities in terms of policy proposals, then religious system variables, such as church-society linkages, the degree of differentiation between the church and political structures, and the types of religious action roles being defined for members in their contacts with society, need to be included. In short, we may have to involve ourselves in more complicated types of thinking and research in order to handle complex problems.

3. I do not hold, of course, that all of the national churches stand at the same point in their developmental paths. My recent study of development in the churches of Argentina, Brazil, Chile, Colombia, and Mexico makes this theme explicit. I refer to my article, "Church 'Development' in Latin America: A Five-Country Comparison," *Journal of Developing Areas*, Vol. I, No. 4 (July, 1967), pp. 461–76.

4. I deal at length with the relationships between religious structures and social change in my forthcoming book *Religion, Social Control, and Modernization: Catholicism in Latin America* (Englewood Cliffs, New Jersey: Prentice-Hall, Inc., in press).

5. J. Lloyd Mecham, *Church and State in Latin America: A History of Politico-Ecclesiastical Relations* (revised edition; Chapel Hill, North Carolina: The University of North Carolina Press, 1966), p. 211.

6. *Ibid.*, p. 211.

7. Federico G. Gil, *The Political System of Chile* (Boston: Houghton Mifflin Company, 1966), p. 43.

8. Mecham, *op cit.*, p. 215.

9. *Ibid.*, p. 122.

10. *Ibid.*, p. 125.

11. *Ibid.*, p. 125.

12. Richard N. Adams, "The Renaissance of the Guatemalan Church," ms. mimeo.

13. William C. Thiesenhusen, *Chile's Experiments in Agrarian Reform* (Madison, Wisconsin: The University of Wisconsin Press, 1966), esp. chaps. ii through v.

14. This typology is intended to bear some integral ties with my earlier typology of religious elites. See Ivan Vallier, "Religious Elites: Differentiations and Developments in Roman Catholicism," in Seymour M. Lipset and Aldo Solari, eds., *Elites in Latin America* (New York: Oxford University Press, 1967), esp. pp. 203–224.

15. Thomas Bruneau, "Autonomy and Change in the Brazilian Catholic Church," ms. typed, chap. ii.

16. The emerging configurations of the laity's demands and their significance for structural change in the church are reported for three countries in Ivan Vallier and Rocco Caporale, "The Roman Catholic Laity in France, Chile, and the United States: Differentiations and Cleavages," *Information Documentation on the Conciliar Church* (IDOC), Part I and Part II, February, 1968.

17. Some of these problems, I judge, can be resolved through comparative studies that give attention to explicit formal units, such as a national hierarchy or the diocese, and then set about to show how the institutional features of the church vary from place to place and how these variations are linked to or are caused by situational conditions. For a systematic approach to these problems see Ivan Vallier, "Comparative Studies of Roman Catholicism: Dioceses as Strategic Units," *Social Compass*, in press.

NOTES TO CHAPTER 3:

The Church in Latin America: A Historical Survey

1. Renato Poblete, "Religión de Masas," *Revista Mensaje*, Vol. CXLIV (November, 1965), Santiago, Chile.

2. Leandro Tormo, *La Historia de la Iglesia en América Latina* (Fribourg: FERES, 1962), I, 166.

3. Hubert Herring, *A History of Latin America from the Beginning to the Present* (New York: Knopf, 1955), p. 169.

4. Antonio de Egaña, S.J., *Historia de la Iglesia en la América Española —Hemisferio Sur* (Madrid: Ed. Católica, 1966), p. 191.

5. Herring, *op. cit.*, p. 183.

6. *Ibid.*, p. 183.

7. Herring, *ibid.*, p. 193.

8. R. Vargas Ugarte, S.J., *El Episcopado en los Tiempos de la Emancipación Sud Americana* (Buenos Aires, 1965), p. 305.

9. Agustín Piaggio, *Influencia del Clero en la Independencia Argentina* (Buenos Aires, 1912), pp. 23 ff.

10. Pedro de Leturia, S.J., *Encíclica Pío VII sobre Revolución Americana*, p. 37.

11. Tormo, *op. cit.*, III, 65 ff.

12. François Houtart, *La Iglesia Latinoamericana en la Hora del Concilio*, 2nd ed. (Bogatá: FERES, 1963).

13. Bilan du Monde, *Enciclopedie Catholique du Monde Chrétien* (Tournai: S. A. Casterman, 1964).

14. Bilan du Monde, *op. cit.*, I, 378, 379.

15. Eduardo Hamuy, "Comportamiento Electoral" (Unpublished ms.; Faculty of Economics, University of Chile, Santiago, 1966).

16. Vatican II, Pastoral Constitution on the Church in the Modern World.

17. Tormo, *op. cit.*, III, 65 ff.

NOTES TO CHAPTER 4:

South America's Multifaceted Catholicism

1. See Earl T. Glauert, "Ricardo Rojas and the Emergence of Argentine Cultural Nationalism," *Hispanic American Historical Review*, Vol. XLIII, No. 1 (February, 1963), esp. p. 5. A valuable survey presenting

interpretations that sometimes differ from those set forth in the present article is John J. Kennedy, *Catholicism, Nationalism and Democracy in Argentina* (Notre Dame, Ind., 1958).

2. Gálvez, *El solar de la raza* (5th ed.; Madrid, 1920), pp. 13, 14, 11, 21.

3. Lugones, *La grande Argentina* (2nd ed.; Buenos Aires, 1962), p. 180.

4. Meinvielle, *Política argentina, 1943–1956* (Buenos Aires, 1956), p. 15.

5. *Ibid.*, p. 324.

6. *Ibid.*, p. 37.

7. *Ibid.*, pp. 16–17.

8. *Ibid.*, p 43.

9. *Ibid.*, p. 8. When General Juan Carlos Onganía seized the Argentine presidency in 1966 through a *golpe del estado*, many right-wing Catholic nationalists enthusiastically heralded him as their new savior and revealed that their attitudes had changed little, if at all, from those expressed by ardent reactionary nationalists in the 1920's.

10. See F. B. Pike, "Aspects of Class Relations in Chile, 1850–1960," *Hispanic American Historical Review*, Vol. XLIII, No. 1 (February, 1963), pp. 14–33.

11. See James O. Morris, *Elites, Intellectuals and Consensus: A Study of the Social Question and the Industrial Relations System in Chile* (Ithaca, N. Y., 1967). Professor Morris' analysis of the Concha program is less favorable than that suggested here.

12. See F. B. Pike, *Chile and the United States, 1880–1962* (Notre Dame, Ind., 1963), p. 207.

13. Morales, "Socialismo y catolicismo," *El Mercurio* (a leading Santiago daily), July 8, 1932.

14. See F. B. Pike (ed.), *The Conflict between Church and State in Latin America* (New York, 1964), pp. 196–217.

15. On the church's partially successful movement to resist the anticlerical programs backed by Peruvian liberals, see F. B. Pike, "Heresy, Real and Alleged, in Peru: An Aspect of the Conservative-Liberal Struggle, 1830–1875," *Hispanic American Historical Review*, Vol. XLVII, No. 1 (February, 1967), pp. 50–74.

16. See F. B. Pike, *The Modern History of Peru* (London, 1967), chaps. vii and viii.

17. Two typical doctoral theses of the period, written at the Catholic University, which extol fascism and the corporate state are Raúl Ferrero Rebagliati, *Marxismo y nacionalismo: estado nacional corporativo* (Lima, 1937), and Carlos Radicati de Primeglio, *De las antiguas a las modernas corporaciones* (Lima, 1937).

18. Confederación Iberoamericana de Estudiantes Católicos, Rama Peruana, Congreso Iberoamericano de Estudiantes Católicos, 2°, Lima, 1939: *Documentos, conclusiones* (Lima, 1941), pp. 158, 172.

19. Riva Agüero, "Sobre dos recientes opúsculos de Jorge del Vecchio," in Riva Agüero and Carlos Miró Quesada Laos, *Dos estudios sobre Italia contemporánea* (Lima, 1937), p. 53.

20. Riva Agüero, writing in *Revista de la Universidad Católica del Perú*, Vol. IX, Nos. 8–9 (November–December, 1941), p. 466.

21. "La última conferencia de Riva Agüero," *ibid.*, Vol. XIII, No. 1 (April, 1945).

22. See F. B. Pike, "Peru and the Quest for Reform by Compromise," *Inter-American Economic Affairs*, Vol. XX, No. 4 (Spring, 1967), esp. pp. 23–27.

23. Valcárcel, *Tempestad en los andes* (Lima, 1927), p. 116.

24. See Valcárcel, *Ruta cultural del Perú* (México, D.F., 1945) and José Carlos Mariátegui, "El proceso del gamonalismo," a 1927 supplement to the Lima periodical *Amauta*. Founded by the brilliant and unorthodox Marxist Mariátegui, *Amauta* was published between 1926 and 1930. It was the most significant intellectual journal of the period with a socialist, leftist, Indianist orientation.

25. See F. B. Pike, "The Catholic Church and Modernization in Peru and Chile," *Journal of International Affairs*, Vol. XX, No. 2 (Summer, 1966), pp. 272–88, and "The Modernized Church in Peru: Two Aspects," *The Review of Politics*, Vol. XXVI, No. 3 (July, 1964), pp. 307–318.

26. Fuentes, "A Changing Church in a Changing Latin America," *Book Week, Sunday Herald Tribune* (New York), April 24, 1966.

27. The church's role in Chilean land reform is skilfully explained by William C. Thiesenhusen in "Chilean Agrarian Reform: The Possibility of Gradualist Turnover of Land," *Inter-American Economic Affairs*, Vol. XX, No. 1 (Summer, 1966), and *Chile's Experiments in Agrarian Reform* (Madison, 1966).

28. The contributions of Jurgens to Peruvian land reform are described in *Vanguardia*, a Lima weekly, April 15, 1963.

29. Statistics of the Federación Nacional de Cooperativas del Crédito del Perú, published in the Lima newspaper *El Comercio*, September 18, 1963.

30. See Vekemans, "Economic Development, Social Change, and Cultural Mutation in Latin America," in William V. D'Antonio and F. B. Pike (eds.), *Religion, Revolution and Reform: New Forces for Change in Latin America* (New York, 1964), pp. 129–42.

31. See Encina, *Nuestra inferioridad económica* (Santiago, 1912), and Capelo, *Sociología de Lima* (Lima, 1900), esp. Vol. II, p. 180.

32. The Conservative candidate was Héctor Rodríguez de la Sotta. For the quotation see Alberto Edwards and Eduardo Frei, *Historia de los partidos políticos chilenos* (Santiago, 1949), p. 266.

33. *Carta pastoral de Pedro Pascual Farfán con motivo de la próxima festividad de Santa Rosa de Lima* (Lima, 1937).

34. See Ramiro Delgado García, "Perspectives of Family Planning Programs in Latin America," in J. Mayone Stycos and Jorge Arias (eds.), *Population Dilemma in Latin America* (Washington, D.C., 1966), pp. 214–27.

35. Discurso del Excmo. Sr. Arzobispo . . . para la Asamblea Arquidiocesana de Acción Católica con motivo de conmemorarse el 25 aniversario de la fundación de la Acción Católica Peruana," *El Amigo del Clero* (Lima), Ano XLIX, Nos. 1626–27 (November–December, 1960), p. 324.

36. For the advanced social position taken by Dammert Bellido, see his "Orientación para la acción de la Iglesia," *ibid.*, Nos. 1610–12 (July, August, September, 1959), pp. 275–94.

37. A few of the more significant works concerned with the new attitudes of the Catholic church in Peru toward social justice include: *Carta pastoral del episcopada peruana sobre algunos aspectos de la cuestión social en el Perú* (Lima, 1958); Discurso . . . de . . . Monseñor Juan Landázuri Ricketts," *El Amigo del Clero*, Nos. 1610–12 (July, August, September, 1959), esp. pp. 213–14, an important declaration by the Cardinal-Archbishop; *Política deber cristiano* (Lima, 1963), a collection of essays by Víctor Andrés Belaúnde, Carlos Cueto Fernandini, Raúl Ferrero, Ernesto Alayza Grundy, and Rev. Felipe McGregor, S.J.; *Primera Semana Social, Exigencias sociales del catolicismo en el Perú* (Lima, 1959); and Ricardo Talavera Campos, "El pensamiento católico acerca de la propiedad," the winning essay in a contest sponsored by the Catholic University in Lima to honor Pope John XXIII's encyclical *Mater et Magistra* and published in abbreviated form in the Lima periodical *Mensajero Agrícola*, No. 161 (August–September, 1963). The new spirit of the Catholic leaders is also reflected in the literature of Peru's Christian Democratic party. See the works of party leader Héctor Cornejo Chávez, *Con los pobres de América* (Lima, 1962), *Nuevos principios para un nuevo Perú* (Lima, 1960), and *Que se propone la democracia cristiana* (Lima, 1962). Also useful are two works by important members of the Christian Democratic party, Alfonso Benavides Correa, *Rumbos contemporáneos del pensamiento político: ensayos de interpretación de las corrientes ideológicas y régimenes políticos en su perfíl teórico y operancia real* (Lima, 1957), and Lino Rodríguez-Arias Bustamante, comp., **La** democracia cristiana y América Latina: testimonios de una posición social revolucionaria (Lima, 1961).

Time, Persons, Doctrine

1. See Fidel Araneda Bravo, *Obispos, sacerdotes y frailes* (Santiago, 1962).

2. See Reinhard Bendix, *Work and Authority in Industry: Ideologies of Management in the Course of Industrialization* (New York: Wiley, 1956), especially chap. ii, pp. 86–116.

3. This and parts of the preceding are based on Alejandro Magnet's excellent *El Padre Hurtado* (Santiago: Editorial del Pacífico, 1954); see esp. pp. 36, *et seq*.

4. James O. Morris, *Elites, Intellectuals and Consensus: A Study of the Social Question and the Industrial Relations System in Chile* (Ithaca, N. Y.: New York State School of Industrial and Labor Relations, 1967).

5. See Robert A. White, S.J., "The Mexican Agrarian Movement of Emiliano Zapata," in Henry A. Landsberger (ed.), *Latin American Peasant Movements* (Cornell University Press, 1969). White bases himself, among other sources, on Paul Murray, *The Catholic Church in Mexico* (Mexico, D.F.: Editorial E.P.M., 1964), pp. 334–68.

6. See Alejandro Magnet, *op. cit.*

7. Pastoral, December 8, 1922, as quoted in Alejandro Magnet, *op. cit.*, p. 100.

8. "Pastoral que el Iltmo. y Rvdmo. Señor doctor don Mariano Casanova, Arzobispo de Santiago de Chile, dirige al clero y fieles al publicar la Encíclica de nuestro Santísimo Padre León XIII sobre la condición de los obreros," (Santiago: Edición del Arzobispado, Imprenta Cervantes, 1891).

9. "La acción social," Pastoral del Ilmo. y Rvdo. Sr. Arzobispo de Santiago, Dr. Crescente Errázuriz, Edición de la Unión Social de Católicos de Chile (Chile, 1921). This is not the pastoral of December 8, 1922, to which we have already referred, dealing with political problems.

10. "Verdadera y única solución de la cuestión social," Carta pastoral colectiva que el episcopado dirige a los sacerdotes y fieles de la nación (Chile, 1932).

11. This relatively unoriginal style was typical of the Chilean episcopate until the late forties, as has been noted in Fr. Mario Zañartu, S.J., "Roman Catholic Ethic and Economic Development," (Ph.D. dissertation, Columbia University, New York, N. Y., 1962).

12. "La verdadera y única solución . . . ," pp. 47–48.

13. "Instrucción pastoral acerca de los problemas sociales," published in *Revista Católica*, No. 942, January–February, 1949. In this pastoral

there is reference to an earlier one dated January, 1947, but this we have been unable to trace.

14. See Henry A. Landsberger and Fernando Canitrot M., *Iglesia, Intelectuales y Campesinos* (Santiago: Editorial del Pacífico, 1967), pp. 63–75.

15. "La iglesia y el problema del campesinado chileno," Publicación del Secretariado General del Episcopado de Chile (Santiago, 1962).

16. "El deber social y política en la hora presente," Publicación del Secretariado General del Episcopado de Chile (Santiago, 1962).

17. The Chilean Radical party, like that of France, was founded at the end of the nineteenth century on the basis of anticlericalism. By the mid forties, this part of its platform was more in the realm of rhetoric and tradition than a matter of practice, but it remained.

18. The quotation used by the bishops is from *Mater et Magistra*, an English version of which was published by The American Press, New York, N. Y., 1961. For the sentence cited by the Chilean Episcopal Conference, see page 63.

NOTES TO CHAPTER 8:

The Church and Revolutionary Change

1. See the monthly magazine, *Mensaje*, especially the two numbers which are dedicated to the development of a Christian perspective on and program for revolution: *Revolución en América Latina*, December, 1962; and *Reformas Revolucionarias en América Latina*, October, 1963.

2. "Christian Participation in the Latin American Revolution," in C. Lacy (ed.), *Christianity Amid Rising Men and Nations* (New York: Association Press, 1965), pp. 91–118.

3. See his "Paternalism, Pluralism and Christian Democratic Reform Movements in Latin America," in D'Antonio and Pike (eds.), *Religion, Revolution and Reform*, (New York, 1964), pp. 25 ff. Also his books, *La Verdad Tiene Su Hora* (Santiago, 1955), and *Pensamiento y Acción* (Santiago, 1958).

4. The Frei government has published a report of its achievements during its first year in power entitled *Revolución en Libertad* (Santiago, 1965).

5. Herein lies one of the main reasons for the present crisis of political ideologies in Latin America. As most Christian social thought in the past has been of this type, those political movements, such as Christian

Democracy, which have functioned in terms of the more traditional categories, face the same problem.

6. Rio de Janeiro, 1964.

7. His political speeches and declarations during the last year of his life have just been published in a booklet, *Camilo Torres* (Medellín, Antorcha, 1966). A group of Catholic laymen who were closely associated with him have presented the story of the deterioration of his relations with the hierarchy, in "El 'Caso' del Padre Camilo Torres," *Inquietudes*, No. 5, Bogotá.

8. For evidence of this in the work of the Centro Belarmino, see the discussions of the "revolución CRISTIANA" in Nos. 117 and 119 of *Mensaje*; also the article by a Uruguayan Catholic lawyer, Héctor Borrat, "La Revolución de 'Mensaje,' " *Cristianismo y Sociedad*, Vol. III, pp. 26 ff.

9. It is very difficult for me to provide much assistance for those who are interested in locating material for further study of this movement. My observations here are based primarily on personal contact, over a number of years, with people related to it; also on several mimeographed declarations by the organization which have never been published. More recently, the attitude of the military government in Brazil toward Popular Action has further complicated this effort at documentation.

10. See his "Análisis Psico-social de la Situación Pre-revolucionaria de América Latina," *Mensaje*, No. 115, pp. 647–55.

11. This is most evident in Frei's *La Verdad Tiene Su Hora*, chap. iii.

12. *Religion, Revolution and Reform*, p. 136.

13. *Ibid.*, pp. 137, 140.

14. *Memento dos Vivos* (Rio de Janeiro: Tempo Brasileiro, 1966).

The Legal Status of the Church in Latin America

1. John Lloyd Mecham, *Church and State in Latin America* (rev. ed.; Chapel Hill, 1966), Fredrick B. Pike (ed.), *The Conflict between Church and State in Latin America* (New York, 1964).

2. This is maintained by Dalmacio Vélez Sarsfield, *Derecho Público Eclesiástico* (Buenos Aires, 1871).

3. Most important of all was the question of appointment of the bishops.

4. Juan Casiello, *Iglesia y Estado en la Argentina* (Buenos Aires, 1948), pp. 58–59.

5. At the present time it appears that the Colombian government is again considering possible changes in the concordat. The Colombian hierarchy is also reported to be considering possible further revisions.

6. Articles 27 and 130.

7. My own conversations with certain of the younger native-born Mexican clergy have suggested, however, that there is a readiness to endorse the "Mexican experience." Whether or not this attitude represents a general tendency is not clear.

8. Article 10.

9. Article 5.

10. Article 36.

11. Article 61.

12. Article 36.

13. Article 54.

14. Articles 2,67 (19,20), 76, 86 (8,9). The 1853 constitution is cited, although the short-lived 1949 revision was in effect as of the 1950 date.

15. Articles 3, 22, 72, 94, 142.

16. Articles 66, 109.

17. Articles 3, 46, 51, 62.

18. Articles 123, 154, 232, 233, 234, 235.

19. Article 85 as of the date given. In connection with the discussion of the Venezuelan treaty of 1964, the corresponding constitutional article is 130.

20. In the Alvear administration there were difficulties over the filling of the Buenos Aires see. These extended from 1923 into 1925.

21. *La Iglesia y El Estado* (Buenos Aires, 1929).

22. Chapter ii, 20.

23. Certain background documents are included in Miguel Angel Zavala Ortiz, *Negociaciones para el Acuerdo entre la Santa Sede y la República Argentina* (Buenos Aires, 1966).

24. The full text is in *Acta Apostolicae Sedis*, An. et Vol. LIX, No. 2 (February 28, 1967), pp. 127–30.

25. Fracción Parlamentaria de Copei, *El Convenio Con La Santa Sede* (Caracas, 1964).

26. The full text is in *Acta Apostolicae Sedis*, An. et Vol. LVI, No. 15 (November 30, 1964), pp. 925–32.

27. Zavala Ortiz, *op. cit.*, p. 43.

28. *Ibid.*, p. 38.

NOTES TO CHAPTER 10:

The History, Structure, and Present Activities of CELAM

1. Since in Rome there was no official meeting, the Holy See prolonged these same titles and offices for another year.

2. With the accidental and tragic death of Bishop Manuel Larraín on June 22, 1966, the presidency *ad interim* passed to the first vice-president, Dom Avelar Brandão Vilela. At the tenth meeting of CELAM in Mar del Plata in 1966, Dom Avelar was chosen president of CELAM to complete the 1966–67 period. Bishop Pablo Muñóz Vega became first vice-president and Bishop Mark G. McGrath, Bishop of Santiago de Veraguas, Panama, became second vice-president.

NOTES TO CHAPTER 11:

The Rise of Catholic Radicalism in Brazil

1. An extended version of this paper will constitute two chapters of Emanuel de Kadt, *Catholic Radicals in Brazil: A Study of the Movimento de Educação de Base*, to be published in 1970 by Oxford University Press for the Royal Institute of International Affairs. The present paper was originally written in mid-1967, and has since been revised. The comments of various Brazilian friends have been extremely useful, as were those of Tom Bruneau. I am especially grateful to my friend Pierre Furter for his extensive suggestions.

In 1967 and 1968, during the period when the grip of the military on Brazil was most relaxed, much was heard in the country of protests against government policies or police actions from a wide range of people connected with the Catholic church. There are reasons to believe that the tightening of government control and the further whittling down of civil and political liberties from December, 1968, were at least partly directed against the supposedly excessive opposition of the church to official policies. As little as four years earlier, during the last months of the Goulart government, the vast majority of churchmen were conservative, or at best cautiously reformist, and two months after the coup of April, 1964, Brazil's bishops hailed the military as the saviors of the country.

When the official and semi-official pronouncements of Brazilian churchmen gradually became more critical of the military government, there were many in Brazil who thought back to the days before the coup when the hierarchy had quite strongly opposed those radicals who regarded themselves inspired by Christian ideals. It is perhaps not altogether fanciful to suggest that in proper "dialectical manner" some of the latter's views, fought first by the bishops and then by the military, came to be accepted within the ecclesiastical establishment. This paper attempts to deal with an important link in the development of those ideas: the emergence of radicalism among Brazil's Catholic students.

At the outset, however, I should like to utter some words of caution. Much that is relevant to that development is not being touched upon in this paper, or is mentioned merely in passing. Nothing is said, for example, about early attempts at liturgical renewal, hardly any attention is paid to the general position of the hierarchy, and very little space is devoted to equivalent ideas outside the student milieu. Such other aspects would have to be brought into the picture if it is to be made complete; moreover, an examination of the secular student movement is relevant for comparative purposes. These points ought to be borne in mind. Nevertheless, it is fair to say that what happened in Catholic student circles was essential to the emergence of radicalism among Brazilian Catholics, and to the consolidation of an increasingly influential radical minority in Brazil's Catholic church: hence the presentation of the following, clearly limited analysis.

2. Useful material on the social situation in the colonial church can be found in Gilberto Freyre, *The Masters and the Slaves*, tr. by Samuel Putnam (New York, 1945); see especially pp. 191–92, 433–37, and 441–42. The same author's *New World in the Tropics* (New York, 1963), may also be consulted. A valuable general survey for the colonial period is the chapter by Américo Jacobina Lacombe, "A Igreja no Brasil Colonial," *História Geral da Civilização Brasileira, A Época Colonial*, Vol. II, ed. by Sergio Buarque de Holanda (São Paulo, 1960).

3. For a discussion of this period, see Clarence H. Haring, "The Church-State Conflict in Nineteenth-Century Brazil," in: Fredrick B. Pike (ed.), *The Conflict between Church and State in Latin America* (New York, 1964); also João Cruz Costa, *A History of Ideas in Brazil*, Suzette Macedo (trans.) (Berkeley and London, 1964), chaps. iii and iv. A general discussion of the church under the empire can be found in the classic work on church-state relations in Latin America since independence: J. Lloyd Mecham, *Church and State in Latin America* (rev. ed.; Chapel Hill, N. C., 1966) chap. xii.

4. Júlio Maria, "A Religiaõ. Ordens Religiosas. Instituiçoĕs pias e beneficentes no Brasil. Memória," in *Livro do centenário (1500–1900)* (Rio, 1900), Vol. I, pt. 2. The quotations are from pp. 127 and 128, respectively.

5. See Cruz Costa, *op. cit.*, pp. 249–57. For a detailed study, see Mário

da Silva Brito, *Antecedentes da Semana de Arte Moderna* (Rio, 1964).

6. See the enlightening article by Francisco Iglésias, "Estudo sôbre o pensamento reacionário: Jackson de Figueiredo," *Rev. Bras. Cien. Soc.*, Vol. II, No. 2 (July, 1962), to which my discussions of Jackson and of Alceu Amoroso Lima, which follows, are much indebted. See also Cruz Costa, *op. cit.*, pp. 256–61.

7. See the massive biography, written with all the love—and some of the bias—of a disciple, by Irmã Maria Regina do Santo Rosário, *O Cardeal Leme* (Rio, 1962), pp. 61–84.

8. *Ibid.*, pp. 173–88.

9. *Ibid.*, pp. 309–22. This method has been followed in elections ever since. For a recent example, cf. my "Religion, the Church and Social Change in Brazil," in Claudio Veliz (ed.), *The Politics of Conformity in Latin America* (London, 1967), p. 207.

10. A general discussion of Catholic Action can be found in Yves Congar, O.P., *Lay People in the Church* (London, 1957), especially chap. V. A book dedicated to the situation in Australia also contains valuable background information; cf. Tom Truman, *Catholic Action and Politics* (rev. ed.; London, 1960).

11. See Irmã Regina, *op. cit.*, pp. 299–308 and 334–49.

12. See Frei Romeu Dale, *JUC do Brasil, Uma Nova Experiência de Ação Católica* (mimeographed; 1962), p. 4. This historical analysis, prepared at the time of JUC's crisis with the hierarchy, discussed later, has been a helpful guide.

13. *Ibid.*, p. 8.

14. Secretariado Nacional da JUC, *Anais do VIII Conselho Nacional de Dirigentes* (Rio, 1958), pp. 107 f.

15. This concept, as will become clear, has obvious affinities with that of *projeto histórico*, which was very much in the air during this period. The latter was popularized through the publications of the *Instituto Superior de Estudos Brasileiros* (ISEB), by such nationalist intellectuals as Hélio Jaguaribe, Candido Mendes, Álvaro Vieira Pinto, and Roland Corbisier. For a general discussion—which somewhat underplays the differences among the group—see Herminio Martins, "Ideology and Development: 'Developmental Nationalism' in Brazil," in *The Sociological Review Monograph 11* (Keele), February, 1967. Almery was, at this time, also influenced by the thought of Jacques Maritain.

16. Pe. Almery Bezerra, "Da Necessidade de um Ideal Histórico," in JUC, *Boletim Nacional No. 2, Anais do IX Conselho Nacional*, December, 1959, pp. 37–40.

17. Pierre Furter, *Educação e Reflexão* (Petrópolis, 1966), p. 39, is an

excellent analysis of relevant educational problems by a sympathetic outside observer.

18. For a long time social scientists have failed to see the distinction
between a "utopia," seen as an ideal construct based on certain political
or philosophical notions to serve as a guide for purposeful social change,
and "utopics," the belief in the *actual* possibility of constructing an ideal
society, free from evil, power, "contradictions," etc. They have usually
either attacked all utopias or engaged in utopics themselves. Martin Buber
implicitly made the distinction in his *Paths in Utopia* (Boston, 1958), p.
10. More recently, Wilbert Moore proposed the revival of utopian thought
in his "The Utility of Utopias," presidential address to the American
Sociological Association in 1966, reprinted in *Amer. Sociol. Rev.*, December, 1966. Extremely useful also are the excellent discussions of the topic
by Pierre Furter. See his "Utopie et Marxisme selon Ernst Bloch," *Arch.
Sociol. Relig.*, No. 21, 1966; Ch. 3 of his *Educação e Reflexão* (op. cit.),
and his outstanding discussion of the thought of Bloch, *L'Imagination
Creatrice, la Violence et le Changement Social*, CIDOC Cuaderno No.
14, (Cuernavaca, Mexico, 1968). I have looked at the problem in relation
to a few other Latin American cases in "Paternalism and Populism: Catholics in Latin America," *Jn. of Contemp. Hist.*, Vol. II, No. 4 (October,
1967).

19. Pe. Fernando Bastos de Ávila, *Neo-capitalismo, Socialismo, Soli-
darismo* (2d ed.; Rio, 1963), pp. 11 f.

20. Reproduced in *Cristianismo Hoje* (Rio, n.d. [1962]), p. 21.

21. Cf. Leonard D. Therry, "Dominant Power Components in the
Brazilian University Student Movement, prior to April, 1964," *Jn. Inter-
American Studies*, VII (No. 1), Jan., 1965, pp. 33 f., who lists these
translations.

22. See Note 15.

23. Regional Centro-Oeste, "Algumas diretrizes de um ideal histórico
Cristão para o povo brasileiro," in JUC, *Boletim 4, I: Ideal Histórico* (Rio,
n.d.), pp. 27–32 (referred to hereafter as JUC, *Ideal Histórico*).

24. Dale, *op. cit.*, p. 14. For a theoretical statement of the position
held on the secular left of the student movement, see Álvaro Vieira Pinto,
A questão da universidade (Rio, n.d. [1962]). A Catholic view can be
found in JUC, *Boletim Informativo No. 2*, n.d. (1963), pp. 18–21.

25. JUC, *Ideal Histórico*, p. 6.

26. JUC, *Boletim Informativo No. 2*, pp. 19 f.

27. See Sonia Seganfreddo, *UNE, Instrumento de Subversão* (Rio,
1963), pp. 6 ff. Though this is a polemical, thoroughly reactionary, and at
many points inaccurate account of the history and activities of UNE, the
careful reader can use the information it contains to his benefit. It touches
at various points on the role of *JUCistas* in UNE.

28. The manifesto is reproduced in *Cristianismo Hoje*, pp. 89–98. See, in the same volume, Pe. Vaz's defense both of the manifesto and of his own indirect role in its formulation (pp. 55–68).

29. JUC, *Boletim Informativo No. 2* (1963), pp. 15, 7, respectively.

30. Dale, *op. cit.*, p. 18.

31. The full text can be found in *Revista Ecclesiastica Brasileira*, Vol. 21, fasc. 4, December, 1961.

32. Pe. Sena, "Reflexões sôbre o Ideal Histórico," JUC, *Ideal Histórico*, p. 15.

33. Dale, *op. cit.*, pp. 34 f.

34. A general view of the dynamics of an emerging "youth-consciousness" in Brazil can be found in Pierre Furter, "Caminhos e Descaminhos de uma política da Juventude," *Paz e Terra*, No. 3 (1967).

35. Dale, *op. cit.*, p. 27.

36. At the Vatican Council, the problem of the role of the laity was given a thorough airing, and the discussions, where quite radical opinions on the matter were expressed, had an influence among the laity at least as great as the more "equilibrated" final document, the *Decree on the Apostolate of the Laity*, or the relevant sections in *Lumen Gentium* or *Gaudium et Spes*. For a discussion which clearly reflects the views of the people treated in these paragraphs by someone who was greatly involved during the whole period, see Luiz Alberto Gomez de Souza, *O Cristão e o Mundo* (Petrópolis RJ, 1965).

37. The lack of wider social relevance of the earlier orientation may be inferred from an article in a pamphlet commemorating the fifth anniversary of JEC in Belo Horizonte: *5 Anos de JEC* (Belo Horizonte, 1958), pp. 18–21. Then the main preoccupation was, clearly, religious. Student readers were urged to deepen their faith. The list of authors that was suggested as fundamental to a more humane vision of Christianity is instructive. Of twenty-one names two are younger contemporary Brazilian priests with direct influence on the movement. Seven are saints, church fathers, or founders of religious orders. Most of the others are such Catholic literary figures as Graham Greene or Chesterton; only three, Jacques Maritain, Simone Weil, and Father Lebret, were people whose main concern was with the social rather than the personal or spiritual.

38. On the social composition of AP, there is an almost complete lack of reliable evidence. There is also no really trustworthy information on size, scope, or operation. Thomas G. Sanders, in his excellent paper "Catholicism and Development: The Catholic Left in Brazil," in Kalman H. Silvert (ed.), *Churches and States* (New York, 1967), p. 96, states that early in 1964 AP had about three thousand members—without, however, giving any source. The coup of 1964 scattered the movement and its documentation and scotched all moves to obtain objective statistical data on it.

One thus has to rely largely on those who remember it, hardly a secure method. One of those impressions, which Mrs. Maria Brandão, a sociologist from the University of Bahia, kindly conveyed to me, relates to the social composition of AP. She suggested that the young AP militants came mainly from traditional upper- or middle-class families. To them the movement represented an "acceptable" protest, however radical, because of its implied tie with Christianity. Youngsters from urban working-class families tended, according to Mrs. Brandão, to join Marxist organizations, especially POLOP.

39. The use of the concept "populist" here merits some explanation, especially as the usage differs in important respects from that usually given to it by Brazilian political scientists (cf. O. Ianni, *Política e Revolução Social no Brasil* (Rio, 1965), p. 40, or Francisco C. Weffort, "Le Populisme dans la Politique brésilienne," *Les Temps Modernes*, Vol. 23, No. 257, October, 1967, a usage introduced into the English-speaking academic community by Torquato di Tella's article "Populism and Reform in Latin America," in Claudio Veliz (ed.), *Obstacles to Change in Latin America* (London, 1965). I have hesitated to challenge the Brazilian (Latin American) usage outright, because this would almost inevitably compound the already-existing terminological confusion. Yet I have done so from the conviction that there is a significant phenomenon usually designated by the term "populism" which is in essential respects different from what some Latin Americans have lately begun to call *populismo*, a shorthand notation for Germani's *nacionalismo popular*. *Populismo* refers to the political movements of which Getulismo and Peronismo were the prototypes. There is no need to duplicate in this already Weberian note di Tella's excellent discussion of this political phenomenon. Populism, on the other hand, was first used in connection with the *Narodnik* movement which developed in Russia in the second half of the nineteenth century. Movements with similar characteristics have since been observed in many places, recently especially in the Third World. This is demonstrated in the proceedings of a conference held in London in May, 1967, the collected papers of which have appeared in a volume edited by Ghita Ionescu and Ernest Gellner, *Populism* (London, 1969). As the radical Catholic movements clearly fall into the pattern, I have preferred to voice my difference. Populism, then, is used here to refer to an almost invariably oppositional social movement, led by elements from the intelligentsia whose main preoccupation is the life situation of the downtrodden groups in society, "the people" caught in the mill of social change. The people's wisdom and purity are contrasted to the evil and corruption of the elites. The political manipulation of the people must be avoided at all costs; while the populist leadership considers it may have something to offer to the people, it also feels it has much to learn from them. For a further

discussion, see my article "Paternalism and Populism: Catholics in Latin America," *loc. cit.*, and the forthcoming volume *Catholic Radicals in Brazil, passim*.

40. A rather comic confusion between JUC and the embryonic AP can be found in Seganfreddo, *op. cit.*, pp. 102 ff., where she cites preparatory documents for AP's founding meeting as referring to JUC.

41. In his interesting, but overly ideological and at times very obscure book on the Catholic left in Brazil, *Memento dos Vivos, A Esquerda Católica no Brasil* (Rio, 1966), Mendes completely ignores the historical relationship between JUC and AP. The former is merely mentioned once in passing, in a quite negative way (p. 51).

42. For an analysis of the development of Teilhard's thought on the subject, see Robert Coffy, *Teilhard de Chardin et le Socialisme*, Chronique sociale de France (Lyon, 1966), which, despite its title, deals exclusively with the idea of socialization. A relevant bibliography is to be found in it on p. 15.

43. AP, *Documento Base* (January, 1963), section i, para. 1.

44. Pe. Henrique de Lima Vaz, "Consciência e responsabilidade histórica," in *Cristianismo Hoje* (*op. cit.*), p. 72.

45. Vaz, quoted by Sanders, *op. cit.*, p. 93. Sanders' discussion of the philosophy of historical consciousness may be profitably consulted.

46. Pe. Henrique de Lima Vaz, *Uma reflexão sôbre Ação e Ideologia* (typescript, 1962).

47. Karl Rahner, "Christentum als Religion der absoluten Zukunft," in Erich Kellner (ed.), *Christentum und Marxismus—Heute* (Vienna, Frankfurt, Zürich, 1966), pp. 202 ff. See also Vaz's own subsequent article "O Absoluto e a História," *Paz e Terra*, No. 2 (1966).

48. *Documento Base*, section ii, para. 3, p. 3.

49. See Note 18.

50. AP, *Documento Base*, "Introduction."

51. In an interesting and valuable article, "Existencialismo e Juventude Brasileira," *Paz e Terra* No. 3 (n.d. [1967]), Conrado Detrez also notes the convergence of various currents of thought in the wider context of the ideas currently prevalent among Brazilian youth. His assertion that existentialist doctrines found no specific Brazilian formulations (as did Comtean positivism and Marxism) seems to be contradicted by his analysis, as well as by the fragmentary evidence which I have presented here.

52. See his *Le Personnalisme* (Paris, 1950), especially chap. ii. I have used the Portuguese translation by João Bénard da Costa, *O Personalismo* (Lisbon, 1964). An excellent analysis of the thought of Mounier can be found in Roy Pierce, *Contemporary French Political Thought* (London, 1966), chap. iii.

53. *O Personalismo*, pp. 65 and 66, respectively.

54. *Ibid.*, p. 104. See also p. 56.
55. *Ibid.*, p. 22.
56. Cf. the point made by Shaull on pp. 145 ff.
57. *Documento Base*, section iv.
58. *Ibid.*
59. Mario Alves, "A Burguesia Nacional e a Crise Brasileira," *Estudos Socials*, Vol. IV, No. 15, December, 1962, p. 244.
60. The reality of these obstacles to success has been perceived neither by Candido Mendes, *op. cit.*, nor by Richard Shaull, in the present volume, who overestimates the actual impact of AP when he speaks of it as an "explosive force" (see page 152 above).
61. A point well made by Mendes, *op. cit.*, pp. 178–85.
62. *Document* discussed at Encontro Nacional of AP, Salvador, February, 1963 (typescript).
63. The following paragraph is based both on information obtained from a person actively engaged, until April, 1964, in the organization of rural unions of radical Christian orientation (interviewed in December, 1965) and from a draft paper, discussing the problems of the *frente Única* (typescript), drawn up by the AP leadership early in 1964.
64. See Paulo Freire, *Educação como prática da liberdade* (Rio, 1967); also the excellent introduction by Francisco C. Weffort.
65. My forthcoming book, *Catholic Radicals in Brazil*, is centered on a study of MEB. For a brief discussion of the movement by its secretary-general, see Marina Bandeira's report in John M. Considine, M.M. (ed.), *The Church in the New Latin America* (Notre Dame, 1964), pp. 74–82. Further remarks can be found in my paper, "Religion, the Church and Social Change in Brazil," *loc. cit.*, pp. 216–18.
66. *Op. cit.*, p. 190. His discussion of the theory and philosophy of *cultura popular* is very interesting indeed, despite the fact that his ideas are obscured by a profusion of jargon.
67. *Ibid.*, pp. 182 ff. For an orthodox Marxist view of the subject, see Carlos Estevam, *A questão da cultura popular* (Rio, 1963).

INDEX